Is evil a problem?

Q₁ what does it prevent us
from achieving?

A1 A state of non-evil?
= NO BAD THINGS

BUT 'BAD THINGS' RELATE TO PURPOSE

SO
= NO BAD PURPOSES

BUT ONE PERSONS 'BAD'
MAY BE ANOTHER PERSONS GOOD

Other volumes are in preparation

THE PROBLEM OF EVIL

Edited by

MARILYN McCORD ADAMS

and

ROBERT MERRIHEW ADAMS

OXFORD UNIVERSITY PRESS
1990

Oxford University Press, Walton Street, Oxford OX2 6DP
Oxford New York Toronto
Delhi Bombay Calcutta Madras Karachi
Petaling Jaya Singapore Hong Kong Tokyo
Nairobi Dar es Salaam Cape Town
Melbourne Auckland
and associated companies in
Berlin Ibadan

Oxford is a trade mark of Oxford University Press

Published in the United States
by Oxford University Press, New York

British Library Cataloguing in Publication Data
The problem of evil.—(Oxford readings in philosophy).
1. Evil
I. Adams, Marilyn McCord   II. Adams, Robert Merrihew
111.84
ISBN 0–19–824867–9
ISBN 0–19–824866–0 (Pbk)

Library of Congress Cataloging in Publication Data
The Problem of evil / edited by Marilyn McCord Adams and Robert
Merrihew Adams.
p.   cm.—(Oxford readings in philosophy)
Includes bibliographical references.
1. Good and evil.   2. Theodicy.   I. Adams, Marilyn McCord.
II. Adams, Robert Merrihew.   III. Series.
BJ1401.P76 1990 216—dc20   90–34004
ISBN 0–19–824867–9
ISBN 0–19–824866–0 (Pbk.)

Printed and bound in
Great Britain by Bookcraft (Bath) Ltd,
Midsomer Norton, Avon

For William P. Alston

CONTENTS

INTRODUCTION

Ordinary English reserves the term 'evil' for what is *morally* sinister, but philosophers and theologians have for centuries lumped all of life's 'minuses' together under that rubric, giving 'evil' a very wide signification. They have distinguished 'moral evils', such as wars and crimes and self-destructive vices and the damage they cause in human life, from 'natural evils', such as diseases and the destructive effects of earthquakes and tornadoes. The inevitability of death itself is regarded by many as one of the greatest of natural evils. Anyone who reads or hears the news of the world knows of the existence of evils in this broad sense, and virtually all of us have, or will have, some agonizing experience of them in our own lives. Several problems, of different kinds, can be found in these facts.

Clearly, the entrenchment of evils in our world poses a *practical* problem for living things generally: how to survive in such a seemingly hostile environment. Human beings, moreover, all face the *existential* problem of whether and how a life laced with suffering and punctuated by death can have any positive meaning. Evils, in the amounts and of the kinds and with the distribution found in our world, make urgent the question, what sort of posture a person ought to adopt to the basic conditions of human existence. Should one see evils as a challenge the overcoming of which adds zest to life in a basically good world? Or should one see life as nightmarish far beyond human powers to affect? Should one endure it with Stoic resignation, doing what one can to ease the pain? Or should one rebel against it in fierce opposition?

Both practical and existential problems have a *theoretical* dimension. Their solution calls for theories about the structure of the world and the place of human beings in it, for explanations that locate the origin and/or explain the occurrence of evils, for accounts that suggest appropriate and effective human responses to them. Both science and religion have stepped into this role. As with all theories, their proposals have to be evaluated and reassessed against the data along the parameters of consistency, explanatory power, and (theoretical and practical) fruitfulness.

Most discussions in Western philosophy (as indeed all the essays of this volume) have focused on the theoretical problem of evil as it arises within the context of biblical religion. It is often seen as the *logical* problem whether the theistic belief

(1) God exists, and is omnipotent, omniscient, and perfectly good,

is logically consistent with

(2) Evils exist.

For initially it seems that

(P1) A perfectly good being would always eliminate evil so far as it could;

(P2) An omniscient being would know all about evils;

and

(P3) There are *no limits* to what an omnipotent being can do.

But the conjunction of (1), (2), (P1), (P2), and (P3) forms an inconsistent quintet, so that it is possible to infer from any four the denial of the fifth. In particular, the last four entail the denial of the first, while the first combines with the last three to entail the denial of the second. Given (P1), (P2), and (P3), it seems to follow that either God does not exist or evil does not; and few have been prepared to deny the existence of evil!

Such reasoning may be taken two ways, however. On the one hand, it may be construed *aporetically*, as generating a puzzle. One may remain convinced of the compatibility of (1) and (2), and yet see the above arguments as imposing, on anyone who rejects them, the burden of explaining how the prima-facie plausible premisses are not all so acceptable, the inferences not so evident as they seem. Approached this way, the philosophical problem of evil gives crisp focus to a philosophical difficulty i nderstanding the relationship between God and evil, one that arises not b ause there is an explicit logical contradiction between (1) and (2),[1] but because our pre-analytic understandings of 'perfectly good', 'omniscient', and 'omnipotent' construe the maximizations straightforwardly, in terms of (P1), (P2), and (P3), respectively. When taken aporetically, such arguments present a constructive challenge to probe more deeply into the logical relations among these propositions, to offer more rigorous and subtle analyses of the divine perfections. (P1), (P2), and (P3) are not held to have anything more than *initial* plausibility in their favour. And the aporetic inconsistent quintet serves the positive function of structuring the discussion and enabling one to pin-point and contrast various resolutions in a precise way. Even those who (like many of the great medieval philosophers) accepted (2) as empirically obvious and held (1) as demonstrable *a priori* or

[1] Cf. Alvin Plantinga, 'Self-Profile', in James E. Tomberlin and Peter van Inwagen (eds.), *Profiles: Alvin Plantinga* (Dordrecht: Reidel, 1985), 38.

as a non-negotiable item of faith, could recognize a problem of under-standing *how* (1) and (2) are compossible—of *articulating* (1), (2), and one's understanding of the divine attributes in such a way as to *exhibit* their compossibility.

In the modern period, however, there has been a trend of using such considerations *atheologically* to mount an argument from evil to *disprove* the existence of God (and hence the truth of biblical religion).[2] Standing in this tradition, J. L. Mackie sets out to show, in his classic article 'Evil and Omnipotence' (Chapter I of this volume), 'not that religious beliefs lack rational support, but that they are *positively irrational*' by showing that 'the several parts of the essential theological doctrine'—namely, (1) and (2)—'are inconsistent with one another' (p. 25).[3] Recognizing that they are not explicitly contradictory, Mackie relies on (P1) and (P3) to argue for an implicit contradiction between (1) and (2). On Mackie's deployment of the argument, (P1) and (P3) are advanced, not as pre-analytic guesses as to what is meant by 'omnipotence' and 'perfect goodness', but as principles having presumption in their favour. He assigns the theologian the burden of proving that a modification of (P1) and/or (P3) that would leave (1) and (2) consistent would not 'seriously affect the essential core of the theistic position' (p. 37).

In what follows, we shall use the term 'theodicy' broadly to cover any theistic response to questions about how theism can be true in view of the existence of evils. Theodicies whose main or exclusive aim is to rebut particular objections to theism may be called *defences*, while those which attempt a fuller positive account of divine goodness, its purposes in allowing, or its methods in overcoming evils may be called *explanatory theodicies*. We shall consider only theodicies that accept proposition (1) in a fairly traditional sense. In particular we shall not discuss theodicies based on the most radical revisions of the conceptions of God's power and the nature of divine action in the world—for instance, those that ascribe to God an extensive power to 'persuade' but no power at all to compel. Such theodicies have been much discussed by theologians, but have been comparatively neglected, thus far, in the contemporary philosophical debate to which we offer here an introduction.[4]

---

[2] A major landmark in this trend is David Hume's *Dialogues Concerning Natural Religion*, pt. 10.

[3] Italics ours. Parenthetical page references in this Introduction are to the present volume.

[4] For literature about them, see section 10 of the Bibliography below.

THE BEST OF ALL POSSIBLE WORLDS AND THE DEFEAT OF EVILS

In his influential paper 'Hume on Evil' (Chapter II of this volume), Nelson Pike examines the Humean atheistic argument from evil, and finds that it requires reformulation. Contrary to (P1), Pike maintains, our ordinary moral intuitions support the following view:

As a general statement, a being who permits (or brings about) an instance of suffering might be perfectly good providing only that there is a morally sufficient reason for his action. (p. 41)

If God had a *morally sufficient reason* for permitting (bringing about) instances of suffering, then His non-prevention of such evils would not count against His perfect goodness. To generate a logical contradiction from (1) and (2), one would have to appeal to

(P4) It is logically impossible for an omniscient, omnipotent being to have a morally sufficient reason for permitting (bringing about) evils,

a premiss whose plausibility derives from the fact that morally legitimate excuses usually arise from the agent's ignorance or weakness.

Having thus clarified the atheistic argument from evil, Pike offers the believer what may be labelled an '*epistemic* defence' against it. Assuming that (2) refers not merely to some evil or other but to evils in the amounts and of the kinds found in the actual world, Pike rules out as unpromising the piece-work approach of arguing that this sort of evil could be logically connected with this sort of good (e.g. injury with forgiveness) and that sort with some other sort of good (e.g. danger with courage). If the atheologian cannot prove (P4) by enumerating putative excuses for permitting (bringing about) evils and rejecting them one by one, because he 'could never claim to have examined all the possibilities' (p. 41), so also it is hopeless to list the evils and display the logically necessary connection of each with great enough particular goods. Far more promising, Pike thinks, is the search for a single good that could at once provide a 'general' morally sufficient reason for the permission of all the evils.

Taking his inspiration from Leibniz, Pike proposes the Best of All Possible Worlds (= BPW) as such a comprehensive good. By 'possible world' is meant a complex state of affairs, whether (as for Plantinga) a completely determinate, maximal consistent state of affairs, or (as for Leibniz and perhaps for Pike) an aggregate of finite or created things together with their whole history. What is important for present purposes is that the least variation in world history constitutes a different possible world. According to Leibniz, what God does in creating is to actualize a possible world. But, he reasons,

(P5) God, being a perfectly good, omniscient, and omnipotent being, would create the BPW,

and it may be that

(P6) The BPW contains instances of suffering as logically indispensable components.

Pike argues that if (P5) and (P6) were true, they would state a morally sufficient reason—namely, the aim of creating the BPW—that even an omniscient and omnipotent being could have for permitting (or even bringing about) evils. Thus, the conjunction of (P5) and (P6) entails the falsity of (P4); just as the conjunction of (1) with (P5 and P6) entails (2) (pp. 45–6).

If we could *know* (P5) and (P6) to be true, or even possible, we would be in a position not only to refute the above atheistic argument from evil (by showing (P4) to be false), but also to demonstrate the compossibility of (1) and (2) (let us call this a '*demonstrative* defence'). The trouble is that (P6) seems to be a proposition that is not even possibly true unless it is necessarily true. Seeing no way to establish the truth (or hence even the possibility) of (P6) apart from (P5) and an *a priori* proof for the existence of God (such as Leibniz thought he had), Pike would have to admit that these materials from the BPW theodicy do not entitle us to the positive assertion that (1) and (2) are compossible. But since the atheist is in no better position to show (P6) false than the theist is to prove it true, Pike can conclude that the atheist is not entitled to his claim of inconsistency either: for all he or the theist knows (P6) is true and (P4) is false (pp. 46–8).

There is more to be said, however, about the tenability of the view that the BPW may contain evil. Much of the interest of the idea of a BPW, in connection with the problem of evil, derives from the following consideration. If there is a BPW and it includes an evil, we may say that that world is the better for including the evil. A world that lacked the evil would be a different world—and an inferior one, since we are supposing that the world that contains the evil is the best. This evil would thus be necessary for a very great good (indeed, the greatest good)—and not just causally necessary, in the way that a painful medical procedure may be causally necessary for a great benefit to someone's health, but necessary as a constitutive or integral part of the good to be obtained. Even an omnipotent being, therefore, for whom merely causal requirements do not provide compelling reasons, would have a reason for causing or permitting such an evil to occur.

We may wonder, however, whether something bad can really contribute, in a non-causal way, to the goodness of a whole of which it is a part. This is an issue about how the value of a whole is related to the value of its parts. If we think of a whole as the sum of its parts, we may be tempted to suppose that the only way in which a whole that has a bad part could be good is by having a quite separate good part whose value is great enough to outweigh the badness of the bad part. On this view, the whole might be good, but its value would have to fall somewhere between the values of the good and bad parts; and one would necessarily get a better whole by omitting the bad part. This is a case of what Roderick Chisholm, in his address on 'The Defeat of Good and Evil' (Chapter III of this collection), calls the 'balancing off' of evil by good. It is clear that if this is the only way in which the value of a whole can be related to the value of its parts, a world containing an evil cannot be the best possible; for one would get a better world by omitting the evil.

A number of philosophers (among them Chisholm and G. E. Moore) have maintained that there is another way in which the value of a whole, and specifically of a state of affairs, can be related to the value of its parts. Consider the following states of affairs:

(A) Jones thinking about a report (false, as it happens, though Jones believes it true) of a misfortune having befallen Smith;
(B) Jones feeling *happy* about what Jones is thinking about;
(C) Jones feeling *un*happy about what Jones is thinking about.

All the following claims seem plausible: feeling happy is good; feeling unhappy is bad; nevertheless it is better for a person to feel unhappy about a misfortune he or she believes to have befallen someone else, than to feel happy about it. And this is not just because feeling unhappy about someone else's misfortune is likely to have better consequences than feeling happy about it. We think it is *intrinsically* better to feel unhappy about another person's distress than to feel happy about it.

If these claims are true, it follows that (B) is good and (C) is bad, but the complex state of affairs consisting of (A)+(C) is better than that consisting of (A)+(B). It appears that the complex (A)+(C) is the better for containing the evil (C), and the complex (A)+(B) is the worse for containing the good (B). In terms defined by Chisholm in Chapter III, the goodness of (B) is at least *partially defeated* by the inferior value of (A)+(B), and the badness of (C) is at least *partially defeated* by the superior value of (A)+(C). If (A)+(B) as a whole is bad (as seems likely), Chisholm would say that the goodness of (B) is simply *defeated* by the badness of (A)+(B). Likewise the badness of (C) is simply *defeated* by the goodness of (A)+(C), if the latter is indeed good as a whole (as may be more doubtful).

An evil could be included in the BPW if its badness were defeated, in something like Chisholm's sense, by the goodness of that world; and in Chisholm's view that is the only way in which the BPW could include an evil. It is debated, however, whether it is really tenable to claim that evil might, for all we know, be globally defeated in this way by good. Four issues for a BPW theodicy will be noted here, beginning with two doubts that are raised about the very idea of a Best of All Possible Worlds.

(i) Perhaps there is no best among possible worlds. The maximum value might belong to several worlds (as Augustine thought), or there might (as Thomas Aquinas believed)[5] be no limit to the value of the worlds that God could create. Either of these hypotheses would impose complications on a BPW theodicy, but neither would radically subvert it. For if we think that, for all we know, the BPW might include an evil, we can equally well suppose that *all* possible worlds whose values exceed a certain level might contain evils. It has been argued, moreover, that theodicy might actually be helped by the assumption that every possible world, no matter how excellent, is inferior to others that are even better. For in that case the observation that God could have actualized a better world (a better total state of affairs) could not reasonably be used as a moral criticism of God, since it would have been true no matter what God did.[6]

(ii) The BPW theodicy, however, could hardly survive abandonment of the assumption that possible worlds can be compared as better and worse, in themselves and as wholes; and this assumption is questioned. The worlds, in these discussions, are conceived as extremely comprehensive *states of affairs*; and Chisholm's account of the defeat of good and evil depends on the assignment of values to states of affairs. Many ethical theorists evaluate states of affairs, including the most comprehensive, as better and worse in themselves; typical consequentialists are particularly committed to the possible truth of such evaluations. But at least one eminent philosopher has recently argued that states of affairs in general are not good or bad, better or worse, in themselves, though they can be good or bad, better or worse, *for* particular persons or projects, and can ground diverse moral assessments of particular agents.[7] And even if states of affairs can ordinarily have values in themselves, there might be some reason why such extraordinary states of affairs as possible worlds cannot.

---

[5] Augustine, *De Libero Arbitrio* [*On Free Choice of Will*], Bk. III, ch. IX, 94–9; Thomas Aquinas, *Summa Theologiae*, pt. I, qu. 25, art. 6.

[6] This is the most persuasive part of the argument of George Schlesinger's much discussed article, 'The Problem of Evil and the Problem of Suffering', *American Philosophical Quarterly*, 1 (1964), 244–7.

[7] Philippa Foot, 'Utilitarianism and the Virtues', *Proceedings and Addresses of the American Philosophical Association*, 57 (1983–4), 273–83. Foot's argument is explicitly intended as the foundation of a critique of consequentialism.

(iii) A well-known paper by Terence Penelhum (Chapter IV of this anthology), framed with specific reference to the views of Pike and Chisholm, shows one way in which someone who grants that there is a best among possible worlds might still doubt that it could really contain those evils that are actual. Penelhum argues (a) that the scheme of values that theists ascribe to God must agree with that which they hold for themselves, and (b) that the religious beliefs of most theists include ethical commitments that sharply limit what they could consistently regard as goods by which evils might be defeated. It follows (c) that evils not defeasible by those goods could not be defeated at all, or included in the BPW, according to the theists' ethical principles.

Possibilities for the defeat of evils, and hence for theodicy, may be both enlarged and limited in different ways by specific features of theistic theories of value. Inasmuch as theists believe that God, and certain relationships with God, are goods far surpassing all others, they may see the world as containing goods that can defeat greater evils than could be defeated on other views. (Ideas related to this point are developed by Diogenes Allen and Marilyn Adams in Chapters XI and XII below.) But Penelhum emphasizes the *limits* that theists' ethics may impose on their theodicy.

Specifically he claims that 'certain forms of spiritual life and relationship have the highest place' in a *Christian* system of values, and that Christians are therefore committed to 'regarding all evils as justified, if God exists, by the possibility of some spiritual benefit of which they are the necessary condition' (p. 80). But there might be reason to think that some evils (e.g. animal pain) are not defeasible by such goods. Penelhum's paper does not defend a definite conclusion about the existence or non-existence of God, but we shall see the example of animal pain used, by William Rowe, in an explicitly atheistic argument in Chapter VII of the present collection.

Questions can be raised about the adequacy and the implications of Penelhum's views about the ethical commitments of Christianity. In asking them, we shall not be quarrelling with his observations about the structure of the problem of evil, but trying to relate the problem to specific theological positions in the way that he has argued is necessary. Must Christians really suppose that 'spiritual benefits' are the only goods by which the suffering of any creature could be defeated? Does that suggest too anthropocentric a view of God's purposes? And how high a value can Christians consistently assign to certain aesthetic or quasi-aesthetic goods—a type of good that Penelhum might (but perhaps need not) be interpreted as disparaging?[8]

[8] The issues of anthropocentrism and aesthetic value in relation to the problem of evil are taken up by Diogenes Allen in Chapter XI below.

Aesthetic values are particularly interesting in relation to the defeat of good and evil because the aesthetic value of quite a large whole so often depends on an opposite value of one or more of its parts. Such aesthetic benefits as beautiful singing and 'a charming pink flush', as Penelhum argues, are surely not weighty enough to defeat (or balance off) the evils of tuberculosis. But if we think of the possible 'beauty' (or even the 'meaningfulness') of human lives, or perhaps of communal histories, as wholes, we are dealing with an aesthetic or quasi-aesthetic value which it is not obviously wrong to rank among the highest from a moral or a Christian point of view.

(iv) Suppose we grant, not only that there is a best among possible worlds, but also that it may, for all we know, contain such evils as actually occur. It is still not beyond question that the creation of the BPW would provide God with a morally sufficient reason for causing or allowing those evils to occur. Here we touch one of the most fundamental disagreements in ethical theory. *Consequentialists* are committed to the view that one ought always to do what will have the best results on the whole; and they must presumably conclude that any being who could create the BPW would have a morally sufficient reason to do so, despite any evils that would be actualized thereby. But many other ethical theorists think it is sometimes wrong to do something, even though it is necessary for obtaining the best result on the whole. They believe, as popular morality puts it, that 'the end does not always justify the means'. Suppose the BPW would contain one innocent creature whose life was absolutely miserable; might it not be *unjust* to that creature to cause or allow such misery even for the sake of creating the BPW? If so, a non-consequentialist might argue, God would not have a morally sufficient reason for causing or permitting that evil, despite its inclusion in the BPW.

On the other hand, rejection of consequentialism might also have some advantages for theodicy. The assumption that a God who could create the BPW must do so in order to be perfectly good lays a burden on theodicy, inasmuch as many find it implausible to suppose that the actual world is the best possible. And it can be argued that Christians and Jews have reason to reject the assumption because their conception of God's goodness emphasizes *grace*, or unmerited love, rather than the production of the best results. If one regards grace, as a disposition to love that is independent of the merit of the beloved, as part of the divine perfection, it would be somewhat incongruous to think that choosing to make and to love less excellent creatures than one could have must manifest some imperfection. Historically, in saying 'What is man that thou art mindful of him, and the son of man that thou dost care for him?' (Psalm 8: 4) Jews and Christians have thanked and praised God for creating and caring for them, while apparently acknowledging that God could have made better things instead of them. This implies a conception of a divine goodness that is not concerned to maximize value, and that therefore would not necessarily choose to actualize the BPW.[9] Related both to this argument and to Penelhum's argument is the fact that Jewish and Christian conceptions of divine goodness have generally been more concerned with God's love and beneficence toward human individuals than with the global excellence of the world as an artefact. The idea of the defeat of evil by good within individual lives may therefore be more important for Christian and Jewish theodicy than the hypothesis that we live in the Best of All Possible Worlds.

PLANTINGA'S FREE WILL DEFENCE

We have not touched, thus far, on one of the main traditional themes of theodicy, the idea that (some or all) evil originates in wrong or evil choices of a being or beings distinct from God. In dualistic theodicies, such as those of Zoroastrianism and Manichaeism, the good God is not omnipotent and is opposed by a malevolent being of comparable power. Monotheistic religious traditions have generally rejected such dualism, but have often suggested that evil springs from the free will of *creatures*—that is, of beings created by an omnipotent God. The creatures, moreover, unlike the anti-God of dualistic traditions, are not essentially evil.

This hypothesis about the origin of evil has been employed for various purposes in the history of theodicy. Sometimes it has been used to distance God from *responsibility* for the existence of evil. Some or all evil, it is said, is not *caused*, but only *permitted*, by God. God did not *intend* that there should be any evil at all. In the beginning, according to the traditional story of 'the Fall', God created only good things, including humans and angels, rational creatures who were appropriately allowed to control many things by their free choice. They were set in Utopian environments, and God's preference was that they should use their free will only to choose what is right and good. Their freedom meant, however, that it was up to them whether they chose right or wrong. In fact they often chose wrong, and this was the origin of all the evil in the world. The existence of evil is therefore

---

[9] This line of argument is developed by Robert M. Adams, 'Must God Create the Best?' *Philosophical Review*, 81 (1972), 317–32, and criticized by Philip L. Quinn, 'God, Moral Perfection, and Possible Worlds', in Frederick Sontag and M. Darrol Bryant (eds.), *God: The Contemporary Discussion* (New York: Rose of Sharon Press, 1982), 197–215.

our fault, not God's, and is consistent with God's perfect goodness. A major attraction of this sort of story is that in it God appears less ambivalent about evil, more unambiguously opposed to it, than in a BPW theodicy, in which it is apt to seem that those evils that are integral parts of the BPW are *intended* by God, and that God *prefers* on the whole that they should occur, in order that the BPW should be actualized.

Despite the intrinsic interest of these ideas, the various questions that have been raised about both the plausibility and the ethical implications of the story of the Fall need not detain us here. For the best-known contemporary development of a Free Will Defence is Alvin Plantinga's, represented in this collection by Chapter V. And while Plantinga sometimes alludes to the story of the Fall, the main line of his argument can be presented (and will be here) without any use of the story or its associated themes of the 'original righteousness' and 'original bliss' of the first free creatures, and without any implication that the actuality of a world containing evils may not have been fully intended by God, or that the distinction between what one causes and what one permits is morally important. The importance of the free will of creatures for Plantinga is not that it distances God from the causation of evils, but that it may limit what God can achieve. Like BPW defences, Plantinga argues that a perfectly good God may have caused or permitted evils in order to achieve a good enough result obtainable in no other way.

His version of the Free Will Defence differs from BPW defences, however, in at least two ways: (i) The valued result on which his arguments turn is not the BPW as such, but the existence of a (very good) world in which creatures *freely* do good. Indeed Plantinga is explicitly not committed to there being a best among possible worlds (p. 87). (ii) He also does not try to show that evils may have been absolutely necessary for greater goods in such a way as to be defeated, in something like Chisholm's sense, by the goods. His claim is rather that, by virtue of facts about free will, the occurrence of the greater goods without the evils, while perhaps possible in itself, may have been unobtainable even by an omnipotent God.

As to the ethics of the matter, Plantinga assumes (i) that 'A world containing creatures who are [free in some matters of moral significance] (and freely perform more good than evil actions) is more valuable, all else being equal, than a world containing no free creatures at all' (p. 85). He is therefore also committed to the assumption (ii) that possible worlds as wholes can be evaluated as more and less valuable, at least along some parameters. In addition, his defence seems committed to the proposition (iii) that it is consistent with perfect goodness for God to actualize a world, despite any evils it contains, if it is good enough as a whole, on the relevant parameters, and better, on those parameters, than any that God could have actualized without the evils. Assumptions (ii) and (iii), of course, must also be numbered among the assumptions of BPW theodicies.

These ethical assumptions are controversial, but Plantinga's contribution is mainly focused on the more metaphysical issues involved in defending the claim that he regards as 'really characteristic and central to the Free Will Defence . . . that God, though omnipotent, could not have created just any possible world he pleased' (p. 87). How could that be true? Plantinga's answer to this question depends on his incompatibilist view of the nature of free action.

Philosophers disagree as to whether free action is compatible with causal determinism. According to *compatibilists*, an action is free, whether or not it was causally determined, provided only that it was done by an agent whose faculties were operating normally, and was done because the agent chose or preferred to do it. It is relatively uncontroversial that many actions satisfy these requirements. According to *incompatibilist* theories of free action, on the other hand, a free action must not only have been done because an agent whose faculties were operating normally chose or preferred to do it; the agent's choice or preference must also not have been causally determined (though it may certainly have been influenced) by other events or states of affairs. It is highly controversial whether any actions satisfy this additional requirement.

Plantinga believes that our normal conception of free action is incompatibilist. What his argument commits him to, however, is just that there could be creatures free in an incompatibilist sense (whether or not it is the normal sense), and that that would be a very good thing (at least if they did more good than evil). Because it is the most relevant sense for his Free Will Defence, we shall henceforth use 'free' and 'freely' in an incompatibilist sense, unless otherwise indicated. It will be convenient also to follow Plantinga (p. 85) in saying that a person who is both free to act rightly and free to act wrongly, from a moral point of view, in some one respect, is *significantly free* in that respect.

On the basis of an incompatibilist conception of freedom we can give a preliminary explanation of how an omnipotent God could be unable to create a possible world containing free creatures but not containing evils. For any possibly free action A, we can say that even an omnipotent God could not cause a creature to do A freely. For in order to do that, God would have to *cause* the creature to do A. And if God causes the creature to do A, the creature does not do A *freely*. This suggests that in order to have creatures who freely abstain from wrongdoing, an omnipotent God would have to leave it up to them whether they do right or wrong, and might thus e unable to prevent their wrongdoing while maintaining their freedom. Plantinga's argument makes use of this idea.

He sees a further complication to be dealt with, however, before he can dismiss Mackie's contention that God had 'the . . . possibility of making beings who would act freely but always go right'.[10] For even if no one can causally determine (or, in Plantinga's terminology, *strongly actualize*) another agent's free action, a subtler alternative might be available to God. In *weak actualization* God uses knowledge of what a creature would freely do under certain conditions to achieve the desired outcome without causally determining the creature's choice. This could happen, Plantinga suggests, if 'God knows that if he creates you free with respect to A in some set S of circumstances, you will refrain from A'. If God then creates you in S with that freedom, you will of course refrain from A. In this case, Plantinga holds, your refraining from A is free because God does not *cause* you to refrain; but God does 'in a broader sense' bring it about that you refrain (pp. 90–1). Plantinga must therefore consider whether God could not *weakly actualize* a world in which significantly free creatures would always do right—a world containing plenty of moral good but no evil.

He replies that whether God could do that depends on the facts about what the various possible free creatures would freely do in the various possible situations in which they could be placed. If God could weakly actualize sinless free creatures, it would be by knowing that certain possible creatures would always do right if created free in certain situations, and so creating them in such situations. But God cannot have this knowledge unless it is true about some possible creatures that they would always do right if created free in certain situations. Plantinga argues that it is possible that this condition is not satisfied.

As we have described it thus far, his argument deals with a highly *abstract* form of the problem of evil, in that it purports to explain only how an omnipotent, omniscient God might be perfectly good in actualizing a world containing *some* evil. It can be adapted, however, to deal with the more *concrete* problem of how God might have a good enough reason for actualizing a world containing the amount of evil that the actual world contains. It can be argued that God might be unable to actualize any of those (indefinitely many) possible worlds that contain significantly free creatures, and that are at least as good as the actual world with respect to the amount and balance of moral good and evil occurring in them, but contain less evil altogether than the actual world does. That follows if it could possibly be true about every such world W that if God did everything

---

[10] p. 33 below; quoted by Plantinga, p. 86 below.

God would have to do in (weakly) actualizing W, W would not in fact resul
because some creature would fail to perform at least one of the free action
that make W what it is. It might be thought consistent with perfec
goodness, in that case, to create the actual world with all its evil. This seem
to us to be the main line of argument proposed by Plantinga in sections *
and 10 of Chapter V.[11]

The most widely discussed objection to the metaphysics of Plantinga'
argument attacks his assumption of the possible truth of *counterfactuals o
freedom*, which say what certain possible creatures would freely do unde
conditions that will never be actualized. He regards such propositions, i
true, as *contingently* true; some philosophers ask what would explain thei
truth. God cannot cause them to be true, if the actions in question are to be
free. And those that are about possible creatures who will never exist car
hardly be caused to be true by actions of the (non-existent) creatures
Doubts are also raised about what it would be for the propositions to be
true. Many philosophers (unlike Plantinga) think that counterfactual conditional facts need some reduction; the truth of such a conditional, it is
suggested, consists in a logically or causally necessary connection between
the antecedent and the consequent. But either sort of necessary connection
would be inconsistent with the freedom of the action under discussion, and
thus with Plantinga's use of these conditional hypotheses. This objection
has been pressed in several forms, and Plantinga and others have responded to
it.

Robert Merrihew Adams, in an essay reprinted as Chapter VI of this
anthology, presents and defends the objection. He draws on a similar
debate in philosophical theology in the sixteenth and seventeenth centuries
about whether it is possible for God to have what has historically been
called 'middle knowledge', which is knowledge of what every possible free
creature would freely do in any situation in which that creature might
possibly find itself. This is the sort of knowledge on which God is supposed
to rely in weakly actualizing states of affairs. Obviously middle knowledge
is not possible if the relevant conditionals cannot be true.

Plantinga argues that the assumption of the possible truth of counterfactuals of freedom is not indispensable to the Free Will Defence (pp. 99–
100). And it is true that if no such propositions are true, divine projects of
weak actualization face an uncertainty that could cause any of them to fail.

[11] If we are right about this, the hypothesis that *all* evil is due to the sins of free creatures,
which Plantinga introduces in section 10, is an unnecessary complication which plays no essential
part in the main line of argument. Cf. Robert M. Adams, 'Plantinga on the Problem of Evil', in
Tomberlin and van Inwagen (eds.), *Profiles: Alvin Plantinga*, pp. 235 f. Other approaches to the
relation (important to the Free Will Defence) between moral and natural evils are represented in
the items cited in section 6 of the Bibliography.

It might be true that if God followed a certain procedure P in making significantly free creatures, they would *probably* always freely do right. But they also *might* sin. Neither 'If God followed P, free creatures *would* always do right' nor 'If God followed P, free creatures *would* sometimes do wrong' would be true. God could try to make significantly free but sinless creatures by following P, but could fail in the attempt. Thus even an omnipotent God's best attempt to weakly actualize a morally perfect world could end in failure. This conclusion seems to favour a Free Will Defence, but we would need a fuller development of the Defence on the assumption of the falsity of the relevant conditionals.

In particular, it is not obvious how Plantinga's argument regarding the *amount* of evil is to be rendered independent of the possible truth of the conditionals. For if virtually any combination of the relevant counterfactuals about free actions could possibly be true, as he supposes, then there is no net balance of moral virtue in significantly free creatures that could not happen to be unobtainable by an omnipotent God with less evil than the actual world contains. But if these conditionals are all false, then even an omniscient God must base decisions on what free creatures 'would probably do' under the various possible conditions. It would take much discussion of such probabilities to determine whether a world containing as much evil as the actual world does could possibly have resulted from God's 'best attempt' to realize a desirable state of affairs.[12]

Even philosophers who agree with Plantinga that counterfactuals of freedom can in principle be true may of course doubt the truth of those that are important to his defence (as R. Adams points out in the concluding section of Chapter VI). How plausible is it, for instance, that if God had placed significantly free creatures in more idyllic circumstances, with less evil on the whole, than in the actual world, then (no matter how God went about this) the balance of moral good over moral evil in their behaviour would have been less favourable than it is in the actual world? Plantinga's main answer to such questions is clear. The Free Will Defence that we are discussing was developed as a solution to the *logical* problem of evil. It is an answer to the charge that the existence of an omnipotent, omniscient, perfectly good God is *logically inconsistent* with the facts of evil. In response, Plantinga develops a hypothesis about what free creatures would do in various situations. The hypothesis, he contends, is such that if it were true, an omnipotent, omniscient God could be perfectly good in actualizing a world containing evil (or even as much evil as there is in the actual world). In order to accomplish the purpose of showing the *consistency* of theism

---

[12] Cf. R. M. Adams, 'Plantinga on the Problem of Evil', pp. 234 f., and Plantinga, 'Self-Profile', p. 50 in Tomberlin and van Inwagen (eds.), *Profiles: Alvin Plantinga*.

with the facts of evil, the hypothesis about what free creatures would do 'need not be true or known to be true; it need not be so much as plausible. All that is required of it is that it be consistent with [theism]', which of course requires that it be possible in itself (p. 84).

THE EVIDENTIAL PROBLEM OF EVIL

Our discussion thus far has indeed been mainly concerned with questions bearing on the *consistency* of theism with the facts of evil. Recently, however, the opinion has become more prevalent that the most serious form of the problem of evil has to do with the evidential rather than the purely logical relation between evil and theism. Even if it is *possible* that God has a morally sufficient reason for creating the sort of world we experience, it is charged, the facts of evil constitute *evidence* against the hypothesis that the world was created, and is governed, by an omnipotent, omniscient, perfectly good God. This evidence, according to some philosophers, provides the basis of an inductive or empirical argument that shows theism to be *implausible*. These issues of plausibility are addressed in various ways in Chapters VII–XII of the present collection.

William Rowe's forceful development of an empirical argument against theism in Chapter VII turns on the conception of 'intense suffering which an omnipotent, omniscient being could have prevented without thereby losing some greater good or permitting some evil equally bad or worse' (p. 127). By way of abbreviation, it will be convenient to follow Rowe in referring to such suffering as 'pointless' (without meaning to beg any questions as to whether it necessarily is pointless in a non-technical sense). Rowe claims that God (an omnipotent, omniscient, wholly good being) would prevent all suffering that is pointless in this sense, and therefore there would be none if God existed. Some theists (perhaps including the authors of Chapters X–XII below) might question this claim. But those who grant it must conclude, as Rowe does, that if pointless suffering exists, God does not, and hence that any evidence for the existence of pointless suffering is evidence against the existence of God.

Rowe finds such evidence in what he regards as *apparently* pointless suffering. For instance, when a fawn dies slowly of burns suffered in a forest fire, 'there does not appear to be any greater good' that omnipotence could have served best by not preventing the fawn's agony (p. 130). He acknowledges that there could in fact be such a good even though it is not apparent to us. That is why the argument does not have demonstrative force, and cannot do more than establish a probability. But in Rowe's opinion, the great number and variety of instances of 'apparently pointless' suffering in our experience makes it quite implausible to maintain that no genuinely pointless suffering exists, and thus constitutes compelling evidence against the existence of God.

Theists may respond to this argument in several ways. In a piecemeal approach, they may try to find greater goods that could plausibly be thought to defeat the evil of particular sorts of suffering that have been thought to be pointless. If they succeed in a number of important cases, that may also increase the plausibility of supposing that defeating goods are present even for sufferings for which we have not yet discovered any—and hence of supposing that there is no genuinely pointless suffering. With regard to the misfortunes of animals they may try, for instance, to show that animals and other physical and biological systems, as we know them, could not exist and act out their own natures without many incidents that are damaging to their individual interests. The existence and autonomous (though not usually voluntary) activity of such creatures themselves, it is argued, are great enough goods to defeat the evils they suffer.[13]

Some theodicists propose a more general solution, attempting to sever the whole epistemological root of empirical arguments from evil. In an influential exemplar of this approach (Chapter VIII of this collection), responding specifically to Rowe's argument for the existence of pointless suffering, Stephen Wykstra argues for the following Condition of Reasonable Epistemic Access (CORNEA, for short):

On the basis of cognized situation s, human H is entitled to claim 'It appears that p' only if it is reasonable for H to believe that, given her cognitive faculties and the use she has made of them, if p were not the case, s would likely be different than it is in some way discernible by her. (p. 152)

Wykstra claims that, on the basis of CORNEA, we are not entitled to Rowe's claim that it appears that some suffering is pointless. He argues that if there were outweighing goods 'connected in the requisite way' to the sufferings Rowe takes as evidence, it is not very likely 'that this should be apparent to us', in view of the fact that the goods at issue are such as would be purposed by a being whose vision, wisdom, and powers vastly exceed our understanding (p. 155).

Rowe has taken Wykstra's objection very seriously, and responded to it in a paper reprinted here as Chapter IX. Rowe accepts CORNEA as an

---

[13] For the richly suggestive beginnings of an argument along these lines, in a modernized Aristotelian dress, see Austin Farrer, *Love Almighty and Ills Unlimited* (London: Collins, 1961), chs. 4 and 5.

appealing principle, in view of much recent work in epistemology. He argues, however, that it is indeed likely that, if God existed, our situation with regard to suffering would be different in ways discernible by us. Rowe's and Wykstra's arguments provide an important entry into the issue, currently much debated, whether sufferings, or more broadly evils, constitute evidence of any sort against the existence of God.

HICK'S SOUL-MAKING THEODICY

In his book *Evil and the God of Love* (parts of which constitute Chapter X of this collection), John Hick approaches the argument from evil aporetically, offering a theodicy which is definitely of the explanatory type and which attempts to meet both logical and empirical problems at once. It is not an attempt to *justify* the ways of God, as if God owed humans an explanation or had obligations to us in creation. Hick's aim is rather to *understand* how it is that evils in the amounts and of the kinds found in this world coexist with God, who is omnipotent and omniscient by nature and whose character is love. In keeping with most traditions of theodicy, Hick thinks this understanding will be found in *moral* considerations that explain *why* God would permit such evils.

He seeks it in terms of a divine goal that essentially involves significantly free creatures.[14] More explicitly than Plantinga, however, he declines to use the traditional story of the Fall to distance God from responsibility for the origin of evil. Indeed he offers a critique of Fall theodicies, arguing that the notion of perfect free creatures introducing evil by perverse misuse of free choice is incredible or even unintelligible.[15] In Hick's own theodicy the idea of free will is subordinated to that of 'soul-making', from which his approach takes its usual name.

God's primary creative project, as Hick envisions it, culminates in a process of spiritual development in which autonomous created persons, with their own free participation, are perfected, fashioned into God's likeness, formed towards the pattern of Christ (pp. 168–9, 171). Hick emphasizes that his concept of the goal is individualistic: he is not posing a progressive development of the human race as a whole (a thesis he finds empirically unsupportable), but only of individuals in every age and time (p. 169). (In keeping with his conception of God's goals, Hick is not

---

[14] Hick's understanding of freedom may be different from Plantinga's, however. Cf. Hick, *Evil and the God of Love*, rev. edn. (New York: Harper & Row, 1978), ch. 13.
[15] Ibid.

committed to assigning values to possible worlds as wholes.) He sees God's choice of such a developmental process, with all its pains, as underwritten by one or both of two assumptions. Sometimes Hick mentions the *metaphysical* presupposition that human *persons* cannot be 'ready made' perfect by divine fiat, 'but only through the uncompelled responses and willing co-operation of human individuals in their actions and reactions in the world in which God has placed them' (p. 168). More prominently, Hick commends the *value-judgement*:

one who has attained to goodness by meeting and eventually mastering temptations, and thus by rightly making responsible choices in concrete situations, is good in a richer and more valuable sense than would be one created *ab initio* in a state either of innocence or of virtue. (p. 168–9)

Nowhere does he note that if the metaphysical thesis is true, the value comparison loses its point.

Hick then tries to explain divine permission of suffering-generating features of this world in terms of their being necessary for the spiritual growth and development of souls (pp. 170–1). Hick's approach here is *piecemeal*, taking up the major types of evil—moral evil, pain, higher forms of human suffering—in turn and indicating how each is a consequence of the soul-making project and the environment required for it. Not surprisingly, it runs into the difficulty that led Pike and Plantinga to approach matters 'on a quite general level':[16] namely, that it is not possible fully to account for evils in the *amounts* and with the *distribution* found in this world (pp. 180–5). Hick meets this difficulty with the ingenious solution that the very occurrence of 'dysteleological' evils creates a context of mystery which is itself conducive to soul-making (pp. 185–8).

Even if such evils *contribute* to, their amounts, kinds, and distributions being *necessary for*, the environment of soul-making, a cost-benefit analysis would have to be done to show how permission of them could be compossible with Omnipotent Love. At first glance, it seems obvious that so far from facilitating spiritual progress, conditions in this world severely deface the image of Christ in many, and effectively obstruct growth into His likeness. Moreover, of the souls that do make progress, few reach the perfection of which Hick speaks by the time of their death. As Hick insists that Omnipotent Love would not accept failure in any soul It created, he must either (i) claim that all souls make progress in this world, whether we recognize it or not; or (ii) assert that the process of soul-making continues beyond the grave. The first (i) undermines the strategy of Hick's soul-making theodicy: for if we cannot recognize progress and regress, then we

---

[16] Cf. Plantinga, 'Self-Profile', pp. 34–5.

are epistemically in a poor position to tell whether or how various features of the world contribute to the maturation of souls. In fact, Hick happily embraces the eschatological scenario (ii).

If souls make better progress in alternative post-mortem environments, however, we may ask why God did not place us in such settings from the beginning. Hick might appeal to the above-mentioned value-judgement and repeat that God puts a positive value on the moral struggle engendered by our present environment; alternatively, he might contend that it is metaphysically impossible for mature human beings to exist apart from beginnings in this sort of environment (as much as without initial life in the womb). The latter claim about human nature would be difficult to establish, and both answers would be subject to renewed cost-benefit analyses as to whether the soul-making project could be worth all the suffering it involves. Hick's reply seems ultimately to be that the glory of the eschatological consummation will justify these means.[17]

SPIRITUAL EXERCISES

Most philosophical discussion of the problem of evil focuses on reasons-why God might permit evils. Our two remaining authors, however, argue that pressing the why-question can be unfruitful. They also direct our attention (as Hick does in part) to the relation of evils to specifically religious values.

Diogenes Allen (in Chapter XI) rehearses Epictetus' warning that focus on such theoretical why-questions is *spiritually* inadvisable because it prevents us from learning from suffering (and so obstructs our solution of the practical and existential problems of evil). In fact, Allen argues, suffering has instrumental value as the occasion for a kind of *soul-making* that is neglected in Hick's account (pp. 203–6). Borrowing from the Stoics and other spiritual writers, Allen describes three types of *actions* the taking of which *makes it reasonable* for the performer not to take his or her suffering as evidence against divine love (pp. 189–93).

All three approaches begin with the belief that divine goodness is shown by its production of a harmoniously ordered cosmos in which humans play a part by exercising their natural abilities, even though that order does not 'cater' to the well-being of living creatures.

(i) The Stoic Epictetus makes the further assumption that human abilities and human suffering are well matched, so that a person can meet any

[17] Hick, *Evil and the God of Love*, pp. 363 f.

adversity with dignity and without being crushed or degraded by it (pp. 192, 200). The recommended Stoic action takes suffering as an occasion to reflect on the truly small place of humans in the world, and to respond to this reality with an act of acceptance, which is the beginning of humility. At the same time, human ability to discern order in the cosmos and to recognize and accept our vulnerability to disease, aging, decay, and death, makes it possible for us to transcend nature, and gives us reason to thank God for His goodness in giving us the abilities we need to accept and bear our place with dignity (pp. 193–5).

(ii) Allen finds some spiritual writers referring to a second type of action: a humble person with an entrenched belief in God's love may yield herself to natural suffering as to a reality that obeys God, and (it is claimed) through this act of submission a gracious presence, a feeling of divine love and of felicity beyond all calculation is experienced. Persons who perform this second act believe suffering logically compossible with divine love because simultaneous with the experience of it (pp. 195–7).

(iii) The third action is one taken in the face of what Simone Weil calls 'affliction'. This is an extreme suffering that contradicts Epictetus' optimistic estimate of human capacity for dignity. For it goes beyond pain and anguish to damage or destroy social relations and even self-respect (pp. 198–9). Nevertheless, Weil was convinced, as she reflected on the cross of Christ, (a) that affliction is contact with the incommensurate good of divine love, as with a friend whose grip is so tight as to be painful (p. 201). Further, she maintains (b) that affliction has instrumental value as an opportunity to love God for Himself (pp. 203, 208).

Allen's claim is not only that the spiritually mature are able to cope with suffering and affliction at the practical level by meeting them with actions of acceptance, praise, and love (pp. 203, 207–8). In addition, those who perform such spiritual exercises may reasonably find no logical incompossibility between such experiences and God's love for them, and thereby resolve the theoretical problem raised by human suffering and affliction. Moreover, because the experience of divine love is recognized in the presence of suffering, this assurance of compossibility rests on no eschatological appeal the way Hick's approach does (pp. 203–6).

Allen's sensitive treatment leaves the scope of the alleged theoretical resolution unclear. At one level, it amounts to a substitution of alternative attribute analyses for (P1) and (P3) above. Early in his paper Allen contrasts two understandings of divine goodness: (i) a 'Humean' one according to which omnipotent goodness would have to show itself, not only in ordering the cosmos into a harmonious whole, but by choosing an arrangement which would 'cater' to the welfare of living things; and (ii) a

Stoic one according to which God shows Himself to be good by ordering the cosmos into a harmonious whole, and/or to have been good to human beings by giving them the abilities which if exercised enable us to meet suffering and death with dignity (pp. 190–3). In reviewing his second and third types of spiritual action, he notes (iii) an understanding of divine love which is not taken to imply any insurance against human suffering or affliction, but which implies (a) harmonious ordering of the cosmos, (b) endowment of humans with abilities to recognize the order, and to engage in spiritual exercises, and (c) God's presence with those who suffer, a presence which can be recognized and/or experienced by those who perform the actions of acceptance, praise, and love (p. 206). Since these alternative understandings of divine goodness and love carry no implications about human welfare in the sense of immunity to suffering, affliction, and death, human vulnerability to the latter is not incompatible with omnipotent goodness and love thus understood.

Sometimes Allen verges on the further claim that the felicitous experience of God's presence through the acceptance of suffering and recognized contact with Him in affliction are an incommensurate good for created persons, and thus guarantee, by constituting, God's incommensurate goodness *to them*. Such persons and others who share their beliefs might be reasonable in finding their suffering and affliction logically compossible not only with divine goodness or love in senses (ii) and (iii) above, but also with incommensurate divine goodness-to or love-for them. Whether divine presence in suffering and in affliction likewise guarantees divine goodness-to or love-for spiritually immature victims, who do not recognize it because they perform none of the three prescribed actions, Allen does not say. If the defeat of suffering and affliction does depend on the victims' response, then presumably the experiences of the spiritually mature do not make reasonable the belief that God is incommensurately good and loving to those who are suffering and afflicted but spiritually immature.

HORRENDOUS SUFFERING DEFEATED

Marilyn McCord Adams (in Chapter XII) argues that the existence of disproportionate suffering makes it *theoretically* unfruitful to press the why-question. She distinguishes the two dimensions of divine goodness we have noted in discussing Allen: 'production of global goods' and 'goodness to' or 'love of individual created persons'. Adapting Chisholm's notions, she contrasts two dimensions of overbalance/defeat: the overbalance/defeat of evil by good on the global scale, and the overbalance/defeat of evil by good within the context of an individual person's life; and she separates two problems of evil parallel to these. Where Weil identifies the disproportionate evil of affliction, M. Adams defines the category of *horrendous* evils: evils the participation in which (either as agent or as victim) by a person x constitutes objective prima-facie reason to believe that x's life cannot be a great good to x on the whole—in contrast to evils whose negative value seems obviously defeasible within the context of the individual's life.

M. Adams complains that Pike and Plantinga have addressed themselves only to the first problem of evil, defending divine goodness along the first dimension by suggesting logically possible strategies for the global defeat of evils. But given the existence of horrendous evils, establishing God's excellence as a producer of global goods does not automatically solve the second problem. For, on her understanding, God cannot be said to be good or loving to any created persons within whose lives horrendous evils remain undefeated. And yet, she contends parallel to Weil (p. 200), where horrors are concerned, not only are we ignorant of the actual reason-why God permits them; we cannot even think of any plausible candidate reasons-why compatible with the second dimension of divine goodness.

M. Adams's alternative strategy for solving the second problem of evil is to focus on the question of *how* God could defeat horrendous evils, not only within the context of the world as a whole, but within the framework of the individual participant's life. According to her, the latter defeat would involve God's giving participants in horrors lives that were great goods to them on the whole and within which horrors were made meaningful. Insisting that no package of non-transcendent goods could overbalance, much less defeat horrendous evils, M. Adams joins Hick and Allen in appealing to the created person's relation to God, the incommensurate good. Where Allen focuses on spiritual giants, M. Adams shares Hick's conviction that divine love can be vouched safe to every created person, despite his or her participation in horrors and regardless of lack of spiritual progress before death, and so she reintroduces the eschatological perspective.

The beatific vision, an explicit and overwhelmingly felicitous vision of God, is an incommensurate good for any created person and would thus 'overbalance' even horrendous evils and ensure that that person's life was a great good to him or her on the whole. But horrors could also be defeated by being made meaningful through integration into that person's, on the whole overwhelmingly felicitous, relationship with God. Whereas Allen follows Weil in regarding affliction itself as *contact* with the incommensurate good, M. Adams draws on the suggestions of mystical literature that all suffering (horrendous or otherwise) is itself a *mystical identification* with the suffering of Christ and/or a *vision* into the inner life of God, whether it is recognized as such at the time or not. As a point of intimate contact with God, all suffering will have a positive aspect, although as suffering it will have an (even horrendously) evil aspect as well. M. Adams suggests that when participants in horrors view them retrospectively from the vantage-point of the beatific vision, they will find positive meaning in them, because they will not wish away from their life histories any occasions of intimacy with God. Likewise, Julian of Norwich envisions a heavenly divine welcome in which God greets the elect with the words, 'Thank you for your suffering, the suffering of your youth.' She claims that such divine gratitude is a good incommensurate with both temporal goods and earthly woes, and so by Chisholm's criteria would defeat the latter.

I

EVIL AND OMNIPOTENCE

J. L. MACKIE

The traditional arguments for the existence of God have been fairly thoroughly criticised by philosophers. But the theologian can, if he wishes, accept this criticism. He can admit that no rational proof of God's existence is possible. And he can still retain all that is essential to his position, by holding that God's existence is known in some other, non-rational way. I think, however, that a more telling criticism can be made by way of the traditional problem of evil. Here it can be shown, not that religious beliefs lack rational support, but that they are positively irrational, that the several parts of the essential theological doctrine are inconsistent with one another, so that the theologian can maintain his position as a whole only by a much more extreme rejection of reason than in the former case. He must now be prepared to believe, not merely what cannot be proved, but what can be *disproved* from other beliefs that he also holds.

The problem of evil, in the sense in which I shall be using the phrase, is a problem only for someone who believes that there is a God who is both omnipotent and wholly good. And it is a logical problem, the problem of clarifying and reconciling a number of beliefs: it is not a scientific problem that might be solved by further observations, or a practical problem that might be solved by a decision or an action. These points are obvious; I mention them only because they are sometimes ignored by theologians, who sometimes parry a statement of the problem with such remarks as 'Well, can you solve the problem yourself?' or 'This is a mystery which may be revealed to us later' or 'Evil is something to be faced and overcome, not to be merely discussed'.

In its simplest form the problem is this: God is omnipotent; God is wholly good; and yet evil exists. There seems to be some contradiction between these three propositions, so that if any two of them were true the third would be false. But at the same time all three are essential parts of most theological positions: the theologian, it seems, at once *must* adhere and *cannot consistently* adhere to all three. (The problem does not arise only for

J. L. Mackie, 'Evil and Omnipotence', first published in *Mind*, 64 (1955), pp. 200–12. Reprinted by permission of Oxford University Press.

theists, but I shall discuss it in the form in which it presents itself for ordinary theism.)

However, the contradiction does not arise immediately; to show it we need some additional premises, or perhaps some quasi-logical rules connecting the terms 'good', 'evil', and 'omnipotent'. These additional principles are that good is opposed to evil, in such a way that a good thing always eliminates evil as far as it can, and that there are no limits to what an omnipotent thing can do. From these it follows that a good omnipotent thing eliminates evil completely, and then the propositions that a good omnipotent thing exists, and that evil exists, are incompatible.

A. ADEQUATE SOLUTIONS

Now once the problem is fully stated it is clear that it can be solved, in the sense that the problem will not arise if one gives up at least one of the propositions that constitute it. If you are prepared to say that God is not wholly good, or not quite omnipotent, or that evil does not exist, or that good is not opposed to the kind of evil that exists, or that there are limits to what an omnipotent thing can do, then the problem of evil will not arise for you.

There are, then, quite a number of adequate solutions of the problem of evil, and some of these have been adopted, or almost adopted, by various thinkers. For example, a few have been prepared to deny God's omnipotence, and rather more have been prepared to keep the term 'omnipotence' but severely to restrict its meaning, recording quite a number of things that an omnipotent being cannot do. Some have said that evil is an illusion, perhaps because they held that the whole world of temporal, changing things is an illusion, and that what we call evil belongs only to this world, or perhaps because they held that although temporal things *are* much as we see them, those that we call evil are not really evil. Some have said that what we call evil is merely the privation of good, that evil in a positive sense, evil that would really be opposed to good, does not exist. Many have agreed with Pope that disorder is harmony not understood, and that partial evil is universal good. Whether any of these views is *true* is, of course, another question. But each of them gives an adequate solution of the problem of evil in the sense that if you accept it this problem does not arise for you, though you may, of course, have *other* problems to face.

But often enough these adequate solutions are only *almost* adopted. The thinkers who restrict God's power, but keep the term 'omnipotence', may reasonably be suspected of thinking, in other contexts, that his power is really unlimited. Those who say that evil is an illusion may also be thinking, inconsistently, that this illusion is itself an evil. Those who say that 'evil' is merely privation of good may also be thinking, inconsistently, that privation of good is an evil. (The fallacy here is akin to some forms of the 'naturalistic fallacy' in ethics, where some think, for example, that 'good' is just what contributes to evolutionary progress, and that evolutionary progress is itself good.) If Pope meant what he said in the first line of his couplet, that 'disorder' is only harmony not understood, the 'partial evil' of the second line must, for consistency, mean 'that which, taken in isolation, falsely appears to be evil', but it would more naturally mean 'that which, in isolation, really is evil'. The second line, in fact, hesitates between two views, that 'partial evil' isn't really evil, since only the universal quality is real, and that 'partial evil' is really an evil, but only a little one.

In addition, therefore, to adequate solutions, we must recognise unsatisfactory inconsistent solutions, in which there is only a half-hearted or temporary rejection of one of the propositions which together constitute the problem. In these, one of the constituent propositions is explicitly rejected, but it is covertly re-asserted or assumed elsewhere in the system.

B. FALLACIOUS SOLUTIONS

Besides these half-hearted solutions, which explicitly reject but implicitly assert one of the constituent propositions, there are definitely fallacious solutions which explicitly maintain all the constituent propositions, but implicitly reject at least one of them in the course of the argument that explains away the problem of evil.

There are, in fact, many so-called solutions which purport to remove the contradiction without abandoning any of its constituent propositions. These must be fallacious, as we can see from the very statement of the problem, but it is not so easy to see in each case precisely where the fallacy lies. I suggest that in all cases the fallacy has the general form suggested above: in order to solve the problem one (or perhaps more) of its constituent propositions is given up, but in such a way that it appears to have been retained, and can therefore be asserted without qualification in other contexts. Sometimes there is a further complication: the supposed solution moves to and fro between, say, two of the constituent propositions, at one point asserting the first of these but covertly abandoning the second, at another point asserting the second but covertly abandoning the first. These fallacious solutions often turn upon some equivocation with the words 'good' and 'evil', or upon some vagueness about the way in which good and evil are opposed to one another, or about how much is meant by 'omnipotence'. I propose to examine some of these so-called solutions, and to exhibit their fallacies in detail. Incidentally, I shall also be considering whether an adequate solution could be reached by a minor modification of one or more of the constituent propositions, which would, however, still satisfy all the essential requirements of ordinary theism.

1. 'Good cannot exist without evil' or 'Evil is necessary as a counterpart to good.'

It is sometimes suggested that evil is necessary as a counterpart to good, that if there were no evil there could be no good either, and that this solves the problem of evil. It is true that it points to an answer to the question 'Why should there be evil?' But it does so only by qualifying some of the propositions that constitute the problem.

First, it sets a limit to what God can do, saying that God *cannot* create good without simultaneously creating evil, and this means either that God is not omnipotent or that there are *some* limits to what an omnipotent thing can do. It may be replied that these limits are always presupposed, that omnipotence has never meant the power to do what is logically impossible, and on the present view the existence of good without evil would be a logical impossibility. This interpretation of omnipotence may, indeed, be accepted as a modification of our original account which does not reject anything that is essential to theism, and I shall in general assume it in the subsequent discussion. It is, perhaps, the most common theistic view, but I think that some theists at least have maintained that God can do what is logically impossible. Many theists, at any rate, have held that logic itself is created or laid down by God, that logic is the way in which God arbitrarily chooses to think. (This is, of course, parallel to the ethical view that morally right actions are those which God arbitrarily chooses to command, and the two views encounter similar difficulties.) And *this* account of logic is clearly inconsistent with the view that God is bound by logical necessities—unless it is possible for an omnipotent being to bind himself, an issue which we shall consider later, when we come to the Paradox of Omnipotence. This solution of the problem of evil cannot, therefore, be consistently adopted along with the view that logic is self created by God.

But, secondly, this solution denies that evil is opposed to good in our original sense. If good and evil are counterparts, a good thing will not 'eliminate evil as far as it can'. Indeed, this view suggests that good and evil are not strictly qualities of things at all. Perhaps the suggestion is that good and evil are related in much the same way as great and small. Certainly, when the term 'great' is used relatively as a condensation of 'greater than so-and-so', and 'small' is used correspondingly, greatness and smallness are counterparts and cannot exist without each other. But in this sense greatness is not a quality, not an intrinsic feature of anything; and it would be absurd to think of a movement in favour of greatness and against smallness in this sense. Such a movement would be self-defeating, since relative greatness can be promoted only by a simultaneous promotion of relative smallness. I feel sure that no theists would be content to regard God's goodness as analogous to this—as if what he supports were not the *good* but the *better*, and as if he had the paradoxical aim that all things should be better than other things.

This point is obscured by the fact that 'great' and 'small' seem to have an absolute as well as a relative sense. I cannot discuss here whether there is absolute magnitude or not, but if there is, there could be an absolute sense for 'great', it could mean of at least a certain size, and it would make sense to speak of all things getting bigger, of a universe that was expanding all over, and therefore it would make sense to speak of promoting greatness. But in *this* sense great and small are not logically necessary counterparts: either quality could exist without the other. There would be no logical impossibility in everything's being small or in everything's being great.

Neither in the absolute nor in the relative sense, then, of 'great' and 'small' do these terms provide an analogy of the sort that would be needed to support this solution of the problem of evil. In neither case are greatness and smallness *both* necessary counterparts *and* mutually opposed forces or possible objects for support and attack.

It may be replied that good and evil are necessary counterparts in the same way as any quality and its logical opposite: redness can occur, it is suggested, only if non-redness also occurs. But unless evil is merely the privation of good, they are not logical opposites, and some further argument would be needed to show that they are counterparts in the same way as genuine logical opposites. Let us assume that this could be given. There is still doubt of the correctness of the metaphysical principle that a quality must have a real opposite: I suggest that it is not really impossible that everything should be, say, red, that the truth is merely that if everything were red we should not notice redness, and so we should have no word 'red'; we observe and give names to qualities only if they have real opposites. If so, the principle that a term must have an opposite would belong only to our language or to our thought, and would not be an ontological principle, and, correspondingly, the rule that good cannot exist without evil would not state a logical necessity of a sort that God would just have to put up with. God might have made everything good, though *we* should not have noticed it if he had.

But, finally, even if we concede that this *is* an ontological principle, it will provide a solution for the problem of evil only if one is prepared to say, 'Evil exists, but only just enough evil to serve as the counterpart of good.' I doubt whether any theist will accept this. After all, the *ontological* requirement that non-redness should occur would be satisfied even if all the universe, except for a minute speck, were red, and, if there were a corresponding requirement for evil as a counterpart to good, a minute dose of evil would presumably do. But theists are not usually willing to say, in all contexts, that all the evil that occurs is a minute and necessary dose.

2. 'Evil is necessary as a means to good.'

It is sometimes suggested that evil is necessary for good not as a counterpart but as a means. In its simple form this has little plausibility as a solution of the problem of evil, since it obviously implies a severe restriction of God's power. It would be a *causal* law that you cannot have a certain end without a certain means, so that if God has to introduce evil as a means to good, he must be subject to at least some causal laws. This certainly conflicts with what a theist normally means by omnipotence. This view of God as limited by causal laws also conflicts with the view that causal laws are themselves made by God, which is more widely held than the corresponding view about the laws of logic. This conflict would, indeed, be resolved if it were possible for an omnipotent being to bind himself, and this possibility has still to be considered. Unless a favourable answer can be given to this question, the suggestion that evil is necessary as a means to good solves the problem of evil only by denying one of its constituent propositions, either that God is omnipotent or that 'omnipotent' means what it says.

3. 'The universe is better with some evil in it than it could be if there were no evil.'

Much more important is a solution which at first seems to be a mere variant of the previous one, that evil may contribute to the goodness of a whole in which it is found, so that the universe as a whole is better as it is, with some evil in it, than it would be if there were no evil. This solution may be developed in either of two ways. It may be supported by an aesthetic analogy, by the fact that contrasts heighten beauty, that in a musical work, for example, there may occur discords which somehow add to the beauty of the work as a whole. Alternatively, it may be worked out in connexion with the notion of progress, that the best possible organisations of the universe will not be static, but progressive, that the gradual overcoming of evil by good is really a finer thing than would be the eternal unchallenged supremacy of good.

In either case, this solution usually starts from the assumption that the evil whose existence gives rise to the problem of evil is primarily what is called physical evil, that is to say, pain. In Hume's rather half-hearted presentation of the problem of evil, the evils that he stresses are pain and disease, and those who reply to him argue that the existence of pain and disease makes possible the existence of sympathy, benevolence, heroism, and the gradually successful struggle of doctors and reformers to overcome these evils. In fact, theists often seize the opportunity to accuse those who stress the problem of evil of taking a low, materialistic view of good and evil, equating these with pleasure and pain, and of ignoring the more spiritual goods which can arise in the struggle against evils.

But let us see exactly what is being done here. Let us call pain and misery 'first order evil' or 'evil (1)'. What contrasts with this, namely, pleasure and happiness, will be called 'first order good' or 'good (1)'. Distinct from this is 'second order good' or 'good (2)' which somehow emerges in a complex situation in which evil (1) is a necessary component—logically, not merely causally, necessary. (Exactly *how* it emerges does not matter: in the crudest version of this solution good (2) is simply the heightening of happiness by the contrast with misery, in other versions it includes sympathy with suffering, heroism in facing danger, and the gradual decrease of first order evil and increase of first order good.) It is also being assumed that second order good is more important than first order good or evil, in particular that it more than outweighs the first order evil it involves.

Now this is a particularly subtle attempt to solve the problem of evil. It defends God's goodness and omnipotence on the ground that (on a sufficiently long view) this is the best of all logically possible worlds, because it includes the important second order goods, and yet it admits that real evils, namely first order evils, exist. But does it still hold that good and evil are opposed? Not, clearly, in the sense that we set out originally: good does not tend to eliminate evil in general. Instead, we have a modified, a more complex pattern. First order good (*e.g.* happiness) *contrasts with* first order evil (*e.g.* misery): these two are opposed in a fairly mechanical way; some second order goods (*e.g.* benevolence) try to maximise first order good and minimise first order evil; but God's goodness is not this, it is rather the will to maximise *second* order good. We might, therefore, call God's goodness an example of a third order goodness, or good (3). While this account is different from our original one, it might well be held to be an improvement on it, to give a more accurate description of the way in which good is opposed to evil, and to be consistent with the essential theist position.

There might, however, be several objections to this solution.

First, some might argue that such qualities as benevolence—and *a fortiori* the third order goodness which promotes benevolence—have a merely derivative value, that they are not higher sorts of good, but merely means to good (1), that is, to happiness, so that it would be absurd for God to keep misery in existence in order to make possible the virtues of benevolence, heroism, etc. The theist who adopts the present solution must, of course, deny this, but he can do so with some plausibility, so I should not press this objection.

Secondly, it follows from this solution that God is not in our sense benevolent or sympathetic: he is not concerned to minimise evil (1), but only to promote good (2); and this might be a disturbing conclusion for some theists.

But, thirdly, the fatal objection is this. Our analysis shows clearly the possibility of the existence of a *second* order evil, an evil (2) contrasting with good (2) as evil (1) contrasts with good (1). This would include malevolence, cruelty, callousness, cowardice, and states in which good (1) is decreasing and evil (1) increasing. And just as good (2) is held to be the important kind of good, the kind that God is concerned to promote, so evil (2) will, by analogy, be the important kind of evil, the kind which God, if he were wholly good and omnipotent, would eliminate. And yet evil (2) plainly exists, and indeed most theists (in other contexts) stress its existence more than that of evil (1). We should, therefore, state the problem of evil in terms of second order evil, and against this form of the problem the present solution is useless.

An attempt might be made to use this solution again, at a higher level, to explain the occurrence of evil (2): indeed the next main solution that we shall examine does just this, with the help of some new notions. Without any fresh notions, such a solution would have little plausibility: for example, we could hardly say that the really important good was a good (3), such as the increase of benevolence in proportion to cruelty, which logically required for its occurrence the occurrence of some second order evil. But even if evil (2) could be explained in this way, it is fairly clear that there would be third order evils contrasting with this third order good: and we should be well on the way to an infinite regress, where the solution of a problem of evil, stated in terms of evil (n), indicated the existence of an evil (n+1), and a further problem to be solved.

4. 'Evil is due to human freewill.'

Perhaps the most important proposed solution of the problem of evil is that evil is not to be ascribed to God at all, but to the independent actions of human beings, supposed to have been endowed by God with freedom of the will. This solution may be combined with the preceding one: first order evil (*e.g.* pain) may be justified as a logically necessary component in second order good (*e.g.* sympathy) while second order evil (*e.g.* cruelty) is not *justified*, but is so ascribed to human beings that God cannot be held responsible for it. This combination evades my third criticism of the preceding solution.

The freewill solution also involves the preceding solution at a higher level. To explain why a wholly good God gave men freewill although it would lead to some important evils, it must be argued that it is better on the whole that men should act freely, and sometimes err, than that they should be innocent automata, acting rightly in a wholly determined way. Freedom, that is to say, is now treated as a third order good, and as being more valuable than second order goods (such as sympathy and heroism) would be if they were deterministically produced, and it is being assumed that second order evils, such as cruelty, are logically necessary accompaniments of freedom, just as pain is a logically necessary pre-condition of sympathy.

I think that this solution is unsatisfactory primarily because of the incoherence of the notion of freedom of the will: but I cannot discuss this topic adequately here, although some of my criticisms will touch upon it.

First I should query the assumption that second order evils are logically necessary accompaniments of freedom. I should ask this: if God has made men such that in their free choices they sometimes prefer what is good and sometimes what is evil, why could he not have made men such that they always freely choose the good? If there is no logical impossibility in a man's freely choosing the good on one, or on several, occasions, there cannot be a logical impossibility in his freely choosing the good on every occasion. God was not, then, faced with a choice between making innocent automata and making beings who, in acting freely, would sometimes go wrong: there was open to him the obviously better possibility of making beings who would act freely but always go right. Clearly, his failure to avail himself of this possibility is inconsistent with his being both omnipotent and wholly good.

If it is replied that this objection is absurd, that the making of some wrong choices is logically necessary for freedom, it would seem that 'freedom' must here mean complete randomness or indeterminacy, including randomness with regard to the alternatives good and evil, in other words that men's choices and consequent actions can be 'free' only if they are not determined by their characters. Only on this assumption can God escape the responsibility for men's actions; for if he made them as they are, but did not determine their wrong choices, this can only be because the wrong choices are not determined by men as they are. But then if freedom is randomness, how can it be a characteristic of *will*? And, still more, how can it be the most important good? What value or merit would there be in free choices if these were random actions which were not determined by the nature of the agent?

I conclude that to make this solution plausible two different senses of 'freedom' must be confused, one sense which will justify the view that freedom is a third order good, more valuable than other goods would be without it, and another sense, sheer randomness, to prevent us from ascribing to God a decision to make men such that they sometimes go wrong when he might have made them such that they would always freely go right.

This criticism is sufficient to dispose of this solution. But besides this there is a fundamental difficulty in the notion of an omnipotent God creating men with free will, for if men's wills are really free this must mean that even God cannot control them, that is, that God is no longer omnipotent. It may be objected that God's gift of freedom to men does not mean that he *cannot* control their wills, but that he always *refrains* from controlling their wills. But why, we may ask, should God refrain from controlling evil wills? Why should he not leave men free to will rightly, but intervene when he sees them beginning to will wrongly? If God could do this, but does not, and if he is wholly good, the only explanation could be that even a wrong free act of will is not really evil, that its freedom is a value which outweighs its wrongness, so that there would be a loss of value if God took away the wrongness and the freedom together. But this is utterly opposed to what theists say about sin in other contexts. The present solution of the problem of evil, then, can be maintained only in the form that God has made men so free that he *cannot* control their wills.

This leads us to what I call the Paradox of Omnipotence: can an omnipotent being make things which he cannot subsequently control? Or, what is practically equivalent to this, can an omnipotent being make rules which then bind himself? (These are practically equivalent because any such rules could be regarded as setting certain things beyond his control, and *vice versa*.) The second of these formulations is relevant to the suggestions that we have already met, that an omnipotent God creates the rules of logic or causal laws, and is then bound by them.

It is clear that this is a paradox: the questions cannot be answered satisfactorily either in the affirmative or in the negative. If we answer 'Yes', it follows that if God actually makes things which he cannot control, or makes rules which bind himself, he is not omnipotent once he has made them: there are *then* things which he cannot do. But if we answer 'No', we are immediately asserting that there are things which he cannot do, that is to say that he is already not omnipotent.

It cannot be replied that the question which sets this paradox is not a proper question. It would make perfectly good sense to say that a human mechanic has made a machine which he cannot control: if there is any difficulty about the question it lies in the notion of omnipotence itself.

This, incidentally, shows that although we have approached this paradox from the free will theory, it is equally a problem for a theological determinist. No one thinks that machines have free will, yet they may well be beyond the control of their makers. The determinist might reply that anyone who makes anything determines its ways of acting, and so determines its subsequent behaviour: even the human mechanic does this by his *choice* of materials and structure for his machine, though he does not know all about either of these: the mechanic thus determines, though he may not foresee, his machine's actions. And since God is omniscient, and since his creation of things is total, he both determines and foresees the ways in which his creatures will act. We may grant this, but it is beside the point. The question is not whether God *originally* determined the future actions of his creatures, but whether he can *subsequently* control their actions, or whether he was able in his original creation to put things beyond his subsequent control. Even on determinist principles the answers 'Yes' and 'No' are equally irreconcilable with God's omnipotence.

Before suggesting a solution of this paradox, I would point out that there is a parallel Paradox of Sovereignty. Can a legal sovereign make a law restricting its own future legislative power? For example, could the British parliament make a law forbidding any future parliament to socialise banking, and also forbidding the future repeal of this law itself? Or could the British parliament, which was legally sovereign in Australia in, say, 1899, pass a valid law, or series of laws, which made it no longer sovereign in 1933? Again, neither the affirmative nor the negative answer is really satisfactory. If we were to answer 'Yes', we should be admitting the validity of a law which, if it were actually made, would mean that parliament was no longer sovereign. If we were to answer 'No', we should be admitting that there is a law, not logically absurd, which parliament cannot validly make, that is, that parliament is not now a legal sovereign. This paradox can be solved in the following way. We should distinguish between first order laws, that is laws governing the actions of individuals and bodies other than the legislature, and second order laws, that is laws about laws, laws governing the actions of the legislature itself. Correspondingly, we should distinguish two orders of sovereignty, first order sovereignty (sovereignty (1)) which is unlimited authority to make first order laws, and second order sovereignty (sovereignty (2)) which is unlimited authority to make second order laws. If we say that parliament is sovereign we might mean that any parliament at any time has sovereignty (1), or we might mean that parliament has both sovereignty (1) and sovereignty (2) at present, but we cannot without contradiction mean both that the present parliament has sovereignty (2) and that every parliament at every time has sovereignty (1), for if the present parliament has sovereignty (2) it may use it to take away the sovereignty (1) of later parliaments. What the paradox shows is that we cannot ascribe to any continuing institution legal sovereignty in an inclusive sense.

The analogy between omnipotence and sovereignty shows that the paradox of omnipotence can be solved in a similar way. We must distinguish between first order omnipotence (omnipotence (1)), that is unlimited power to act, and second order omnipotence (omnipotence (2)), that is unlimited power to determine what powers to act things shall have. Then we could consistently say that God all the time has omnipotence (1), but if so no beings at any time have powers to act independently of God. Or we could say that God at one time had omnipotence (2), and used it to assign independent powers to act to certain things, so that God thereafter did not have omnipotence (1). But what the paradox shows is that we cannot consistently ascribe to any continuing being omnipotence in an inclusive sense.

An alternative solution of this paradox would be simply to deny that God is a continuing being, that any times can be assigned to his actions at all. But on this assumption (which also has difficulties of its own) no meaning can be given to the assertion that God made men with wills so free that he could not control them. The paradox of omnipotence can be avoided by putting God outside time, but the freewill solution of the problem of evil cannot be saved in this way, and equally it remains impossible to hold that an omnipotent God *binds himself* by causal or logical laws.

CONCLUSION

Of the proposed solutions of the problem of evil which we have examined, none has stood up to criticism. There may be other solutions which require examination, but this study strongly suggests that there is no valid solution of the problem which does not modify at least one of the constituent propositions in a way which would seriously affect the essential core of the theistic position.

Quite apart from the problem of evil, the paradox of omnipotence has shown that God's omnipotence must in any case be restricted in one way or another, that unqualified omnipotence cannot be ascribed to any being that continues through time. And if God and his actions are not in time, can omnipotence, or power of any sort, be meaningfully ascribed to him?

II

HUME ON EVIL

NELSON PIKE

In Parts X and XI of the *Dialogues Concerning Natural Religion*, Hume sets forth his views on the traditional theological problem of evil. Hume's remarks on this topic seem to me to contain a rich mixture of insight and oversight. It will be my purpose in this paper to disentangle these contrasting elements of his discussion.[1]

PHILO'S FIRST POSITION

(1) God, according to the traditional Christian view put forward by Cleanthes in the *Dialogues*, is all-powerful, all-knowing, and perfectly good. And it is clear that for Cleanthes, the terms 'powerful', 'knowing', and 'good' apply to God in exactly the same sense in which these terms apply to men. Philo argues as follows (pp. 61–9): If God is to be all-powerful, all-knowing, and perfectly good (using all key terms in their ordinary sense), then to claim that God exists is to preclude the possibility of admitting that there occur instances of evil; that is, is to preclude the possibility of admitting that there occur instances of suffering, pain, superstition, wickedness, and so forth.[2] The statements 'God exists' and 'There occur instances of suffering' are logically incompatible. Of course, no one could deny that there occur instances of suffering. Such a denial would

Nelson Pike, 'Hume on Evil', first published in *The Philosophical Review*, 72 (1963), pp. 180–97. Reprinted by permission of the Managing Editor and the author.

---

[1] All references to Hume's *Dialogues Concerning Natural Religion* will be to the Hafner Library of Classics edition, ed. by H. D. Aiken (New York, 1955).

[2] It is clear that, for Philo, the term 'evil' is used simply as a tag for the class containing all instances of suffering, pain, and so on. Philo offers no analysis of 'evil' nor does his challenge to Cleanthes rest in the least on the particularities of the logic of this term. On p. 69, e.g., Philo formulates his challenge to Cleanthes without using 'evil'. Here he speaks only of *misery*. In what is to follow, I shall (following Hume) make little use of 'evil'. Also, I shall use 'suffering' as short for 'suffering, pain, superstition, wickedness, and so on'.

plainly conflict with common experience.[3] Thus it follows from obvious fact that God (having the attributes assigned to him by Cleanthes) does not exist.

This argument against the existence of God has enjoyed considerable popularity since Hume wrote the *Dialogues*. Concerning the traditional theological problem of evil, F. H. Bradley comments as follows:

> The trouble has come from the idea that the Absolute is a moral person. If you start from that basis, then the relation of evil to the Absolute presents at once an irreducible dilemma. The problem then becomes insoluble, but not because it is obscure or in any way mysterious. To any one who has the sense and courage to see things as they are, and is resolved not to mystify others or himself, *there is really no question to discuss. The dilemma is plainly insoluble because it is based on a clear self-contradiction.*[4]

John Stuart Mill,[5] J. E. McTaggart,[6] Antony Flew,[7] H. D. Aiken,[8] J. L. Mackie,[9] C. J. Ducasse,[10] and H. J. McCloskey[11] are but a very few of the many others who have echoed Philo's finalistic dismissal of traditional theism after making reference to the logical incompatibility of 'God exists' and 'There occur instances of suffering'. W. T. Stace refers to Hume's discussion of the matter as follows:

> (Assuming that 'good' and 'powerful' are used in theology as they are used in ordinary discourse), we have to say that Hume was right. The charge has never been answered and never will be. The simultaneous attribution of all-power and all-goodness to the Creator of the whole world is logically incompatible with the existence of evil and pain in the world, for which reason the conception of a finite God, who is not all-powerful . . . has become popular in some quarters.[12]

In the first and second sections of this paper, I shall argue that the argument against the existence of God presented in Part X of the *Dialogues* is quite unconvincing. It is not at all clear that 'God exists' and 'There occur instances of suffering' are logically incompatible statements.

(2) Moving now to the details of the matter, we may, I think, formulate Philo's first challenge to Cleanthes as follows:

---

[3] Had Philo been dealing with 'evil' (defined in some special way) instead of 'suffering', this move in the argument might not have been open to him.

[4] *Appearance and Reality* (Oxford, 1930), 174. Italics mine.

[5] *Theism* (New York, 1957), 40. See also *The Utility of Religion* (New York, 1957), 73 ff.

[6] *Some Dogmas of Religion* (London, 1906), 212–13.

[7] 'Theology and Falsification', in Flew and MacIntyre (eds.), *New Essays in Philosophical Theology* (New York, 1955), 108.

[8] 'God and Evil: Some Relations between Faith and Morals', *Ethics*, 68 (1958), 77–97.

[9] 'Evil and Omnipotence', *Mind*, 64 (1955), 201 [Chapter 1, p. 26, in this collection].

[10] *A Philosophical Scrutiny of Religion* (New York, 1953), ch. 16.

[11] 'God and Evil', *Philosophical Quarterly*, 10 (1960), 97–114.

[12] *Time and Eternity* (Princeton, 1952), 56.

(1) The world contains instances of suffering.
(2) God exists—and is omnipotent and omniscient.
(3) God exists—and is perfectly good.

According to the view advanced by Philo, these three statements constitute an 'inconsistent triad' (p. 66). Any two of them might be held together. But if any two of them are endorsed, the third must be denied. Philo argues that to say of God that he is omnipotent and omniscient is to say that he *could* prevent suffering if he wanted to. Unless God could prevent suffering, he would not qualify as both omnipotent and omniscient. But, Philo continues, to say of God that he is perfectly good is to say that God *would* prevent suffering if he could. A being who would not prevent suffering when it was within his power to do so would not qualify as perfectly good. Thus, to affirm propositions (2) and (3) is to affirm the existence of a being who both could prevent suffering if he wanted to and who would prevent suffering if he could. This, of course, is to deny the truth of proposition (1). By similar reasoning, Philo would insist, to affirm (1) and (2) is to deny the truth of (3). And to affirm (1) and (3) is to deny the truth of (2). But, as conceived by Cleanthes, God is both omnipotent-omniscient and perfectly good. Thus, as understood by Cleanthes, 'God exists' and 'There occur instances of suffering' are logically incompatible statements. Since the latter of these statements is obviously true, the former must be false. Philo reflects: 'Nothing can shake the solidarity of this reasoning, so short, so clear (and) so decisive' (p. 69).

It seems to me that this argument is deficient. I do not think it follows from the claim that a being is perfectly good that he would prevent suffering if he could.

Consider this case. A parent forces a child to take a spoonful of bitter medicine. The parent thus brings about an instance of discomfort—suffering. The parent could have refrained from administering the medicine; and he knew that the child would suffer discomfort if he did administer it. Yet, when we are assured that the parent acted in the interest of the child's health and happiness, the fact that he knowingly caused discomfort is not sufficient to remove the parent from the class of perfectly good beings. If the parent fails to fit into this class, it is not because he caused *this* instance of suffering.

Given only that the parent knowingly caused an instance of discomfort, we are tempted to *blame* him for his action—that is, to exclude him from the class of perfectly good beings. But when the full circumstances are known, blame becomes inappropriate. In this case, there is what I shall call a 'morally sufficient reason' for the parent's action. To say that there is a morally sufficient reason for his action is simply to say that there is a circumstance or condition which, when known, renders *blame* (though, of course, not *responsibility*) for the action inappropriate. As a general statement, a being who permits (or brings about) an instance of suffering might be perfectly good providing only that there is a morally sufficient reason for his action. Thus, it does not follow from the claim that God is perfectly good that he would prevent suffering if he could. God might fail to prevent suffering, or himself bring about suffering, while remaining perfectly good. It is required only that there be a morally sufficient reason for his action.

(3) In the light of these reflections, let us now attempt to put Philo's challenge to Cleanthes in sharper form.

(4) The world contains instances of suffering.

(5) God exists—and is omnipotent, omniscient, and perfectly good.

(6) An omnipotent and omniscient being would have no morally sufficient reason for allowing instances of suffering.

Unlike the first, this sequence is logically tight. Suppose (6) and (4) true. If an omnipotent and omniscient being would have no morally sufficient reason for allowing instances of suffering, then, in a world containing such instances, either there would be no omnipotent and omniscient being or that being would be blameworthy. On either of these last alternatives, proposition (5) would be false. Thus, if (6) and (4) are true, (5) must be false. In similar fashion, suppose (6) and (5) true. If an omnipotent and omniscient being would have no morally sufficient reason for allowing suffering, then, if there existed an omnipotent and omniscient being who was also perfectly good, there would occur no suffering. Thus, if (6) and (5) are true, (4) must be false. Lastly, suppose (5) and (4) true. If there existed an omnipotent and omniscient being who was also perfectly good, then if there occurred suffering, the omnipotent and omniscient being (being also perfectly good) would have to have a morally sufficient reason for permitting it. Thus, if (5) and (4) are true, (6) must be false.

Now, according to Philo (and all others concerned), proposition (4) is surely true. And proposition (6)—well, what about proposition (6)? At this point, two observations are needed.

First, it would not serve Philo's purpose were he to argue the truth of proposition (6) by enumerating a number of reasons for permitting suffering (which might be assigned to an omnipotent and omniscient being) and then by showing that in each case the reason offered is not a morally sufficient reason (when assigned to an omnipotent and omniscient being). Philo could never claim to have examined all of the possibilities. And at any given point in the argument, Cleanthes could always claim that God's reason for permitting suffering is one which Philo has not yet considered. A retreat to unexamined reasons would remain open to Cleanthes regardless of how complete the list of examined reasons seemed to be.

Second, the position held by Philo in Part X of the *Dialogues* demands that he affirm proposition (6) as a *necessary truth*. If this is not already clear, consider the following inconsistent triad.

(7) All swans are white.
(8) Some swans are not large.
(9) All white things are large.

Suppose (9) true, but not necessarily true. Either (7) or (8) must be false. But the conjunction of (7) and (8) is not contradictory. If the conjunction of (7) and (8) were contradictory, then (9) would be a necessary truth. Thus, unless (9) is a necessary truth, the conjunction of (7) and (8) is not contradictory. Note what happens to this antilogism when 'colored' is substituted for 'large'. Now (9) becomes a necessary truth and, correspondingly, (7) and (8) become logically incompatible. The same holds for the inconsistent triad we are now considering. As already discovered, Philo holds that 'There are instances of suffering' (proposition 4) and 'God exists' (proposition 5) are logically incompatible. But (4) and (5) will be logically incompatible only if (6) is a necessary truth. Thus, if Philo is to argue that (4) and (5) are logically incompatible, he must be prepared to affirm (6) as a necessary truth.

We may now reconstitute Philo's challenge to the position held by Cleanthes.

Proposition (4) is obviously true. No one could deny that there occur instances of suffering. But proposition (6) is a necessary truth. An omnipotent and omniscient being would have no morally sufficient reason for allowing instances of suffering—just as a bachelor would have no wife. Thus, there exists no being who is, at once, omnipotent, omniscient, and perfectly good. Proposition (5) must be false.

(4) This is a formidable challenge to Cleanthes' position. Its strength can best be exposed by reflecting on some of the circumstances or conditions which, in ordinary life, and with respect to ordinary agents, are usually counted as morally sufficient reasons for failing to prevent (or relieve) some given instance of suffering. Let me list five such reasons.

First, consider an agent who lacked physical ability to prevent some instance of suffering. Such an agent could claim to have had a morally sufficient reason for not preventing the instance in question.

Second, consider an agent who lacked knowledge of (or the means of knowing about) a given instance of suffering. Such an agent could claim to have had a morally sufficient reason for not preventing the suffering, even if (on all other counts) he had the ability to prevent it.

Third, consider an agent who knew of an instance of suffering and had the physical ability to prevent it, but did not *realize* that he had this ability. Such an agent could usually claim to have had a morally sufficient reason for not preventing the suffering. Example: if I push the button on the wall, the torment of the man in the next room will cease. I have the physical ability to push the button. I know that the man in the next room is in pain. But I do not know that pushing the button will relieve the torment. I do not push the button and thus do not relieve the suffering.

Fourth, consider an agent who had the ability to prevent an instance of suffering, knew of the suffering, knew that he had the ability to prevent it, but did not prevent it because he believed (rightly or wrongly) that to do so would be to fail to effect some future good which would outweigh the negative value of the suffering. Such an agent might well claim to have had a morally sufficient reason for not preventing the suffering. Example: go back to the case of the parent causing discomfort by administering bitter medicine to the child.

Fifth, consider an agent who had the ability to prevent an instance of suffering, knew of the suffering, knew that he had the ability to prevent it, but failed to prevent it because to do so would have involved his preventing a prior good which outweighed the negative value of the suffering. Such an agent might claim to have had a morally sufficient reason for not preventing the suffering. Example: a parent permits a child to eat some birthday cake knowing that his eating the cake will result in the child's feeling slightly ill later in the day. The parent estimates that the child's pleasure of the moment outweighs the discomfort which will result.

Up to this point, Philo would insist, we have not hit on a circumstance or condition which could be used by Cleanthes when constructing a 'theodicy', that is, when attempting to identify the morally sufficient reason God has for permitting instances of suffering.

The first three entries on the list are obviously not available. Each makes explicit mention of some lack of knowledge or power on the part of the agent. Nothing more need be said about them.

A theologian might, however, be tempted to use a reason of the fourth type when constructing a theodicy. He might propose that suffering *results in goods* which outweigh the negative value of the suffering. Famine (hunger) leads man to industry and progress. Disease (pain) leads man to knowledge and understanding. Philo suggests that no theodicy of this kind can be successful (pp. 73–4 and 76). An omnipotent and omniscient being could find other means of bringing about the same results. The mere fact that evils give rise to goods cannot serve as a morally sufficient reason for an omnipotent and omniscient being to permit suffering.

A theologian might also be tempted to use reasons of the fifth type when constructing a theodicy. He might propose that instances of suffering *result from goods* which outweigh the negative value of the suffering. That the world is run in accordance with natural law is good. But any such regular operation will result in suffering. That men have the ability to make free choices is good. But free choice will sometimes result in wrong choice and suffering. Philo argues that it is not at all clear that a world run in accordance with natural law is better than one not so regulated (p. 74). And one might issue a similar challenge with respect to free will. But a more general argument has been offered in the contemporary literature on evil which is exactly analogous to the one suggested by Philo above. According to H. J. McCloskey, an omnipotent and omniscient being could devise a law-governed world which would not include suffering.[13] And according to J. L. Mackie, an omnipotent and omniscient being could create a world containing free agents which would include no suffering or wrong-doing.[14] The import of both of these suggestions is that an omnipotent and omniscient being could create a world containing whatever is good (regularity, free will, and so on) without allowing the suffering which (only factually) results from these goods. The mere fact that suffering results from good cannot serve as a morally sufficient reason for an omnipotent and omniscient being to allow suffering.

Though the above reflections may be far from conclusive, let us grant that, of the morally sufficient reasons so far considered, none could be assigned to an omnipotent and omniscient being. This, of course, is not to say that proposition (6) is true—let alone necessarily true. As mentioned earlier, proposition (6) will not be shown true by an enumerative procedure of the above kind. But consider the matter less rigorously. If none of the reasons so far considered could be assigned to an omnipotent and omniscient being, ought this not to raise a suspicion? Might there not be a principle operating in each of these reasons which guarantees that *no* morally sufficient reason for permitting suffering *could* be assigned to an omnipotent and omniscient being? Such a principle immediately suggests itself. Men are sometimes excused for allowing suffering. But in these cases, men are excused only because they lack the knowledge or power to prevent suffering, or because they lack the knowledge or power to bring about goods (which are causally related to suffering) without also bringing about

---

[13] 'God and Evil', pp. 103–4.
[14] 'Evil and Omnipotence', pp. 208–10 [pp. 33–4 above].

suffering. In other words, men are excusable only because they are limited. Having a morally sufficient reason for permitting suffering *entails* having some lack of knowledge or power. If this principle is sound (and, indeed, it is initially plausible) then proposition (6) must surely be listed as a necessary truth.

But the issue is not yet decided. Demea has offered a theodicy which does not fit any of the forms outlined above. And Philo must be willing to consider all proposals if he is to claim 'decisiveness' for his argument against Cleanthes.

Demea reasons as follows:

This world is but a point in comparison of the universe; this life but a moment in comparison of eternity. The present evil phenomena, therefore, are rectified in other regions, and in some future period of existence. And the eyes of men, being then opened to larger views of things, see the whole connection of general laws, and trace, with adoration, the benevolence and rectitude of the Deity through all mazes and intricacies of his providence [p. 67].

It might be useful if we had a second statement of this theodicy, one taken from a traditional theological source. In Chapter LXXI of the *Summa Contra Gentiles*, St. Thomas argues as follows:

The good of the whole is of more account than the good of the part. Therefore, it belongs to a prudent governor to overlook a lack of goodness in a part, that there may be an increase of goodness in the whole. Thus, the builder hides the foundation of a house underground, that the whole house may stand firm. Now, if evil were taken away from certain parts of the universe, the perfection of the universe would be much diminished, since its beauty results from the ordered unity of good and evil things, seeing that evil arises from the failure of good, and yet certain goods are occasioned from those very evils through the providence of the governor, even as the silent pause gives sweetness to the chant. Therefore, evil should not be excluded from things by the divine providence.

Neither of these statements seems entirely satisfactory. Demea might be suggesting that the world is good on the whole—that the suffering we discover in our world is, as it were, made up for in other regions of creation. God here appears as the husband who beats his wife on occasion but makes up for it with favors at other times. In St. Thomas' statement, there are unmistakable hints of causal reasoning. Certain goods are 'occasioned' by evils, as the foundation of the house permits the house to stand firm. But in both of these statements another theme occurs. Let me state it in my own way without pretense of historical accuracy.

I have a set of ten wooden blocks. There is a T-shaped block, an L-shaped block, an F-shaped block, and so on. No two blocks have the same shape. Let us assign each block a value—say an aesthetic value—making the T-shaped block most valuable and the L-shaped block least valuable. Now the blocks may be fitted together into formations. And let us suppose that the blocks are so shaped that there is one and only one subset of the blocks which will fit together into a square. The L-shaped block is a member of that subset. Further, let us stipulate that any formation of blocks (consisting of two or more blocks fitted together) will have more aesthetic value than any of the blocks taken individually or any subset of the blocks taken as a mere collection. And, as a last assumption, let us say that the square formation has greater aesthetic value than any other logically possible block formation. The L-shaped block is a necessary component of the square formation; that is, the L-shaped block is logically indispensable to the square formation. Thus the L-shaped block is a necessary component of the best of all possible block formations. Hence, the block with the least aesthetic value is logically indispensable to the best of all possible block formations. Without this very block, it would be logically impossible to create the best of all possible block formations.

Working from this model, let us understand Demea's theodicy as follows. Put aside the claim that instances of suffering are *de facto* causes or consequences of greater goods. God, being a perfectly good, omniscient, and omnipotent being, would create the best of all possible worlds. But the best of all possible worlds must contain instances of suffering: they are logically indispensable components. This is why there are instances of suffering in the world which God created.

What shall we say about this theodicy? Philo expresses no opinion on the subject.

Consider this reply to Demea's reasonings. A world containing instances of suffering as necessary components might be the best of all possible worlds. And if a world containing instances of suffering as necessary components were the best of all possible worlds, an omnipotent and omniscient being would have a morally sufficient reason for permitting instances of suffering. But how are we to know that, in fact, instances of suffering are logically indispensable components of the best of all possible worlds? There would appear to be no way of establishing this claim short of assuming that God does in fact exist and then concluding (as did Leibniz) that the world (containing suffering) which he did in fact create is the best of all possible worlds. But, this procedure assumes that God exists. And this latter is precisely the question now at issue.

It seems to me that this reply to Demea's theodicy has considerable merit. First, my hypothetical objector is probably right in suggesting that the only way one could show that the best of all possible worlds must contain instances of suffering would be via the above argument in which the existence of God is assumed. Second, I think my objector is right in allowing that if instances of suffering were logically indispensable components of the best of all possible worlds, this would provide a morally sufficient reason for an omnipotent and omniscient being to permit instances of suffering. And, third, I think that my objector exhibits considerable discretion in not challenging the claim that the best of all possible worlds *might* contain instances of suffering as necessary components. I know of no argument which will show this claim to be true. But on the other hand, I know of no argument which will show this claim to be false. (I shall elaborate this last point directly.)

Thus, as I have said, the above evaluation of the theodicy advanced by Demea seems to have considerable merit. But this evaluation, *if correct*, seems to be sufficient to refute Philo's claim that 'God exists' and 'There occur instances of suffering' are logically incompatible statements. If instances of suffering were necessary components of the best of all possible worlds, then an omnipotent and omniscient being would have a morally sufficient reason for permitting instances of suffering. Thus, if it is *possible* that instances of suffering are necessary components of the best of all possible worlds, then there *might* be a morally sufficient reason for an omnipotent and omniscient being to permit instances of suffering. Thus if the statement 'Instances of suffering are necessary components of the best of all possible worlds' is not contradictory, then proposition (6) is not a necessary truth. And, as we have seen, if proposition (6) is not a necessary truth, then 'God exists' and 'There occur instances of suffering' are not logically incompatible statements.

What shall we say? Is the statement 'Instances of suffering are logically indispensable components of the best of all possible worlds' contradictory? That it is is simply assumed in Philo's first position. But, surely, this is not a trivial assumption. If it is correct, it must be shown to be so; it is not *obviously* correct. And how shall we argue that it is correct? Shall we, for example, assume that any case of suffering contained in any complex of events detracts from the value of the complex? If this principle were analytic, then a world containing an instance of suffering could not be the best of all possible worlds. But G. E. Moore has taught us to be suspicious of any such principle.[15] And John Wisdom has provided a series of counterexamples which tend to show that this very principle is, in fact, not

---

[15] I refer here to Moore's discussion of 'organic unities' in *Principia Ethica* (Cambridge, 1903), 28 ff.

analytic. Example: if I believe (rightly or wrongly) that you are in pain and become unhappy as a result of that belief. The resulting complex would appear to be better by virtue of my unhappiness (suffering) than it would have been had I believed you to be in pain but had not become unhappy (or had become happy) as a result.[16] Philo's argument against the existence of God is not finished. And it is not at all obvious that it is *capable* of effective completion. It is, I submit, far from clear that God and evil could not exist together in the same universe.

PHILO'S SECOND POSITION

At the end of Part X, Philo agrees to 'retire' from his first position. He now concedes that 'God exists' and 'There occur instances of suffering' are not logically incompatible statements (p. 69). (It is clear from the context that this adjustment in Philo's thinking is made only for purposes of argument and not because Hume senses any inadequacy in Philo's first position.) Most contemporary philosophers think that Hume's major contribution to the literature on evil was made in Part X of the *Dialogues*. But it seems to me that what is of really lasting value in Hume's reflections on this subject is to be found not in Part X, but in the discussion in Part XI which follows Philo's 'retirement' from his first position.

(1) Consider, first of all, a theology in which the existence of God is accepted on the basis of what is taken to be a conclusive (*a priori*) demonstration. (A theology in which the existence of God is taken as an item of faith can be considered here as well.) On this view, that God exists is a settled matter, not subject to review or challenge. It is, as it were, axiomatic to further theological debate. According to Philo, evil in the world presents no special problem for a theology of this sort:

> Let us allow that, if the goodness of the Deity (I mean a goodness like the human) could be established on any tolerable reasons *a priori*, these (evil) phenomena, however untoward, would not be sufficient to subvert that principle, but might easily, in some unknown manner, be reconcilable to it [p. 78].

This point, I think, is essentially correct, but it must be put more firmly.

Recalling the remarks advanced when discussing the inconsistent nature of propositions (4) through (6) above, a theologian who accepts the existence of God (either as an item of faith or on the basis of an *a priori* argument) must conclude either that there is some morally sufficient reason

---

[16] 'God and Evil', *Mind*, 44 (1935), 13–14. I have modified Wisdom's example slightly.

for God's allowing suffering in the world, or that there are no instances of suffering in the world. He will, of course, choose the first alternative. Thus, in a theology of the sort now under consideration, the theologian begins by affirming the existence of God and by acknowledging the occurrence of suffering. It follows *logically* that God has some morally sufficient reason for allowing instances of suffering. The conclusion is not, as Philo suggests, that there *might* be a morally sufficient reason for evil. The conclusion is, rather, that there *must be* such a reason. It *could* not be otherwise.

What then of the traditional theological problem of evil? Within a theology of the above type, the problem of evil can only be the problem of discovering a *specific* theodicy which is adequate—that is, of discovering which, if any, of the specific proposals which might be advanced really describes God's morally sufficient reason for allowing instances of suffering. This problem, of course, is not a major one for the theologian. If the problem of evil is simply the problem of uncovering the specific reason for evil—given assurance that there is (and must be) some such reason—it can hardly be counted as a critical problem. Once it is granted that there is some specific reason for evil, there is a sense in which it is no longer vital to find it. A theologian of the type we are now considering might never arrive at a satisfactory theodicy. (Philo's 'unknown' reason might remain forever unknown.) He might condemn as erroneous all existing theodicies and might despair of ever discovering the morally sufficient reason in question. A charge of incompleteness would be the worst that could be leveled at his world view.

(2) Cleanthes is not, of course, a theologian of the sort just described. He does not accept the existence of God as an item of faith, nor on the basis of an *a priori* argument. In the *Dialogues*, Cleanthes supports his theological position with an *a posteriori* argument from design. He argues that 'order' in the universe provides sufficient evidence that the world was created by an omnipotent, omniscient, and perfectly good being.[17] He proposes the existence of God as a quasi-scientific explanatory hypothesis, arguing its truth via the claim that it provides an adequate explanation for observed facts.

Philo has two comments to make regarding the relevance of suffering in the world for a theology of this kind.

---

[17] It is interesting to notice that, in many cases, theologians who have used an argument from design have not attempted to argue that 'order' in the world proves the existence of a perfectly moral being. For example, in St. Thomas' 'fifth way' and in William Paley's *Natural Theology*, 'order' is used to show only that the creator of the world was *intelligent*. There are, however, historical instances of the argument from design being used to prove the goodness as well as the intelligence of a creator. For example, Bishop Berkeley argues this way in the second of the *Dialogues Between Hylas and Philonous*.

The first is a comment with which Philo is obviously well pleased. It is offered at the end of Part X and is repeated no less than three times in Part XI. It is this: even if the existence of God and the occurrence of suffering in the world are logically compatible, one cannot argue from a world containing suffering to the existence of an omnipotent, omniscient, and perfectly good creator. This observation, I think all would agree, is correct. Given only a painting containing vast areas of green, one could not effectively argue that its creator disliked using green. There would be no *logical* conflict in holding that a painter who disliked using green painted a picture containing vast areas of green. But given *only* the picture (and no further information), the hypothesis that its creator disliked using green would be poorly supported indeed.

It is clear that in this first comment Philo has offered a criticism of Cleanthes' *argument* for the existence of God. He explicitly says that this complaint is against Cleanthes' *inference* from a world containing instances of suffering to the existence of an omnipotent, omniscient, and perfectly good creator (p. 73). Philo's second comment, however, is more forceful than this. It is a challenge of the *truth* of Cleanthes' *hypothesis*.

Philo argues as follows:

Look round this universe. What an immense profusion of beings, animated and organized, sensible and active! You admire this prodigious variety and fecundity. But inspect a little more narrowly these living existences, the only beings worth regarding. How hostile and destructive to each other! How insufficient all of them for their own happiness! . . . There is indeed an opposition of pains and pleasures in the feelings of sensible creatures; but are not all the operations of nature carried on by an opposition of principles, of hot and cold, moist and dry, light and heavy! The true conclusion is that the original Source of all things is entirely indifferent to all these principles, and has no more regard to good above ill than to heat above cold, or to drought above moisture, or to light above heavy [p. 79].

Philo claims that *there is* an 'original Source of all things' and that this source is indifferent with respect to matters of good and evil. He pretends to be inferring this conclusion from observed data. This represents a departure from Philo's much professed skepticism in the *Dialogues*. And, no doubt, many of the criticisms of Cleanthes' position which Philo advanced earlier in the *Dialogues* would apply with equal force to the inference Philo has just offered. But I shall not dwell on this last point. I think the center of Philo's remarks in this passage must be located in their skeptical rather than their metaphysical import. Philo has proposed a hypothesis which is counter to the one offered by Cleanthes. And he claims that his hypothesis is the 'true conclusion' to be drawn from the observed data. But the point is not, I think, that Philo's new hypothesis is true, or even probable. The conclusion is, rather, that the hypothesis advanced by Cleanthes is false, or very improbable. When claiming that evil in the world *supports* a hypothesis which is counter to the one offered by Cleanthes, I think Philo simply means to be calling attention to the fact that evil in the world provides *evidence against* Cleanthes' theological position.

Consider the following analogy which, I think, will help expose this point. I am given certain astronomical data. In order to explain the data, I introduce the hypothesis that there exists a planet which has not yet been observed but which will be observable at such and such a place in the sky at such and such a time. No other hypothesis seems as good. The anticipated hour arrives and the telescopes are trained on the designated area. No planet appears. Now, either one of two conclusions may be drawn. First, I might conclude that there is no planet there to be seen. This requires either that I reject the original astronomical data or that I admit that what seemed the best explanation of the data is not, in fact, the true explanation. Second, I might conclude that there is a planet there to be seen, but that something in the observational set-up went amiss. Perhaps the equipment was faulty, perhaps there were clouds, and so on. Which conclusion is correct? The answer is not straightforward. I must check both possibilities.

Suppose I find nothing in the observational set-up which is in the least out of order. My equipment is in good working condition, I find no clouds, and so on. To decide to retain the planet hypothesis in the face of the recalcitrant datum (my failure to observe the planet) is, in part, to decide that there is some circumstance (as yet unknown) which explains the datum *other* than the nonexistence of the planet in question. But a decision to retain the planet hypothesis (in the face of my failure to observe the planet and in the absence of an explicit explanation which 'squares' this failure with the planet hypothesis) is made correctly *only* when the *evidence for* the planet hypothesis is such as to render its negation less plausible than would be the assumption of a (as yet unknown) circumstance which explains the observation failure. This, I think, is part of the very notion of dealing reasonably with an explanatory hypothesis.

Now Cleanthes has introduced the claim that there exists an omnipotent, omniscient, and perfectly good being as a way of explaining 'order' in the world. And Philo, throughout the *Dialogues* (up to and including most of Part XI), has been concerned to show that this procedure provides very little (if any) solid evidence for the existence of God. The inference from the data to the hypothesis is extremely tenuous. Philo is now set for his final thrust at Cleanthes' position. Granting that God and evil are not logically incompatible, the existence of human suffering in the world must still be taken as a recalcitrant datum with respect to Cleanthes' hypothesis.

Suffering, as Philo says, is not what we should antecedently expect in a world created by an omnipotent, omniscient, and perfectly good being (pp. 71–2). Since Cleanthes has offered nothing in the way of an explicit theodicy (that is, an explanation of the recalcitrant datum which would 'square' it with his hypothesis) and since the *evidence for* his hypothesis is extremely weak and generally ineffective, there is pretty good reason for thinking that Cleanthes' hypothesis is false.

This, I think, is the skeptical import of Philo's closing remarks in Part XI. On this reading nothing is said about an 'original Source of all things' which is indifferent with respect to matters of good and evil. Philo is simply making clear the negative force of the fact of evil in the world for a hypothesis such as the one offered by Cleanthes.

It ought not to go unnoticed that Philo's closing attack on Cleanthes' position has extremely limited application. Evil in the world has central negative importance for theology only when theology is approached as a quasi-scientific subject, as by Cleanthes. That it is seldom approached in this way will be evident to anyone who has studied the history of theology. Within most theological positions, the existence of God is taken as an item of faith or embraced on the basis of an *a priori* argument. Under these circumstances, where there is nothing to qualify as a 'hypothesis' capable of having either negative or positive 'evidence', the fact of evil in the world presents no special problem for theology. As Philo himself has suggested, when the existence of God is accepted prior to any rational consideration of the status of evil in the world, the traditional problem of evil reduces to a noncrucial perplexity of relatively minor importance.

III

THE DEFEAT OF GOOD AND EVIL

RODERICK M. CHISHOLM

1. Looking for a topic that would be philosophically live, that would reflect my own interests, and that would be appropriate for the events of 1968, I kept coming back to the nature of evil. When the time came to submit a title, however, courage failed and I settled for 'The Types of Intrinsic Goodness and Badness'. Now I am able to compromise with 'The Defeat of Good and Evil'.

I shall discuss a distinction that seems to me to be of first importance to the theory of value. The distinction was seen by such theodicists as St. Thomas and Hume's Demea. It was seen more clearly by Leibniz in his *Theodicy* and by G. E. Moore in the first and last chapters of *Principia Ethica*. And now, I think, we are able to see the distinction more clearly still as a result of recent work in the logic of preference—the logic of such concepts as *good, bad*, and *better*.

The distinction may be put by contrasting what I shall call 'balancing off' and 'defeating'. It is one thing to say that the goodness—the intrinsic goodness—of a certain situation is *balanced off* by means of some other situation; and it is quite another thing to say that the goodness of a certain situation is *defeated* by means of some other situation. Again, it is one thing to say that the evil—the intrinsic badness—of a certain situation is balanced off by means of some other situation; and it is quite another thing to say that the evil of a certain situation is defeated by means of some other situation.

Before I try to define the distinction precisely, I shall make certain general points about the logic of the terms 'good', 'bad', and 'better', when these are used in connection with intrinsic value. I shall assume that we can know, with respect to some things, that those things are good in themselves; that we can know, with respect to other things, that those things are bad in themselves; that we can know, with respect to still other things, that those things are neither good nor bad in themselves; and that we can know, with

Roderick M. Chisholm, 'The Defeat of Good and Evil', first published in *Proceedings of the American Philosophical Association*, 42 (1968–9), pp. 21–38, and revised by the author for publication in this volume. Copyright © the American Philosophical Association. Used with permission.

respect to many things, that some of them are better in themselves than others. I shall also assume that we all know what is meant by the expressions I have just used. These assumptions may themselves be worthy of discussion but they are not the topic of the present paper.

2. The word 'good', Aristotle said, is predicated in every category.[1] There is a sense in which we may say of a substance that it is good; there is a sense in which we may say of a quantity that it is good; and so, too, of a quality, a relation, a time, and a place. And similarly for 'bad'. But this is not true of the expressions 'intrinsically good' and 'intrinsically bad'—of 'good in itself' and 'bad in itself'.

Consider the things that are said to be intrinsically good or intrinsically bad. If we follow the great traditions in western philosophy, we could readily make two lists—a good list and a bad list. The good list, the list of those things that are intrinsically good, would include such items as these: happiness, love, knowledge, justice, beauty, proportion, good intention, and the exercise of virtue. The bad list, on the other hand, would include such items as these: displeasure, unhappiness, hate, ignorance, injustice, ugliness, disharmony, bad intention, and the exercise of vice. The things on the good list, one might say, are the sorts of things that ought to be. To the extent that they may be found in any possible world, that possible world could be said to rate a plus. The things that are on the bad list, one could then say, are the sorts of things that ought not to be. To the extent that *they* may be found in any possible world, *that* possible world rates a minus.

Without pausing to consider whether these lists are too long or too short, let us note one general point about all the items listed. The *terms* we have used in making up the lists are all abstract—'pleasure', 'displeasure', 'love', 'hate', 'the exercise of virtue', 'the exercise of vice', and so on. What these terms refer to are not individuals or concrete things or substances. They are rather propositional entities, or states of affairs: there being happy individuals or there being unhappy individuals; there being individuals experiencing pleasure or there being individuals experiencing displeasure; there being individuals exercising virtue or there being individuals exercising vice. The things that are intrinsically good and the things that are intrinsically bad are, all of them, states of affairs. We may also put this point by saying that states of affairs are the bearers of intrinsic value.

I am using the expression 'state of affairs' in the way in which Moore and Lewis used it—also, I think, in the way in which Frege used the word '*Gedanke*', in the way in which Meinong used the word '*Objektiv*', in the way in which Wittgenstein used '*Sachverhalt*', and in the way in which

[1] *Ethics*, i. 6.

Russell once used the word 'proposition'. I am assuming, therefore, that there *are* states of affairs, some of which obtain and some of which do not obtain. There being horses, for example, is one that does and there being unicorns is one that doesn't. In place of the verb 'obtains', we could use 'takes place', or 'occurs', or 'is actual', or even 'is true' or 'exists' (but if we use 'exists', then we should say 'There *are* states of affairs that do not exist' and not 'There *exist* states of affairs that do not exist'). I am also assuming that states of affairs stand in logical relations to other states of affairs; one state of affairs, for example, may be said to imply or entail another, and every state of affairs has a negation.

Perhaps we ought to say that the only bearers of intrinsic value are *actual* states of affairs—just those states of affairs that occur, obtain, or exist. Everyone being happy is not a state of affairs that obtains and therefore we are not likely to say of it that it *is* good. We would be more likely to say of it that it *would* be good if it *were* to obtain. We would not try to comfort a pessimistic hedonist by telling him that everyone being happy is something that is intrinsically good. Yet we may say of it that it *is* such that it ought to be, just as we may say of everyone being unhappy that it *is* such that it ought not to be. And it is a useful shorthand to say, of nonactual as well as of actual states of affairs, that they *are* good, or bad, or neutral. It is also a useful shorthand to say, of nonactual states of affairs, that some of them *are* better, intrinsically, than others, rather than saying, more cumbersomely, that some of them are such that they *would* be better than others if only they were to exist.

A state of affairs is not intrinsically good unless it entails one of those states of affairs that are on our good list—unless it entails, for example, that there are individuals experiencing pleasure or that there are individuals behaving virtuously. A state of affairs is not intrinsically bad unless it entails one of those states of affairs that are on our bad list—unless it entails, for example, that there are individuals experiencing displeasure or that there are individuals behaving wickedly. These facts have a very important consequence which, I believe, has not been sufficiently noticed.

The negation of a state of affairs that is intrinsically good will not be a state of affairs that is intrinsically bad, and the negation of a state of affairs that is intrinsically bad will not be a state of affairs that is intrinsically good. There being happy Mexicans and there being Romans who are behaving virtuously are states of affairs that are intrinsically good. But their negations—there not being happy Mexicans and there not being Romans who are behaving virtuously—are not intrinsically bad, for they do not entail the existence of any of the items on our bad list. There not being happy Mexicans, of course, is very different from there being unhappy Mexicans, and there not being Romans who are behaving virtuously is very different from there being Romans who are behaving wickedly. On the other hand, there being unhappy Mexicans and there being Romans who are behaving wickedly *are* states of affairs that are intrinsically bad. And *their* negations—there not being unhappy Mexicans and there not being Romans who are behaving wickedly—are *not* intrinsically good, for they do not entail the existence of any of the items on our good list.

Good states of affairs and bad states of affairs, then, have this feature in common: they have neutral negations, negations that are neither good nor bad. I have used the word 'neutral' and not 'indifferent', since, if we take the word 'indifferent' in one of its familiar philosophical senses, we must distinguish what is intrinsically neutral—that is to say, neither good nor bad—from what is intrinsically indifferent. An indifferent state of affairs, in this familiar sense, would be a state of affairs having the same value as its negation—a state of affairs such that it is no better than its negation and its negation is no better than it. There being stones, for example, whatever its instrumental value may be in this world, is intrinsically indifferent. So far as intrinsic value is concerned, there being stones is no better than there not being stones, and there not being stones is no better than there being stones. But the negations of states of affairs that are good and the negations of states of affairs that are bad, though they are themselves neither good nor bad, are not thus indifferent. For *they* differ in value from their negations. All indifferent states of affairs, therefore, are neutral, but not all neutral states of affairs are indifferent. And though we may say that every state of affairs is good, bad, or neutral, we may not say that every state of affairs is good, bad, or indifferent; for the negations of states of affairs that are good and the negations of states of affairs that are bad are states of affairs that are neither good, bad, nor indifferent.

Professor Sosa and I have worked out what we take to be the proper logic of these concepts and we have suggested how to define them all in terms of the relation of being intrinsically better. The gist of what we have said is this: Two states of affairs may be said to be the *same in value* if neither one is better than the other. An *indifferent* state of affairs, as just noted, is one that is the same in value as its negation. A *neutral* state of affairs, on the other hand, is one that is the same in value as some state of affairs that is indifferent. A *good* state of affairs is one that is better than some state of affairs that is indifferent. And a *bad* state of affairs is one such that some state of affairs that is indifferent is better than it. We have assumed, of course, that the relation of being intrinsically better is one that is asymmetric and transitive. And we have also assumed the following: that all indifferent states of affairs are the same in value; that all good states of affairs are better than their negations; and that all bad states of affairs are worse than their negations.[2]

With these simple points in mind, let us now turn to the difference between balancing off and defeat.

3. Balancing off is clear enough, but let us be explicit so that we may contrast it with defeat. Suppose there is one man, Mr. Jones, experiencing a certain amount of innocent pleasure and there is another man. Mr. Smith, experiencing that same amount of innocent displeasure; Mr. Smith is just as displeased as Mr. Jones is pleased. Given a theory of value such as Jeremy Bentham's, we could say that, since the amount of goodness in this conjunctive state of affairs is the same as the amount of badness, therefore the positive and negative values *counterbalance* each other. If the positive and negative values thus counterbalance each other, then the total state of affairs—Mr. Jones in his innocent pleasure and Mr. Smith in his innocent displeasure—is one that is neutral in value. If we think of the total conjunctive state of affairs as being a whole and of its conjuncts as being proper parts, we could say that one of the parts is better than the whole and that another of the parts is worse than the whole.

Or consider that whole which is Mr. Jones experiencing a certain amount of pleasure and Mr. Robinson experiencing a greater amount of displeasure. Applying Bentham's principles to this case, we could say that the whole is bad inasmuch as the goodness of one of its parts is *outweighed* by the badness of another one of its parts. Here, too, one of the parts is better than the whole. And here, too, the whole, though bad, is better than one of its parts. The whole is worse than its good part and better than its worst part. For that state of affairs which is Jones experiencing a certain amount of pleasure and Robinson experiencing a greater amount of displeasure, though bad, is not as bad as that part which is Robinson experiencing that greater amount of displeasure.

And so it is easy to say what it is for goodness to be balanced off. There will be a whole with a good part and a bad part; these parts will exclude each

---

[2] See Roderick M. Chisholm and Ernest Sosa, 'On the Logic of "Intrinsically better"', *American Philosophical Quarterly*, 3 (1966), 244–9. We set forth a 'value calculus' with the following axioms, reading 'pPq' as 'p is intrinsically better than q':

(A1) $(p)(q)[pPq \supset \sim(qPp)]$

(A2) $(p)(q)(r)\{[\sim(pPq) \& \sim(qPr)] \supset \sim(pPr)\}$

(A3) $(p)(q)\{[\sim(pP\sim p) \& \sim(\sim pPp) \& \sim (qP\sim q) \& \sim (\sim qPq)] \supset [\sim(pPq) \& \sim(qPp)]\}$

(A4) $(p)\{(q)[(\sim(pP\sim q) \& \sim (\sim qPp)) \supset pPq] \supset pP\sim p\}$

(A5) $(p)\{(q)[(\sim(qP\sim q) \& \sim (\sim qPq)) \supset qP\sim p] \supset pP\sim p\}$

I now believe the following axioms should have been added:

(A6) $(p)(q)(r)[(pvq)Pr \supset (pPrvqPr)]$

(A7) $(p)(q)(r)[pP(qvr) \supset (pPqvpPr)]$.

other (neither one will entail the other); the whole itself will not be good, but it will be better than one of its parts. Actually, we needn't even say that the whole has a bad part; for if a whole is not good and is better than one of its parts, then the part that it is better than will be a part that is bad.[3] If the whole is neutral, then the goodness of the part will be counterbalanced; if the whole is bad, then the goodness of the part will be outweighed.

We may put the matter pedantically by saying that the *goodness* of a state of affairs p *is balanced off* by a wider state of affairs q provided that the following is true: q obtains; q entails p; p is good; q is not good; and q entails a state of affairs r such that p does not entail r, r does not entail p, and q is better than r. But it is simpler to say that when goodness is balanced off, then a whole that is not good has a part that is good, and, outside of it, a part that is worse than the whole.

When goodness is thus balanced off, we may be consoled at least by *its* presence in the larger whole.

The balancing off of evil is, of course, analogous. There will be a whole with a good part and a bad part; these parts will exclude each other; the whole itself will not be bad; but it will be worse than its good part. We needn't say, however, that the whole has a good part; for if a whole is not bad and is worse than one of its parts, then the part that it is worse than will be a part that is good. If the whole is neutral, then the badness of the part will be counterbalanced; if the whole is good, then the badness of the part will be outweighed.

We may put the matter pedantically by saying that the *badness* of a state of affairs p *is balanced off* by a wider state of affairs q provided that the following is true: q obtains; q entails p; p is bad; q is not bad; and q entails a state of affairs r such that p does not entail r, r does not entail p, and r is better than q.[4] But it is simpler to say that when evil is balanced off, then a whole that is not bad has a part that is bad and, outside of it, a part that is better than the whole.

When evil is balanced off, we may yet regret or resent *its* presence in the larger whole.

4. Now let us contrast *defeat* with balancing off. I shall first cite a number of examples, beginning with what Brentano called 'pleasure in the bad'.

---

[3] That this is so follows from the axioms and definitions of the value calculus referred to in the previous footnote.

[4] If, in our definition of the balancing off of goodness, we replace 'q is not good' and 'q is better than r', respectively, by 'p is better than q' and 'r is bad', we obtain a definition of the more general concept of the *partial balancing off of goodness*. And if, in our definition of the balancing off of evil, we replace 'q is not bad' and 'r is better than q', respectively, by 'q is better than p' and 'r is good', we obtain a definition of the more general concept of the *partial balancing off of evil*. Just as we may contrast balancing off with defeat, we may also contrast partial balancing off with partial defeat.

Consider the sentence: 'Jones is pleased that Smith is displeased.' We may suppose that Smith being displeased is a state of affairs that is bad. Hence the sentence tells us, with respect to a certain state of affairs that is bad, that that state of affairs is the intentional object of Jones's pleasure. Let us interpret our sentence in such a way that it tells us that Smith's displeasure is, *as such*, the object of Jones's pleasure. That is to say, Jones relishes or savors Smith's displeasure in itself, so to speak, and not in virtue of, or merely in virtue of, what he takes to be its consequences. And refining to a certain extent upon ordinary language, let us so interpret 'Jones is pleased that Smith is displeased' that it does not imply that Smith *is*, in fact, displeased. Jones may be pleased, for all we know, about what he mistakenly thinks to be the fact that Smith is displeased.

We understand 'pleasure in the bad', then, in such a way that we may say: first, that the intentional object of such pleasure is a state of affairs that is bad; secondly, that the pleasure is directed upon this state of affairs itself and not upon what are taken to be its consequences; and, thirdly, that the pleasure may be 'illusory' or 'univeridical'—that is to say, its intentional object may in fact be a state of affairs that does not obtain.

Pleasure in the bad is certainly an unseemly emotion. One might say, as Brentano did, that 'pleasure in the bad is, as pleasure, something that is good, but at the same time, as an incorrect emotion, it is something that is bad'.[5] We may have our example, however, without being this rigid in our ethics. Let us suppose, for the moment, that pleasure in the bad, to the extent that it is pleasure, is good, and to the extent that it is pleasure in the bad, is neither good nor bad. Now we consider the state of affairs expressed by the sentence, 'Jones is pleased that Smith is displeased.' The state of affairs itself is neutral; it is neither good nor bad. It entails a state of affairs that is good; for it entails that Jones is pleased. It does not entail any state of affairs that is bad. (We are assuming, it will be recalled, that Jones's unseemly pleasure over Smith's displeasure may be illusory or unveridical. It may be that Smith is not displeased at all.) And, finally, this neutral state of affairs—Jones being pleased that Smith is displeased—does not entail any state of affairs that is worse than it is. Hence we cannot say that the goodness of Jones being pleased is in any way *balanced off* in the larger neutral situation that entails it. For the larger situation does not entail any *bad* state of affairs which outweighs or counterbalances the goodness of Jones being pleased. But, if the example is acceptable, we may say that the

[5] Franz Brentano, *The Origin of our Knowledge of Right and Wrong* (London: Routledge and Kegan Paul, 1969), translated by Roderick M. Chisholm and Elizabeth Schneewind; p. 90. Compare p. 115 n.

goodness of Jones being pleased is *defeated* by the wider state of affairs that entails it.

If pleasure in the bad illustrates the defeat of goodness, then displeasure in the bad may illustrate the defeat of badness. Consider what St. Thomas says about righteous indignation. He defines the righteously indignant man as one who is 'saddened at the prosperity of the wicked'.[6] But let us modify his definition slightly and say that the righteously indignant man is one who is saddened at what he takes to be the prosperity of the wicked. That he takes the wicked to be prospering, one might say, is a state of affairs that is itself neither good nor bad. That he is saddened is a state of affairs that is bad. But that he is saddened at what he takes to be the prosperity of the wicked, is, according to St. Thomas, a state of affairs that is good, or, at any rate, not a state of affairs that is bad.

Or consider these types of feeling—pleasure in the bad and displeasure in the bad—when the intentional object that is bad is one's own wicked deed instead of the displeasure of another. Contemplation of what I take to be a previous misdeed of mine might be said to be a state of affairs that is neutral. If now we add to it that *good* state which is my taking pleasure in the object of my contemplation, then, some would be tempted to say, the resulting whole becomes *worse* instead of better. And so, if this is true, then, by adding a state of affairs that is good to a state of affairs that is neutral, we obtain a state of affairs that is bad.

Or suppose, again, that the added state is one of displeasure instead of pleasure. We have, as before, my contemplation of what I take to be my previous misdeed and this contemplation is ethically neutral. But now we add to it that *bad* state which is my taking displeasure in the object of my contemplation. Then the result, some will be tempted to say, is the virtuous activity of repentance and therefore the resulting whole is *better* because of the component that is bad. If this is true, then, by adding a state of affairs that is bad to a state of affairs that is neutral, we obtain a state of affairs that is good.

Let us add three further examples—two of them being very familiar.

The unpleasant experience of fear, we may suppose, is a state of affairs that is intrinsically bad. But such experience is necessarily involved in the exercise of courage. And the exercise of courage, we may further suppose, is a virtuous activity that is intrinsically good. We need not pause to consider what else it is that goes with fear to make up courage. For the point of the present example is that the larger whole—the exercise of courage—is *better* intrinsically because of the badness of the part that is bad.

[6] St. Thomas, *Commentary on the Nichomachean Ethics*, Para. 356. See Aristotle's *Ethics*, bk. ii, ch. 7, 1108b.

A certain combination of paints may be ugly. This combination may be entailed by a larger whole that is not ugly or that is even beautiful. And the larger whole may be preferable aesthetically just because of the ugliness of the part that is ugly.

I have said that, when evil is *balanced off* in a larger whole, we may, when considering the larger whole, regret or resent the presence of the evil there. But if these examples are acceptable, then one should say 'Thank goodness for the badness of the part that is bad!' For in each case the badness of the part that is bad makes the whole *better* than what we would have had had the bad part been replaced by its neutral negation.

Finally, consider there being one wicked man and many men who are good. Presumably this state of affairs is one that is neutral or possibly even one that is good. Now consider there being one man who feels pleasure and many men who do not. Here we seem to have a state of affairs that is good—for we are saying of the many men, not that they are in a state of displeasure, but only that they are not in a state of pleasure. And now let us add these two states of affairs together, letting the wicked man be the one who experiences the pleasure and the many good men the ones who do not. I think one may well be tempted to say that this combination of a neutral state of affairs with one that is good results in a whole that is neutral. Here, then, we would have the defeat of goodness. We have a whole that is *worse* for the presence of a part that is good. Contemplating such a whole, we might well regret or resent the presence of the goodness there. For the goodness of the part that is good makes the whole worse than what we would have had had only the good part been replaced by its neutral negation.[7]

5. Let us now try to characterize *defeat* more formally.

We must first say what is meant by a 'part of a state of affairs':

(D1) p is part of a state of affairs q $=_{Df}$ q is necessarily such that (a) if it obtains then p obtains and (b) whoever conceives it conceives p.

We will next summarize our contrast between defeat and balancing off. And then we will set forth some definitions.

When goodness is balanced off, then a whole that is not good has a part

---

[7] The following example is proposed by John Wisdom. Friendship is good; that is to say, two people standing in the relation of friendship to each other is good. Friendship is better for the exercise of tolerance, understanding, and forgiveness. But the exercise of tolerance, understanding, and forgiveness requires the existence of pain and sorrow. And the existence of pain and sorrow is intrinsically bad. Wisdom suggests there could not be 'sorrowing affection without pain nor lamenting affection without degradation'. And the important point is, he realizes, not merely that joint sufferings 'tend under certain circumstances to *cause* greater affection'; it is, rather, that a state of friendship that includes this evil is better, in itself, than one that does not. See John Wisdom, 'God and Evil', *Mind*, 44 (1935), 1–20; the quotations are from p. 19.

that is good and, outside of that part, a part that is worse than the whole itself. When goodness is defeated in a larger whole, then that whole does not thus contain any part that is worse than the whole. We may characterize the *defeat of goodness* this way:

(D2) Some of the goodness of state of affairs p is defeated by q $=_{Df}$ p is a good part of q and better than q; and if q has a bad part that is worse than q, then that bad part is a part of p

(D3) The goodness of p is partially defeated by q $=_{Df}$ Some of the goodness of p is defeated by q, and q is good

(D4) The goodness of p is totally defeated by q $=_{Df}$ Some of the goodness of p is defeated by q, and q is not good.

And so when the goodness of p is defeated by such a larger whole, it will not be the case that the goodness of p is balanced off by that larger whole; we will not find elsewhere in the whole a part that is worse than the whole. When goodness is balanced off, and not defeated, by a whole that is bad, then we may be consoled at least by the presence of the part that is good. But if goodness is ever defeated by a whole that is bad, then we may well regret or resent the presence of the part that is good.

Analogously, when evil is balanced off, then a whole that is not bad has a part that is bad and, outside of that part, a part that is better than the whole itself. But when evil is defeated by a larger whole, then that whole does not contain any part that is better than the whole. We will characterize the *defeat of evil* this way:

(D5) Some of the evil of state of affairs p is defeated by q $=_{Df}$ p is a bad part of q and worse than q; and if q has a good part that is better than q, then that good part is part of p

(D6) The evil of p is partially defeated by q $=_{Df}$ Some of the evil of p is defeated by q, and q is bad

(D7) The evil of p is totally defeated by q $=_{Df}$ Some of the evil of p is defeated by q, and q is not bad

And so when the evil of p is defeated by such a larger whole, it will not be the case that the evil of p is balanced off by that whole; we will not find elsewhere in the whole a part that is better than the whole. When evil is merely balanced off, and not defeated, by a whole that is good, then one may regret or resent its presence in that whole. But if evil is ever defeated by a whole that is good, then, as I have suggested, we may well be thankful for the very part that is bad.

I would say, then, that the *concept* of defeat is entirely clear. It may well be that the examples I have given are not entirely plausible. It may even be, as some will doubtless urge, that the concept is not exemplified at all.

Nevertheless I think the concept is of fundamental importance to the theory of value. Let us consider some of its applications.

6. We may now distinguish several different types of intrinsic goodness and intrinsic badness.

Consider a state of affairs that is intrinsically good. We may ask whether that state of affairs is defeasibly good or indefeasibly good. It will be *defeasibly good* if there is a wider state of affairs by which its goodness would be defeated. It will be *indefeasibly good* if there is no wider state of affairs by which its goodness would be defeated.

Consider, once again, Jones being pleased. According to Bentham's principles, this state of affairs would be indefeasibly good; although there are wider states of affairs in which its goodness would be balanced off, there are no wider states of affairs by which its goodness would be defeated. But according to certain other ethical views, the goodness of Jones being pleased is defeasible and it would in fact be defeated if Jones's pleasure were pleasure in the bad.

We should note that it is one thing to say that Jones's pleasure is only defeasibly good and it is another thing to say that its goodness has in fact been *defeated*. The goodness of his pleasure may be defeasible, since, let us suppose, it would be defeated if the pleasure were pleasure in the bad. But what if his pleasure is not pleasure in the bad? In this case, it may be that, though the goodness of his pleasure is defeasible, it is not in fact defeated.

What, then, of pleasure in the good? Suppose Jones is taking pleasure in Smith's innocent pleasure in the neutral—in Smith's innocent pleasure, say, in the being of stones. Shall we say that the goodness of this pleasure in the good is indefeasible? Kant would not agree. For what if Jones's pleasure were undeserved? Let Jones's pleasure in the good, then, be pleasure that is deserved. Here, surely, we have a state of affairs that is indefeasibly good. Though there are wider states of affairs in which its goodness would be balanced off, there are no wider states of affairs in which its goodness would be defeated.

Hence, with respect to states of affairs that are good, we may distinguish between those that are defeasibly good and those that are indefeasibly good. Then, with respect to those states of affairs that are defeasibly good and are also actual, those defeasibly good states of affairs that actually obtain, we may distinguish between those which are such that their goodness is in fact defeated and those which are such that their goodness is not in fact defeated. We may also distinguish between those which are such that their goodness is known to be defeated and those which are such that their goodness is not known to be defeated. (Hence we may provide a variety of possible uses for the technical philosophical expression, *'prima facie* good'.

We could say that a *prima facie* good is a good that is defeasible; or we could say that it is a good that is in fact defeated; or we could say that it is a good that is defeasible and not known to be defeated.)

What we have been saying holds, *mutatis mutandis*, of evil. With respect to states of affairs that are bad, we may distinguish between those that are defeasibly bad and those that are indefeasibly bad. Then with respect to those states of affairs that are defeasibly bad and also actual, we may distinguish between those which are such that their badness has in fact been defeated and those which are such that their badness has not in fact been defeated. And we may distinguish between those which are such that their badness is known to be defeated and those which are such that their badness is not known to be defeated. (We could then provide analogous uses for '*prima facie* evil.' We could say that a *prima facie* evil is an evil that is defeasible, or that it is an evil that has in fact been defeated, or that it is an evil that is defeasible and not known to be defeated.)

Let us note in passing that it is now possible to distinguish still other types of intrinsic goodness and badness.

We could say, for example, that a state of affairs p is *absolutely good* provided, first, that p is good and provided, further, that *any* possible state of affairs entailing p is better than any possible state of affairs not entailing p, no matter how good or bad the other constituents of those states of affairs may happen to be.[8] Thus Pascal seems to have held that the existence of living things is such an absolute good: a world in which there is life, no matter how it is otherwise constituted, is one that is good and one that is better than any world in which there is no life.

Absolute evil would be analogous. A state of affairs p is *absolutely bad* provided that p is bad and provided that any possible state of affairs entailing p is worse than any possible state of affairs not entailing p. Thus Schopenhauer seems to have held that the existence of suffering is such an absolute evil: *any* world in which there is suffering is one such that 'its nonexistence would be preferable to its existence'.[9]

One could move on to greater heights, and depths. Thus there is, or may be, that which is not only absolutely good but also *diffusively good*. A state of affairs p is diffusively good if p is good and if any logically possible state of affairs containing p is also good. Hence if a state of affairs is diffusively

---

[8] In *The Logic of Preference* (Edinburgh: The University Press, 1963), G. H. von Wright envisages the possibility that a person 'actually welcomes a change to p & -q more than a change to -p and q, irrespective of all other changes which may simultaneously happen to the world', and says 'if this is the case, I shall say that he prefers p to q *absolutely*' (p. 29).

[9] See 'On the Vanity and Suffering of Life', in the Supplements to the Fourth Book of *The World as Will and Idea*.

good, it is not only indefeasibly good but it is also such that its goodness cannot be balanced off. Analogously, a state of affairs p is *diffusively bad* if p is bad and if any logically possible state of affairs containing p is also bad. Hence if a state of affairs p is diffusively bad, it is not only indefeasibly bad but it is also such that its badness cannot be balanced off.

I confess, however, that such distinctions as these are not likely to be of much use to most of us.

7. Before turning to theodicy, let us make certain general points about our *knowledge* of value and of defeat and defeasibility.

Propositions about *instrumental* value are, of course, *a posteriori* and contingent. To know with respect to some state of affairs that it is 'good as a means', or that it is 'bad as a means', is to know something about its causal properties; it is to know something about those states of affairs that would obtain as a result of its obtaining. What is instrumentally good on one occasion may be instrumentally neutral, or instrumentally bad, on another occasion.

Where knowledge of the instrumental value of a state of affairs thus involves knowledge of its *causal* properties, knowledge of the *intrinsic* value of a state of affairs may be likened to knowledge of its logical properties. For statements or propositions about intrinsic value may be said to hold in every possible world and therefore they may be thought of as being necessary. If pleasure is intrinsically good in this world, then it would be intrinsically good in any world in which it might be found. And if pleasure in the bad is intrinsically bad in this world, then it would be intrinsically bad in any world in which it might be found. Hence the kind of knowledge we have of intrinsic value is properly said to be *a priori*.

Statements or propositions about the defeasibility of value will also be necessary and *a priori*. But statements or propositions about defeat, as distinguished from defeasibility, are *a posteriori* and contingent. For to know that the value of a given state of affairs is actually defeated is to know, with respect to some state of affairs which would defeat its value, that that state of affairs in fact obtains.

There is no absurdity in supposing that a rational man might know *a priori*, with respect to some state of affairs p, that p is good, or that p is bad, and yet *not* know whether the value of p is defeasible. He might even believe, mistakenly, that the value of p is indefeasible. This could happen if every state of affairs q, such that q would defeat the value of p, were a state of affairs that he had never even conceived. Suppose, for example, that the goodness of pleasure would be defeated by the pleasure's being undeserved but otherwise not. And suppose there were a man who knew what pleasure is but who didn't know what it is to deserve anything or what it is not to deserve anything. Then he might know that pleasure is intrinsically good and believe, mistakenly, that it is also indefeasibly good.

Hence a reasonable man may be *dogmatic* with respect to questions of intrinsic value ('Is p a state of affairs that is intrinsically good?') and *agnostic* with respect to questions of defeasibility ('Is the goodness of p defeasible?'). If he conceives of some state of affairs q such that q would defeat the value of p, then, of course, he may be dogmatic with respect to the defeasibility of p. But if he does not conceive of any state of affairs q such that q would defeat the value of p, he may well withhold judgment about the indefeasibility of p. To know that the value of p is indefeasible, one needs to know that there is *no* state of affairs q such that q would defeat the value of p. Hence one would have to consider, for *every* possible state of affairs q, just what the total value of p and q would be. And this is hardly possible.

These epistemological observations have one important consequence. There is doubtless a temptation to say that a defeated good is not a good at all and thus to restrict the term 'good' to what I have called indefeasible goods. If we were thus to restrict our use of 'good', we would also restrict our use of 'evil', confining it to those things that are indefeasible evils.[10] Now if the only things that are really good or bad are just those things that I have called indefeasibly good or indefeasibly bad, and if we can never know, with respect to any state of affairs, that that state of affairs *is* indefeasibly good or indefeasibly bad, then it will follow that we cannot know, with respect to any state of affairs at all, that the state of affairs is good or that that state of affairs is bad. And this is an extreme that most of us would be unwilling to accept.

8. Finally, I shall make some brief observations about theodicy. For the concept of defeat has obvious application to the problem of evil.

We may assume that if an omnipotent, omniscient, and benevolent deity were to create a world, then that world would be at least as good as any other possible world. The total state of affairs which would make up such a world would be at least as good as any other possible set of states of affairs that would make up a world. We encounter the problem of evil when we try to answer the simple question: 'Is it possible for a world that is at least as

---

[10] Although, as I have said, St. Thomas seems to be aware of the concept of defeat (see *Summa Theologica*, i. 48. 2), he is also inclined to say, at times, that defeated goods and evils are not goods and evils at all. Thus he says: 'Initially and without qualification something may be judged to be good or evil, yet this decision may have to be reversed when additional circumstances are taken into account' (i. 19. 6); and '. . . something may be good according to a particular judgment which is not good according to a wider judgment, and conversely . . .' (i–ii. 19. 10). Contrast G. E. Moore: 'The part of a valuable whole retains exactly the same value when it is, as when it is not, a part of that whole'; *Principia Ethica*, p. 30.

good as any other logically possible world to include any states of affairs that are intrinsically bad?'

Perhaps we should remind ourselves that it would not be possible for there to be a world containing only states of affairs that are intrinsically good. For every state of affairs is such that every possible world contains either it or its negation. But some states of affairs—there being stones, once again—are intrinsically indifferent and therefore such that both they and their negations are neutral. Therefore every possible world will contain some states of affairs that are intrinsically neutral. Moreover, every bad state of affairs and every good state of affairs is a state of affairs such that its negation is neutral. Hence, for every evil as well as every good, that is *excluded* from a world that is good, that world will include its neutral negation.

Perhaps we should also note that, if God does not create all, he will still function as a *causa deficiens*. For there will then be certain neutral states of affairs—the non-existence of stones as well as the non-existence of the various goods and evils we have discussed—which he will thereby *allow* to exist.

I have said we encounter the problem of evil when we consider the question: 'Is it possible for a world that is at least as good as any other possible world to include any states of affairs that are intrinsically bad?' There is an impressive list of philosophers who seem to believe, not only that the answer to this question is negative, but also that it is very obviously negative.[11] Yet if what I have said about defeat is correct, then the answer to this question is at least not *obviously* negative. For it would seem that a world that is at least as good as any other possible world could contain states of affairs that are intrinsically bad—provided that the badness of each of these states of affairs is defeated.

What if the evils of the world were defeated by some wider state of affairs that is *absolutely good* in the sense we have defined—what if the evils of the world were defeated by a certain state of affairs q such that q is good and such that any possible state of affairs entailing q is better than any possible state of affairs not entailing q? Epicurus said that if God is able but unwilling to *prevent* evil, then he is malevolent. But if the evil in the world is defeated and contained in a larger whole that is absolutely good, one should rather say that, if God had been able but unwilling to *create* such evil, then he would have been malevolent. (What, though, if there were a possible world having the same value as this one but containing no evil? One is

---

[11] For example: John Stuart Mill, F. H. Bradley, J. M. E. McTaggart, C. J. Ducasse, Henry Aiken, Antony Flew, J. L. Mackie, H. J. McCloskey, and W. T. Stace. See the references in Nelson Pike's anthology, *God and Evil* (Englewood Cliffs, NJ: Prentice-Hall, 1964), 86–7.

tempted to say that God should have created that world instead of this one. But why so, if this one is just as good? Creation of the other world, one might say, would be very much like an act of supererogation.)

It is clear, I think, that this is the sort of thing that has been intended by the great theodicists in the history of western thought. It is also clear, I think, that the theodicist *must* appeal to the concept of defeat—that he can deal with the problem of evil *only* by saying that the evils in the world are defeated in the sense that I have tried to describe.[12] The other familiar moves just don't work at all.

But we must not let the theodicist have the last word—not this year anyway.

What possible state of affairs *could* thus serve to defeat the evil that is in the world? The wise theodicist, I should think, would say that he doesn't know. Is it at least *logically* possible with respect to the evil that does exist that that evil is defeated? The most the theodicist has a right to say, I believe, is that it is *epistemically* possible. It may be, for all we know, that the evil in the world is defeated by some state of affairs that is absolutely good. And it may also be, for all we know, that the goodness in the world is defeated by some state of affairs that is absolutely evil.

---

[12] Discussing some unpublished statements of mine on this problem, Terence Penelhum writes: 'Chisholm's suggestion that a theist can hold that every evil is defeated without claiming to know by what, must contend with the fact that in a given form of theism the range of possible defeating factors may be specifically understood and incorporated in its moral requirements.' See Terence Penelhum, 'Divine Goodness and the Problem of Evil', *Religious Studies*, 2 (1966–7), 95–107 [Chapter IV in this collection]; the quotation is on p. 107, [p. 82 below]. Many theists, I would think, could accept the epistemological point made above—namely, that a reasonable man may be dogmatic with respect to questions of intrinsic value and at the same time agnostic with respect to questions of defeasibility.

IV

DIVINE GOODNESS AND THE
PROBLEM OF EVIL

TERENCE PENELHUM

I

The purpose of this paper is not to offer any solution to the problem of evil, or to declare it insoluble. It is rather the more modest one of deciding on its nature. Many writers assume that the problem of evil is one that poses a logical challenge to the theist, rather than a challenge of a moral or scientific sort. If this assumption is correct, and the challenge cannot be met, Christian theism can be shown to be untenable on grounds of inconsistency. This in turn means that it is refutable by philosophers, even if their task is interpreted in the most narrowly analytical fashion. It has recently been argued that the challenge of the problem of evil can be met on logical grounds, and that if the existence of evil is damaging to theism it is not because the recognition of its existence is inconsistent with some essential part of it. I take two examples of this position. The first is in the paper 'Hume on Evil' by Nelson Pike;[1] the second I owe to Professor R. M. Chisholm.[2]

Let us first present the problem of evil in its traditional, logical guise. The argument is that it is inconsistent for anyone to believe both of the following two propositions:

   I. The world is the creation of a God who is omnipotent, omniscient, and wholly good.
   II. The world contains evil.

Terence Penelhum, 'Divine Goodness and the Problem of Evil', first published in *Religious Studies*, 2 (1966–7), pp. 95–107. Reprinted by permission of the author and Cambridge University Press.

[1] Nelson Pike, 'Hume on Evil', *Philosophical Review*, 72, (1963), 180–97 [Chapter II in this collection]. The argument is also presented in his volume *God and Evil* (Prentice-Hall, 1964), 85–102.

[2] I learned of this argument through seminar discussion, and Professor Chisholm is not responsible for any inaccuracies in my account of it or any infelicities in my examples.

Both, especially the first, are highly complex propositions, and it is natural that the problem is often put as one of the apparent inconsistency of holding three or four or more propositions at once. Although the complexity of I is vital, the problem can be stated well enough in this deceptively simple form. Let us begin by recognising two things about the problem as presented. (*a*) Apart from some eminent and disingenuous theologians, proposition II is not itself a challenge to theism. It is a part of it. The existence of evil is not something the facts of life force the theist to admit, in the way in which the facts of the fossil evidence forced some nineteenth century theists to admit the antiquity of the world. The existence of evil is something the theist emphasises. Theists do not see fewer evils in the world than atheists; they see more. It is a necessary truth that they see more. For example, to the theist adultery is not only an offence against another person or persons, but also an offence against a sacrament, and therefore against God; it is therefore a worse offence, because it is a compound of several offences. Atheists can never be against sin, for to atheists there can be no sins, 'sin' being a theological concept that only has application if God exists. Only if this is accepted can the problem of evil be represented as a logical problem. For a charge of inconsistency can only be levelled against the theist if he holds both of the allegedly inconsistent propositions *as part of his belief*. The nineteenth century theist who finally accepted the antiquity of the world could not have been accused of logical inconsistency unless a belief like that of the world's beginning in 4004 B.C. were entailed by his form of theism. (*b*) Given this, it is easy to see why the logical challenge the problem of evil presents is so serious. For the theist, in believing in God, believes *both* that God created the world *and* that much that is in the world is deeply deficient in the light of the very standards God himself embodies. The inconsistency seems to result from two distinguishable functions which the idea of God has. It is an ultimate source of explanations of why things are as they are; it is also the embodiment of the very standards by which many of them are found to be wanting.

II

Let us now turn to Pike's argument. Briefly paraphrased, it runs as follows. Propositions I and II are not of themselves incompatible. To get a logically inconsistent set of beliefs we have to add:

III. A being who is omnipotent and omniscient would have no morally sufficient reason for allowing instances of evil.

I, II, and III are, taken together, logically inconsistent, since any two together entail the falsity of the third. For the inconsistency of theism to be demonstrated, Pike argues, III has to be a necessary truth. Unless it is shown to be a necessary truth it is always open to a theist to say that there is some morally sufficient reason why God allows evil, even though he may have no idea what this reason actually is. He can say that he knows I and II are true (e.g. I by revelation and II by observation); so III is false: even though God is omnipotent and omniscient, there is some (mysterious) morally sufficient reason for the evils which he allows. There just *must* be. This is, Pike argues, a perfectly adequate retort to the charge of inconsistency unless proposition III can be *demonstrated*: i.e. unless there is a demonstration that there *cannot* be any available morally sufficient reason for an omnipotent and omniscient being to allow evils.

But how would one set about demonstrating the truth of III? It cannot be deduced from I or II separately, and in any case to try to do this would be to beg the question. It obviously cannot be deduced from the conjunction of I and II, because it is incompatible with this conjunction. The only apparent way of establishing the truth of III is to show in one case after another that a suggested reason for God's permitting evil is not morally sufficient. But this is not conclusive, since the theist can always deny that the list of suggested reasons is complete. This denial can be based on a simple deduction from I and II taken together, and is compatible with complete agnosticism as to what God's morally sufficient reason or reasons might be. A theist is not, in other words, committed to any particular theodicy. The onus is therefore on the sceptic to show that III is a necessary truth. The theist does not have to make it seem *plausible* that there is a morally sufficient reason for evil in order to evade the inconsistency charge. Rather the sceptic has to make the inconsistency charge take hold by proving that there *cannot* be one.

I think this argument is serious. I shall now summarise Chisholm's argument. The goodness or badness of a state of affairs is, says Chisholm, *defeasible*, if it can (logically) be overridden. This can happen when the state of affairs is combined with another and the resultant complex is of a value which is either neutral or opposite to that of the first state of affairs, and is not reduced by the fact that the first state of affairs is a part of it. It might be held, for example, that the evil of my suffering pain is defeated by my acquisition of fortitude in the face of it; or that the evil of my suffering mental distress is defeated by the fact that my distress is due to contrition for my former sins. Since there is no more good, and perhaps even less good, in my acquiring fortitude in ways other than that of living through occasions that require its exercise, then the pain plus the fortitude is better than either without the other; and since contrition is only possible if some sins have been committed, the contrite sinner may be a better phenomenon, or no worse a phenomenon, than the unhumbled innocent.

The theist can argue in the face of the problem of evil in the following way. Every evil in the world, he can say, is or will be defeated. For every evil there is a state of affairs which, when combined with it, results in a conjoint state of affairs which is *either*

(i) not bad and better than either without the other,

or (ii) good and better than either without the other,

or (iii) good and better than any alternative state of affairs.

God can allow evil situations if their defeat is assured in one of these ways; in fact, his goodness would require him to do so.

Chisholm concludes that the problem of evil as a logical challenge is soluble. The moral problem of evil, as he calls it, is harder. This is the problem of suggesting in given cases what states of affairs actually defeat the evils we find in the world; the problem in other words, of finding a specific theodicy. On this he recommends the agnosticism which Pike implicitly recommends. Pike recommends this by classifying the problem thus understood as a 'noncrucial perplexity of relatively minor importance'.[3]

I would like to suggest that this defence of theism is not successful, since it is not open to the theist to eschew theodicy in the way Pike and Chisholm recommend.

III

Consider the following discussion. To counter the argument that diseases are an indication that the world is not the creation of a wholly good and powerful deity, a believer uses the following obviously bad arguments.

(i) Diseases are a way of reducing populations and preventing undue pressure on world food supplies.

(ii) Some diseases have aesthetically pleasing side-effects: tuberculosis sufferers often acquire a charming pink flush and according to Puccini can often sing better than healthy people.

Both these arguments fail, but for different reasons. The first one fails because it implies what is clearly false, that God could not manage to avoid over-population and food shortage by any means other than allowing epidemics. The second fails because it suggests that aesthetically pleasing side-effects are a morally sufficient reason for allowing the suffering attendant upon diseases. Sceptics often score points against believers by showing that more sophisticated defences end up on examination by committing the same errors. It is very important to stress that the basic

[3] Pike, 'Hume on Evil', p. 197 [p. 52 above].

challenge that these arguments, and others like them, fail to meet is a logical one rather than a moral or scientific one. This is especially hard to bear in mind in the second sort of case, because people who object to defences of this sort have to appeal to moral considerations in presenting their case. Nevertheless it is the consistency of theism that is at issue. In the first case the defence fails because it would only work if God were not omnipotent or were not omniscient; and these attributes are built into the *concept* of God. By saying the world is created by God the believer is ruling out this line of defence from the beginning. In the second case we reject the defence because it could only succeed if we were prepared to agree that minor aesthetic advantages could outweigh major moral and physical disadvantages in the assessment of evils like disease. We reject this evaluation, and in doing so we commit ourselves to saying that any being who placed such aesthetic considerations higher on the scale of choices than the physical ones would not be morally good. And moral goodness is also built into the concept of God. It is therefore inconsistent to present a defence of theism which attributes to God this particular preference.

These cases show, therefore, that for all the moral heat the problem of evil gives rise to it is correct to regard it as a logical issue, even though logical issues frequently do not give rise to heatedness. They also show, if they are as typical in form as I think they are, that the concept of God rules out a very large number of theistic defences, because they entail attributing to God limitations or preferences that are incompatible with his stated attributes. So although it may seem plausible for a theist to say, with Pike and Chisholm, that he does not need to commit himself to any particular theodicy, his very theism commits him at the very least to saying that a large number of possible theodicies are false, viz. all those that commit these errors. This entails the view that whatever reason God may have for allowing evils, it is a reason which is compatible with his omnipotence, omniscience, and his moral goodness. The situations regarding the omnipotence and the omniscience are fairly clear, though they generate interesting perplexities. I would like to concentrate here on the more complex attribute of moral goodness.

It is impossible to emphasise too much how deeply our thinking about religious matters has been affected by the absorption of the ideas of moral goodness and omnipotence into the concept of God. From time to time thinkers suggest that there is a God who is all-good but not all-powerful, or who is all-powerful but not all-good. Such suggestions clearly avoid the problem of evil; but we are merely bored by them. The alternatives are always tacitly restricted to two: either there is a God who is all-powerful and all-good, or there is no God at all. Christianity may not have convinced everybody, but it has certainly made us all very finicky. For (as Findlay has so forcibly reminded us[4]) the only God in whose existence we can evince interest is one whom it would be proper to worship. And worship in the Western world does not now mean the appeasing of an angry god or the encouragement of a weak one. It necessarily includes submission and moral reverence.

This important feature of the logic of theism goes so deep that it can be overlooked or misunderstood. In particular, since the very complexity of the demands made on the concept of deity by most people issues in a tacit rejection of many possible hypotheses intermediate between theism and atheism, there is a tendency for us to overlook the fact that there are a variety of reasons why the concept of God may be thought to have no application. An unbeliever may decide that no being is omnipotent, or that no being is omniscient, or that no being is all-good. Or he may decide that even if there exists a being who is all these things in the eyes of the believers he knows, the policies attributed to him are not such as to merit moral reverence. If he decides this he decides that the object of his friends' worship is not God; God does not exist. This is a *moral* rejection of theism. He may, yet again, reject theism on the ground that no being who was all-powerful, omniscient and all-good *by his friends' standards* would allow the evils that he and his friends both see to exist. *This* would be a logical reason for rejecting theism, even though it would lean, at critical points, on the attribution to God of moral goodness. Let us now explore this attribution with more care.

IV

There is something very odd about suggesting that although someone is morally good I have no idea what he would do in a wide range of situations; though it is quite possible for me to say that I do not know how he would handle some particularly knotty problem. The reason the second is possible is that familiar situations, where the good man's actions are predictable, do not supply precedents that yield ready answers to the knotty problems. In such cases the good man will likely serve as the source of such guidance, his suitability for this role deriving from his rectitude in more readily assessable situations. If this is correct it shows that evaluating someone as morally good may entail a readiness to agree to the wisdom of his decision on a difficult case just because it is he who is making the decision; but it also

---

[4] J. N. Findlay, 'Can God's Existence be Disproved?' in Flew and MacIntyre, *New Essays in Philosophical Theology* (London: SCM, 1955), 47–56.

shows that this cannot cover *all* cases. His very authority derives from our having certified him as good, and this derives from his decisions in straightforward instances. These I acknowledge as good on the basis of *my own* moral standards. If I see that someone else, however consistent or deliberative, acts in straightforward cases in ways that manifest standards different from my own, I will not accept his decisions as a guide, and not evaluate his decisions as morally good. (If I call such a person good I shall refer to his motives not his particular choices, and, what is important here, I shall not regard the reasons he offers for his decisions as morally sound or sufficient, even though I shall not blame him for adhering to them.) The case of God may be different; but I shall put this possibility on one side for the present. What I wish to emphasise at this stage is that the concept of moral goodness, however, blessedly general it may look, nevertheless requires, when actually applied to a particular person and his actions *by* some particular person (in other words, when actually used rather than mentioned) the attribution to the person it is applied to of a fairly specific set of choice-patterns. More than this, these choice-patterns are (and this is a necessary truth, and a familiar one) the choice-patterns *of the speaker*. In calling someone morally good, a speaker must have in mind some set of moral standards which the man he calls good follows in his conduct. In Hare's terms, he must have criteria of goodness which the man he calls good satisfies.[5] And these must be criteria he subscribes to himself (though he need not, of course, act on them—he can show he subscribes to them by feeling guilty at *not* acting on them). For it is inconsistent to say that someone else's decisions are made in accordance with correct moral standards but that one does not subscribe to these standards oneself. It is true that people's criteria of goodness differ. But in calling someone good I have to use *some* set of criteria. And these have, banally, to be my own.

Extrapolating to the divine case is hazardous. But I will nevertheless hazard the following. In calling God good one is not merely applying to him some general epithet of commendation, with no ancillary commitment on what he might be expected to do. Although one cannot require God to do anything, in calling him good one is necessarily expressing the conviction that his behaviour will satisfy a certain set of moral standards; and in this case as in others, it is vacuous to apply the concept of goodness without a fairly detailed idea of what these standards are. These standards are standards which the speaker must regard as applying to himself. If God's actions are approved because it is God who does them, this is the result of his manifesting, in general, the standards to which believers subscribe

---

[5] See *The Language of Morals* (Oxford: Clarendon Press, 1952), ch. 6.

themselves. I wish to conclude from this set of theses that in calling God good a theist is committed to saying that God's reasons for permitting evils must be reasons that are acceptable according to the believer's own set of moral standards. I wish to argue that in some important cases these are sufficiently restrictive to delineate a definite theodicy, even if it is not worked out in practice.

It is true that people's moral standards differ. But if they do, their concepts of God differ also; and, notoriously, one's concept of the will of God will be affected by one's independent moral judgments and the changes in them. Let us imagine two examples. A doctor, who believes in God, may find it hard to decide whether euthanasia is ever morally permissible. If he decides it never is, he will no doubt say euthanasia is contrary to the will of God. Let us now suppose that after some harrowing experiences he comes to believe that euthanasia is in some cases morally right. How will he describe his state of mind? I think it is clear he will not say, 'I used to agree with God that euthanasia is always wrong; but now I see he is mistaken.' He will say, if he retains his belief, that he has reversed his view of what God's will is. If he has changed his mind about euthanasia but not about the divine will he must abandon his theism. Secondly, let us imagine a consistent disciple of Oscar Wilde, who believes that aesthetic values can properly take precedence over ethical ones. We can expect such a person, if he believes in God, to ascribe such standards to him, and not, therefore, to repudiate the aesthetic defence of theism that I outlined earlier. 'Good', we are often reminded, is an evaluative term, and evaluations vary; but the concept of the being who gets the highest possible value-rating will vary with the scale of values of those who award the marks.

It should be emphasised that the word 'evil' is also an evaluative term. It is frequently said that observation will establish that the world contains evil. This is no doubt true, but the judgment that certain observed facts in the world are *to be classed as evils* is an evaluative judgment, however much the presence of those facts is established by observation. The theist can only be accused of inconsistency if the scale of values *he* uses commits him to saying that the facts *he* calls evil are allowed by God without reasons that *his* scale of values allows *him* to call morally sufficient; if the states of affairs *he* calls evil ones are undefeated on *his* scale of values by other facts conjoined with them. And of course the theist commits no logical mistake if he rejects the sceptic's value-scale, and insists that certain apparent evils are not evils at all, and certain apparent goods not goods at all. We must avoid posing the problem as one where the theist is attacked for accepting the existence of certain facts which only the critic regards as evil and ascribing to God reasons which only the critic would refuse to accept as morally good. This is a moral disagreement, not a logical one. We must also avoid the suggestion that the recognition of the evil facts is straightforwardly empirical, and their justification something more besides. If the facts are to pose a problem at all, they have to be accepted by the believer as potential counter-examples; and moral agreement here is too readily assumed. This is one of the many places where Christianity is paying a high price for its social success.

It might be agreed thus far that in ascribing the creation of the world to a being he classifies as all-good, the theist is ascribing to God a scale of values akin to his own, and that this circumscribes the range of possible reasons for allowing evil that he can consistently ascribe to God. But this may seem a long way from admitting that the theist is committed in most or any cases to the choice of one or two such reasons, or from admitting that he cannot in the tough cases resort to agnosticism on the grounds that God knows best and we do not understand.

Let us look at the second first. Certainly it seems reasonable in the case of any person endowed with high moral standing and authority to say that he should be the source of advice, and even to go so far as to say that *his* deciding one way rather than the other may serve, now and again, as a criterion of the correctness of the decision. If this can go for wise men, why not for the deity? Certainly there is a strong theological tradition which argues, against Plato, that some things are right because God does them rather than that God does them because they are right. I think the retort to this for our present purpose is not to contest this possibility, but to allow it and contest its relevance. Certainly I might say that I have accepted the Pope's moral authority and must therefore accept what he says on birth control, even though it runs counter to my own intuitions in these matters. This is allowable, but does have one consequence. Having decided that the authority's decision has to stand, I am not at liberty to leave my principles unaffected. If the Pope's stand on birth control is agreed to, so be it; but then I must sacrifice any principles I previously held with which this value-decision is inconsistent. Or I must show that there are no real inconsistencies, only apparent ones. Then of course those who object to the papal pronouncements have a straightforwardly moral disagreement with me—and it follows at once that their concept of God cannot be mine, or (what comes to the same here) that they think the Pope is not the infallible mouthpiece of the Holy Ghost. We do not need to insist that God's moral authority depends on his decisions' coinciding with our moral intuitions; but we do need to insist that if we accept a purported moral decision as coming from God, our moral intuitions have to be put aside as misleading if they do not coincide with that decision. What is necessary is that the moral principles the theist holds to and the ones he ascribes to God are the same. Here again we have to allow for the fact that an omnipotent and omniscient being will not be in situations that compare precisely with any in which we find ourselves (God, in fact, is never 'in' situations at all); but the principles he follows must be the same. A rich man with no family and a poor man with a large one will no doubt respond differently to the same request for money; yet their moral principles can be identical.

The problem of internal consistency would arise if some moral decision were ascribed to God which was inconsistent with moral principles the theist could not adjust or abandon, because they were previously held by him to have divine sanction. And it would arise also if the only logically possible reasons for the existence of a given evil were inconsistent with such principles. This would show, if it happened, that there are no morally sufficient reasons possible for the evil in question (that it is indefeasible), and that agnosticism regarding the reasons God actually might have does not provide an escape-route for the theist.

How would we know when such a case was before us? The answer, I think, is 'when the system of values adhered to by the believer, and ascribed to God, is one which contains specific guidance on what goods do and do not defeat certain evils, or upon what is and is not a morally sufficient reason for certain evils; when a given evil is agreed to exist, and the goods which might defeat it do not'. If this general answer is agreed to, it will readily be seen that some forms of theism would indeed permit a wide range of instances where a prudent agnosticism on matters of theodicy might be possible, and others would not permit any range at all. One could only argue from this point on with particular theists with particular scales of value. Catholics would have much less room for manœuvre than Unitarians. I propose to discuss the case of a moderately sophisticated biblical Protestant.

V

It would be absurd to attempt a detailed characterisation of Christian ethics here. But two features of it are particularly striking and important. The first is the fact that Christian principles are in many cases rules for assigning priorities in choice, and serve as guides to relatively complex moral situations, not as mere classifications of certain states of affairs as good or bad. To illustrate, let us consider the contrast between Christian ethics and hedonistic ethics. The latter are based upon the fundamentally simple assertions that pleasure is the main or only good and pain the main or only evil. The fundamental principles of Christian ethics, such as the Ten Commandments, deal directly with complex moral situations such as stealing, murder, or adultery, rather than with their ingredients. Notoriously they do not even say unambiguously whether pleasure and pain are good or bad; they direct attention at once onto occasions where we are called upon, as moral agents, to assign a precedence among various possibilities. However good pleasure may be, or however bad frustration may be, if the potential partner in the enterprise is another man's wife, the pleasure is forbidden. The goodness of the pleasure, if any, is defeated by the badness of the violation of the marriage-bond; and the badness, if any, of the frustration, is defeated by the goodness of the observance of it. However good, if at all, the acquisition of property is, the badness of depriving someone to whom it already belongs defeats it. The ethic makes fundamental use of notions such as temptation and resistance, which themselves suggest this sort of complexity of choice. The second feature requiring emphasis here is the fact that as it finds expression in the New Testament, the Christian ethic places uniquely high value on certain personal qualities and relationships, founded upon love. The value assigned to pleasure or pain would seem to depend upon their relationship to these qualities (or to their opposites) in complex situations. Clearly in the Christian tradition pleasure in the infliction of suffering makes the infliction worse, not better; although the same conclusion can be arrived at in a hedonistic ethic, a good deal of casuistic footwork needs to be done to reach it. Christianity obviously rejects the thesis that pleasure is the only good, and does not clearly embrace even the modest thesis that it is good *per se*, i.e. in the absence of bad accompaniments. It even more obviously rejects the principle that pain is the only, or even the greatest, evil, though in enjoining its diminution it would seem to embrace the thesis that it is *per se* bad, i.e. bad when not a means to that which is prized, such as steadfastness, forgiveness or humility.

If these brief characterisations of the ethics associated with one familiar form of theism are correct, it follows, I would suggest, that its adherents are committed to the principles of a familiar form of theodicy, and embroiled thereby in its problems. For they are committed to a moral scheme which requires them to judge the value of certain states of affairs in the light of that of others. This, in turn, will determine their judgments on what are, and (equally importantly) what are not, morally sufficient reasons for certain kinds of action or inaction. As theists they are committed to ascribing this very scheme of moral priorities to God, to ascribing to him, in other words, a set of policies which have to determine what evils have to be allowed by him in his creation. More accurately, they are committed to ascribing to him the particular sorts of reasons which *their* ethic would permit them to regard as sufficient for the evils which his creation can independently be seen to contain. They have to say, in other words, that the universe is run on Christian principles, and when they encounter a state of affairs which, by those principles, is evil, they must in consistency hold that it is permitted by God for reasons which are applications of those principles. This follows from calling God good and this state of affairs evil. More specifically, if certain forms of spiritual life and relationship have the highest place in the application of Christian principles, God too must value them highly, and evils he permits must only *appear* to contravene the ascription of these values to him; when rightly understood they have to be thought of as furthering them. We seem to be involved, therefore, in the traditional theological exercise of regarding all evils as justified, if God exists, by the possibility of some spiritual benefit of which they are the necessary condition.

This is not to say that a commitment to a general theodicy of this sort is tantamount to agreement to any particular theologian's justification of a particular historical evil, like the Lisbon earthquake. It is, however, tantamount to the acceptance of a limited *range* of possible explanations (those that entail ascribing to God a choice good by Christian standards) and the rejection of others. The problem becomes the acute difficulty of internal consistency it is traditionally alleged to be when the permissible range provides no reason that will fit some state of affairs that is admittedly an evil one. (A theodicy emphasising spiritual benefits can perhaps offer reason for human suffering, but seems unable to deal with animal pain, for example. Such an evil may not be in practice the worst, but it may be in theology the most intractable.)

Even this limitation allows a wide range of theological interpretation. Two areas of potential variation should be mentioned. There is, first of all, some ambiguity in the ascription to God of the value-scale of a believer. Our moral principles tell us what to do in certain sets of circumstances. God is not limited by circumstances, but creates them. Some principles tell us what to do in bad circumstances, e.g. the rule that we should forgive injuries. In ascribing such a standard to God we do of course imply that he forgives those who commit offences against him. But do we also imply that he so prizes forgiveness in us that his goodness requires him to provide (or allow) the unpleasant occasions that call for its exercise? Granted that when Smith injures Jones, Jones ought to forgive Smith; is the evil of Smith's injury to Jones justified by the fact that only it, or something like it, could afford Jones an opportunity to show forgiveness? It is at least plausible to argue that a theodicy that would justify the evil by reference to its potential for training men in the right spiritual responses would require us to ascribe to God this very strong sort of adherence to the value of forgiveness; but it is not obviously necessary to do so. Furthermore, the spiritual states most highly prized in the Christian tradition are only possible for free agents; hence the great emphasis on man's freedom of choice in all the major theodicies. This emphasis enables apologists to distinguish between natural evils like pain (evils which can elicit good states of mind but which are not caused by bad states of mind) and moral evils like vengefulness which *are* bad states of mind. The latter can all be blamed on the misuse of human free choice, which is a logically necessary condition of good states of mind like love and forgiveness, or fortitude, which can turn natural evils into ingredients of good situations. From this in turn it follows that the badness of many actual bad states of mind can be regarded as justified by the fact that their very possibility is a necessary condition of the free choice which is logically required for the chance of the good states of mind which have not, on these occasions, materialised. This generates the problem of whether free choice is itself a good which God fosters. It is not obvious what the apologist should say to this. All he *has* to say is that the highest goods in the Christian tradition are states of mind and relationships which cannot exist without free choice; so that the presence of some evils which free choice can lead to (such as revenge instead of forgiveness) is due to the wrong exercise of a faculty which one has to have to achieve the preferred states of mind. This would seem to leave open, and perhaps to render unimportant, the issue of the intrinsic value of free choice itself.

These two areas of potential controversy are enough to show that there is much freedom of theological manœuvre even within the fairly specific value scheme of Christian theism. It is nevertheless true, however, that Christian theism, by calling God omnipotent and omniscient *and* wholly good, requires its adherents to hold that he permits such evils as there are for Christian reasons; and that these involve his being said to allow them in the interests of certain spiritual states in his creatures, who have, to participate in these states, to be capable of free choice. A Christian theist, therefore, is committed to some form or other of the traditional 'free-will defence'.

VI

To sum up: I have argued that any theist, in calling his God good, ascribes to him his own moral principles, and implies that the world is created and governed in a way which ideally represents their exercise. Any evils he admits to being in the world must, he must say, be allowed by God because their presence is at least compatible with the futherance of those ends regarded on the very scale which classes the evils *as* evils, as being supremely good. The existence of any admitted evil not so compatible would refute the believer's theism; for to admit its existence would be to introduce an element of inconsistency into the theist's position. When this is recognised it becomes clear that a theist is committed to a scheme of theodicy in two ways at least. He cannot remain confidently agnostic about the range of purposes for which God would allow evils. And the more specific his moral code is on moral priorities, the more precise he has to be in suggesting possible divine reasons for particular evils. I have suggested that *Christian* theism is quite specific on moral priorities, and that it lays fundamental stress on certain relationships and states of mind. A Christian theist, faced with what he admits to be an evil, has therefore to hold that God allows it because the existence or possibility of it, or of something equally bad, is a necessary condition of some such relationship or state of mind. To admit the existence of an evil which demonstrably cannot have this function would be to admit a proposition inconsistent with Christian theism. For such an evil would be *pointless*. It is logically inconsistent for a theist to admit the existence of a pointless evil.

Pike argued that for the problem of evil to present a logical challenge to the theist, it must be possible to show that his proposition III:

> A being who is omnipotent and omniscient would have no morally sufficient reason for allowing instances of evil

is a necessary truth; and that it is not possible to show it to be one. In all its high generality it is not. I have tried to show, however, that in a given form of theism the concept of a morally sufficient reason may be sufficiently restricted to render it impossible for an omnipotent and omniscient being to have morally sufficient reasons for some evils. If such evils seem to exist in fact, then the problem of evil presents itself to the theist as the logical difficulty it has traditionally been thought to be.

Similarly, Chisholm's suggestion that a theist can hold that every evil is defeated without claiming to know by what, must contend with the fact that in a given form of theism the range of possible defeating factors may be specifically understood and incorporated in its moral requirements. If it should seem that a particular evil is not so defeasible its existence poses a logical difficulty to the theist as it has traditionally been thought to do.

V

GOD, EVIL, AND THE METAPHYSICS OF FREEDOM

ALVIN PLANTINGA

1. THE PROBLEM

In this and the following chapter [of *The Nature of Necessity*] I wish to apply some of the foregoing ideas to two traditional topics in the philosophy of religion: the Problem of Evil (which will occupy this chapter) and the Ontological Argument. Perhaps the former constitutes the most formidable objection to theistic belief—or so, at any rate, it has seemed to many. A multitude of philosophers have held that the existence of evil is at the least an embarrassment for those who accept belief in God.[1] And most contemporary philosophers who hold that evil constitutes a difficulty for theistic belief claim to detect *logical inconsistency* in beliefs a theist typically accepts. So, for example, according to H. J. McCloskey:

Evil is a problem for the theist in that a *contradiction* is involved in the fact of evil, on the one hand, and the belief in the omnipotence and perfection of God on the other.[2]

J. L. Mackie urges the same charge:

I think, however, that a more telling criticism can be made by way of the traditional problem of evil. Here it can be shown, not that religious beliefs lack rational support, but that they are positively irrational, that the several parts of the essential theological doctrine are *inconsistent* with one another.[3]

And Henry David Aiken substantially repeats this allegation.[4]

Now the alleged contradiction arises, of course, when we consider the fact that evil exists together with the belief that God exists and is omniscient,

Alvin Plantinga, 'God, Evil, and the Metaphysics of Freedom' from Ch. 9 (pp. 164–93) of *The Nature of Necessity* (Clarendon Press, 1974). Reprinted by permission of Oxford University Press.

[1] Epicurus, for example, as well as David Hume, some of the French Encyclopedists, F. H. Bradley, J. McTaggart, J. S. Mill, and many others.
[2] 'God and Evil', *Philosophical Quarterly*, 10 (1960), 97 [italics Plantinga's].
[3] 'Evil and Omnipotence', *Mind*, 64 (1955), 200 [Chapter I, p. 25, of this collection; italics Plantinga's].
[4] 'God and Evil', *Ethics*, 68 (1957-8), 79.

omnipotent, and wholly good or morally perfect. Obviously these propositions are not *formally* inconsistent; the resources of logic alone do not enable us to deduce an explicit contradiction from their conjunction. But then presumably the atheologian—he who offers arguments against the existence of God—never meant to hold that there was a formal contradiction here; he meant instead that the conjunction of these two propositions is necessarily false, false in every possible world. To show that he is right, therefore, he must produce a proposition that is at least plausibly thought to be necessary and whose conjunction with our original two formally yields a contradiction.

I have argued elsewhere[5] that it is extremely difficult to find any such proposition. I have also argued[6] that the *Free Will Defence* can be used to show that in fact these propositions are not inconsistent. In what follows I wish to look again at the issues involved in the *Free Will Defence*—this time from the vantage point of the foregoing ideas about *possible worlds*.

2. THE FREE WILL DEFENCE

The Free Will Defence is an effort to show that

(1) God is omnipotent, omniscient, and wholly good

(which I shall take to entail that God exists) is not inconsistent with

(2) There is evil in the world.

That is, the Free Will Defender aims to show that there is a possible world in which (1) and (2) are both true. Now one way to show that a proposition p is consistent with a proposition q is to produce a third proposition r whose conjunction with p is consistent and entails q. r, of course, need not be true or known to be true; it need not be so much as plausible. All that is required of it is that it be consistent with p, and in conjunction with the latter entail q. What the Free Will Defender must do, therefore, is find such a proposition.

But first, some preliminary definitions and distinctions. What does the Free Will Defender mean when he says that people are or may be *free*? If a person S is free with respect to a given action, then he is free to perform that action and free to refrain; no causal laws and antecedent conditions determine either that he will perform the action, or that he will not. It is within his power, at the time in question, to perform the action, and within

---

[5] *God and Other Minds: A Study of the Rational Justification of Belief in God* (Ithaca, NY: Cornell University Press, 1967), ch. 5.

[6] Ibid., ch. 6.

his power to refrain. Consider the state *U* of the universe up to the time he takes or decides to take the action in question. If *S* is free with respect to that action, then it is causally or naturally possible both that *U* hold and *S* *take* (or decide to take) the action, and that *U* hold and *S* *refrain* from it.[7] Further, let us say that an action is *morally significant*, for a given person at a given time, if it would be wrong for him to perform the action then but right to refrain, or vice versa. Keeping a promise, for example, would typically be morally significant, as would refusing induction into the army; having an apple for lunch (instead of an orange) would not. And, a person *goes wrong with respect to a morally significant action* if it is wrong for him to perform it and he does, or wrong for him not to and he does not. Still further, suppose we say that a person is *significantly free*, on a given occasion, if he is then free with respect to an action that is morally significant for him. And finally, we must distinguish between *moral* evil and *natural* evil. The former is evil that results from some human being's going wrong with respect to an action that is morally significant for him; any other evil is natural evil.[8] Suffering due to human cruelty—Hitler's treatment of the Jews, for example—would be an example of the former; suffering resulting from an earthquake or tidal wave, an example of the latter. An analogous distinction is made between moral and natural good.

Given these definitions and distinctions, we can make a preliminary statement of the Free Will Defence as follows. A world containing creatures who are sometimes significantly free (and freely perform more good than evil actions) is more valuable, all else being equal, than a world containing no free creatures at all. Now God can create free creatures, but he cannot *cause* or *determine* them to do only what is right. For if he does so, then they are not significantly free after all; they do not do what is right *freely*. To create creatures capable of *moral good*, therefore, he must create creatures capable of moral evil; and he cannot leave these creatures *free* to perform evil and at the same time prevent them from doing so. God did in fact create significantly free creatures; but some of them went wrong in the exercise of their freedom: this is the source of moral evil. The fact that these free creatures sometimes go wrong, however, counts neither against God's omnipotence nor against his goodness; for he could have forestalled the occurrence of moral evil only by excising the possibility of moral good.

I said earlier that the Free Will Defender tries to find a proposition that is consistent with

---

[7] Of course it does not follow that if *S* is free with respect to some of his actions, then what he will do is in principle unpredictable or unknowable.

[8] This distinction is not very precise (how, exactly, are we to construe 'results from'?); but perhaps it will serve our present purposes.

(1) God is omniscient, omnipotent, and wholly good

and together with (1) entails that there is evil. According to the Free Will Defence, we must find this proposition somewhere in the above story. The heart of the Free Will Defence is the claim that it is *possible* that God could not have created a universe containing moral good (or as much moral good as this one contains) without creating one containing moral evil.

3. THE OBJECTION

A formidable objection goes like this. Surely it is logically possible that there be a world containing significantly free creatures who always do what is right. There is certainly no contradiction or inconsistency in this idea. If so, however, there are possible worlds containing moral good but no moral evil. Now the theist says that God is omnipotent—which means, roughly, that there are no non-logical limits to his power. Accordingly, he could have created just any possible world he chose, including those containing moral good but no moral evil. If it is possible that there be a world containing significantly free creatures who never do what is wrong, then it follows that an omnipotent God could have created such a world. If so, however, the Free Will Defence must be mistaken in its insistence upon the possibility that God, though omnipotent, could not have created a world containing moral good without permitting moral evil. As Mackie puts it:

If God has made men such that in their free choices they sometimes prefer what is good and sometimes what is evil, why could he not have made men such that they always freely choose the good? If there is no logical impossibility in a man's freely choosing the good on one, or on several occasions, there cannot be a logical impossibility in his freely choosing the good on every occasion. God was not, then, faced with a choice between making innocent automata and making beings who, in acting freely, would sometimes go wrong; there was open to him the obviously better possibility of making beings who would act freely but always go right. Clearly, his failure to avail himself of this possibility is inconsistent with his being both omnipotent and wholly good.[9]

Was it within the power of an omnipotent God to create just any logically possible world? This is the important question for the Free Will Defence, and a subtle question it is. Leibniz, as you recall, insisted that *this* world, the actual world, must be the best of all possible worlds. His reasoning is as follows. Before God created anything at all, he was confronted with an enormous range of choices; he could have created or actualized any of the

---

[9] 'Evil and Omnipotence', p. 209 [p. 33 above].

myriads of different possible worlds. Being perfectly good, he must have chosen to create the best world he could; being omnipotent, he was able to create just any possible world he pleased. He must, therefore, have chosen the best of all possible worlds; and hence *this* world, the one he did create, must be (despite appearances) the best possible. Now Mackie agrees with Leibniz that God, if omnipotent, could have created just any world he pleased and would have created the best world he could. But while Leibniz draws the conclusion that *this* world must be the best possible, Mackie concludes instead that there is no omnipotent, wholly good God. For, he says, it is obvious enough that this actual world is not the best possible.

The Free Will Defender disagrees with both Leibniz and Mackie. First, we have the question whether *there is* such a thing as the best of all possible worlds, or even *a* best. Perhaps for any world you pick, there is a better. But what is really characteristic and central to the Free Will Defence is the claim that God, though omnipotent, could not have created just any possible world he pleased; and this is the claim we must investigate.

4. WHICH WORLDS COULD GOD HAVE CREATED?

We speak of God as *creating* the world; yet if it is α the possible world that is in fact actual, conceived as a state of affairs of which we speak, what we say is false. For a thing is created only if there is a time before which it does not exist; and this is patently false of α, as it is of any state of affairs. What God has created are the heavens and the earth and all that they contain; he has not created himself, or numbers, propositions, properties, or states of affairs: these have no beginnings. We can say, however, that God *actualizes* states of affairs; his creative activity results in their being or becoming actual. God has *created* Socrates, but *actualized* the state of affairs consisting in the latter's existence. And God is actualizing but not creating α.

Furthermore, while we may properly say that God actualizes α, it does not follow that he actualizes every state of affairs the latter includes. He does not, as previously mentioned, actualize his own existence; that is to say, he does not create himself. Nor does he create his own properties; hence he does not actualize the state of affairs consisting in the existence of such properties as omniscience, omnipotence, moral excellence, and *being the creator of the heavens and the earth*. But the same is really true of other properties too; God no more creates the property of being red than that of omnipotence. Properties are not creatable: to suppose that they have been created is to suppose that although they exist now, there was a time at which they did not; and this seems clearly false. Again, since God did not create numbers, propositions, pure sets, and the like, he did not actualize the states of affairs consisting in the existence of these things. Nor does he actualize such other necessary states of affairs as *7+5's equalling 12*. Necessary states of affairs do not owe their actuality to the creative activity of God. So if we speak of God as actualizing α, we should not think of him as actualizing every state of affairs α includes. But perhaps we may say that he actualizes every *contingent* state of affairs included in α; and perhaps we may say that God *can* actualize a given possible world *W* only if he can actualize every contingent state of affairs *W* includes. And now we can put our question: can an omnipotent being actualize just any possible world he pleases—that is, is every possible world such that an omnipotent being can actualize it?

Here more distinctions are needed. Although there are any number of possible worlds in which Abraham never met Melchizedek, God can actualize none of them. That is, he can no longer actualize any of them; for Abraham in fact *did* meet Melchizedek (let us suppose) and not even an omnipotent being can bring it about that Abraham did *not* meet Melchizedek; it is too late for that. Take any time *t*; at *t* there will be any number of worlds God cannot actualize; for there will be any number of worlds in which things go differently before *t*. So God cannot actualize any world in which Abraham did not meet Melchizedek; but perhaps God *could have* actualized such worlds. Perhaps we should say that God could have actualized a world *W* if and only if for every contingent state of affairs *S* included by *W*, there is a time at which it is (timelessly) within his power to actualize *S*.[10] And now perhaps the atheologian's claim may be put as follows:

(3) If God is omnipotent, then God could have actualized just any possible world.

But this will not be entirely accurate either—not, at any rate, if God himself is a contingent being. For if he is a contingent being, then there are worlds in which he does not exist; and clearly he could not have actualized any of *these* worlds. Clearly the only worlds within God's power to actualize are those that include his existence. So suppose we restrict our attention to these worlds. (In Chapter X [of *The Nature of Necessity*] I argue that this is no real restriction.) Is it true that

---

[10] To say that God could have actualized *W* suggests that there is some time—some past time—such that God could have performed the action of actualizing *W* at that time. Thus it suggests that actualizing a possible world requires but a moment or at any rate a limited stretch of time. This suggestion must be resisted; perhaps God's actualizing a possible world requires an unlimited span of time; perhaps it requires his action at *every time*, past, present, and future.

(4) If God is omnipotent, then he could have actualized just any world that includes his existence?

Still more distinctions are needed. In particular, we must look more closely at the idea of *freedom*. According to the Free Will Defender, God thought it good to create free persons. And a person is free with respect to an action *A* at a time *t* only if no causal laws and antecedent conditions determine either that he performs *A* at *t* or that he refrains from so doing. This is not a comment upon the ordinary use of the word 'free': that use may or may not coincide with the Free Will Defender's. What God thought good, on this view, was the existence of creatures whose activity is not causally determined—who, like he himself, are centres of creative activity. The freedom of such creatures will no doubt be *limited* by causal laws and antecedent conditions. They will not be free to do just anything; even if I am free, I am not free to run a mile in two minutes. Of course my freedom is also *enhanced* by causal laws; it is only by virtue of such laws that I am free to build a house or walk on the surface of the earth. But if I am free with respect to an action *A*, then causal laws and antecedent conditions determine neither that I take *A* nor that I refrain.

More broadly, if I am free with respect to an action *A* then God does not *bring it about* or *cause it to be the case* either that I take or that I refrain from this action; he neither causes this to be so through the laws he establishes, nor by direct intervention, nor in any other way. For if he *brings it about* or *causes it to be the case* that I take *A*, then I am not free to *refrain* from *A*, in which case I am not free with respect to *A*. Although of course God may cause it to be the case that I *am* free with respect to *A*, he cannot cause it to be the case either that I freely take or that I freely refrain from this action—and this though he is omnipotent.[11] But then it follows that there are plenty of contingent states of affairs such that it is not within the power of God to bring about their actuality, or cause them to be actual. He cannot cause it to be the case that I freely refrain from an action *A*; for if he does so, he causes it to be the case that I refrain from *A*, in which case I do not do so *freely*.

Now I have been using 'brings it about that' as a rough synonym for 'causes it to be the case that'. Suppose we take the term 'actualize' the same way. Then God can actualize a given state of affairs *S* only if he can cause it to be the case that *S*, causes *S* to be actual. And then there will be many contingent states of affairs *S* such that there is no time at which God can actualize *S*. But we said a page back that

[11] Just to simplify matters I shall henceforth take it for granted that *if God exists, he is omnipotent* is a necessary truth.

(5) God could have actualized a given possible world W if and only if for every contingent state of affairs S that W includes, there is a time at which God can actualize S.

Given just the possibility that there are created free agents, it follows that there are any number of possible worlds including God's existence and *also* including a contingent state of affairs S such that there is no time at which God can actualize S. Hence (contrary to (4) and to the atheologian's claim) there are any number of possible worlds that God could not have actualized, even though they include his existence: all those containing a state of affairs consisting in some creature's freely taking or refraining from some action. Since a world containing moral good is such a world, it follows that God could not have actualized any world containing moral good; *a fortiori* he could not have actualized a world containing moral good but no moral evil.

The atheologian's proper retort, I think, is as follows. Suppose we concede that not even God can cause it to be the case that I freely refrain from A. Even so, he *can* cause me to be free with respect to A, and to be in some set S of circumstances including appropriate laws and antecedent conditions. He may also know, furthermore, that *if* he creates me and causes me to be free in these circumstances, I will refrain from A. If so, there is a state of affairs he can actualize, cause to be actual, such that if he does so, then I will freely refrain from A. In a broader sense of 'bring about', therefore, he *can* bring it about that I freely refrain from A. In the narrower sense there are many contingent states of affairs he cannot bring about; what is relevant to the Free Will Defence, however, is not this narrow sense, but the broader one. For what is really at issue is whether for each possible world there are some actions God could have taken such that if he *had*, then that morally perfect world (one including moral good but no moral evil) would have been actual.

Perhaps we can sharpen this point. The narrow sense of 'bring about' is such that the sentence

(6) If God brings it about that I refrain from A, then I do not freely refrain from A

expresses a necessary truth. You are free with respect to an action A only if God does not bring it about or cause it to be the case that you refrain from A. But now suppose God knows that if he creates you free with respect to A in some set S of circumstances, you will refrain from A; suppose further that he brings it about (narrow sense) that you *are* free with respect to A in S; and suppose finally that you do in fact freely refrain from A. Then in a broader sense of 'bring about' we could properly say that God has brought it about that you freely refrain from A. We must make a corresponding distinction, then, between a stronger and a weaker sense of 'actualize'. In the strong sense, God can actualize only what he can *cause* to be actual; in that sense he cannot actualize any state of affairs including the existence of creatures who freely take some action or other. But so far we have no reason for supposing that the same holds for *weak* actualization. And what the atheologian requires for his argument, presumably, is not that every possible world (including the existence of God) is one God could have actualized in the *strong* sense; weak actualization is enough for his purposes. What is at issue is not the question whether each world is such that God could have actualized it in the *strong* sense, but (roughly) whether for each world *W* there is something he could have done—some series of actions he could have taken—such that if he had, *W* would have been actual. For if God is wholly good and it *was* within his power thus to secure the actuality of a perfect world, then presumably he would have done so. Accordingly the Free Will Defender's claim—that God could not have actualized a world containing moral good without actualizing one containing moral evil—is either irrelevant or unsubstantiated: irrelevant if 'actualize' is taken in the strong sense and unsubstantiated otherwise.

Since it is weak actualization that is relevant, let us henceforth use 'actualize' to mean 'weakly actualize'. And so our question is this: could God have actualized just any possible world that includes his existence?

Perhaps we can best proceed by way of an example. Curley Smith, the mayor of Boston, is opposed to the proposed freeway route. From the Highway Department's point of view, his objection is frivolous; he complains that the route would require destruction of the Old North Church along with some other antiquated and structurally unsound buildings. The Director of Highways offers him a bribe of $35,000 to drop his opposition. Unwilling to break with the fine old traditions of Bay State politics, Curley accepts; whereupon the Director spends a sleepless night wondering whether he could have had Curley for $20,000. That is to say, Smedes wonders which of

(7) If Curley had been offered $20,000, he would have accepted the bribe

or

(8) If Curley had been offered $20,000, he would have rejected the bribe

is true.

5. COUNTERFACTUALS

But here an objection arises. (7) and (8), of course, are *counterfactual conditionals*. Subject to all the difficulty and obscurity of that peculiar breed, they contain traps for the unwary. Here, for example, we seem to be assuming that either (7) or (8) must be true. But what is the justification for that? How do we know that at least one of them *is* true? What leads us to suppose that there is an answer to the question what Curley would have done, had he been offered a bribe of $20,000?

This question can be amplified. According to an interesting proposal[12] a counterfactual conditional such as (7) can be explained as follows. Consider those possible worlds that include its antecedent; and then of these consider that one W that is *most similar to* the actual world. (7) is true if and only if its consequent—that is,

(9) Curley took the bribe

is true in W. A counterfactual is true if and only if its antecedent is impossible, or its consequent is true in the world most similar to the actual in which its antecedent is.

This intriguing proposal provokes questions. In the first place, the required notion of similarity is in many respects problematic. What does it mean to say that one possible world is more similar to α than another? In this context, is there such a thing as similarity *überhaupt*, or should we speak only of similarity in given respects? These are good questions; we have no time to linger over them, but let us pause just long enough to note that we do seem to have an intuitive grasp of this notion—the notion of similarity between states of affairs. Secondly, the proposal presumes that for each contingently false proposition *p* there is a possible world including *p* that is uniquely closest (i.e. most similar) to the actual world. So take any such proposition and any proposition *q*: on the proposal in question, either *if p then q* or *if p then ~q* will be true. This may seem a bit strong: *if I had red hair, Napoleon would not have lost the Battle of Waterloo* is obviously false, but *if I had red hair Napoleon would have won the Battle of Waterloo* does not seem much better. (*Even if*, perhaps, but not *if*.) Indeed, take any such proposition *p*: on this view there is some entire possible world W such that the counterfactual *if p had been true, W would have obtained* holds. But is it not unduly extravagant to claim that there is some possible world W such that if I had red hair, W would have been actual? Is there a possible world

---

[12] See Robert Stalnaker, 'A Theory of Conditionals', in N. Rescher, *Studies in Logical Theory* (*American Philosophical Quarterly*, supplementary monograph, 1968), 98.

W^* such that if α had not been actual, W^* would have been? Is there reason to believe that there is a world including the antecedent of (7) and (8) (call it 'A') that is *uniquely closest* to α? Perhaps several worlds include it, each such that none including it is closer.[13] And this leads directly to our question. Perhaps there is a family of closest worlds in which A is true; and perhaps in some of these

(9) Curley accepted the bribe

is true, while in others it is

(10) Curley rejected the bribe

that enjoys that distinction. If so, then perhaps we must conclude that neither (7) nor (8) is true; there is then no such thing as *what Curley would have done* under the envisaged circumstances.

Indeed, perhaps the objector need not rest content with the idle suspicion that there may be such a family of worlds; perhaps he can go further. There are possible worlds W and W^* that include A and are *exactly alike* up to 10.00 a.m., 10 November 1973, the time at which Curley makes his response to the bribe offer; in W Curley accepts the bribe and in W^* he does not. If $t = 10.00$ a.m., 10 November 1973, let us say that W and W^* *share an initial segment up to t*. We could call the t-initial segment of W 'S_w^{-t}' the subscript 'W' indicating that S is a segment of W, and the superscript '$-t$' indicating that this segment terminates at t. (S_w^{+t} would be the unending segment of W that begins at t.) And of course $S_w^{-t} = S_w^{-t}$.

It is not entirely easy to give a rigorous characterization of this notion of an initial segment. It is clear that if W and W^* share an initial segment terminating at t, then for any object x and for any time t^* earlier than t, x exists in W at t^* if and only if x exists in W^* at t^*. But we cannot say that if a thing x has a property P in W at t^*, then x has P in W^* at t^*. For one property Curley has at t^* in W is that of being such that at t he will take the bribe; and of course he does not have *that* property in W^* at t^*. Perhaps there is an intuitive notion of a *non-temporal* property under which we can say that if at t^* x has a non-temporal property P in W then x also has P in W^* at t^*. The problem of course is to say just what this notion of a non-temporal property amounts to; and that is by no means easy. Still the idea of a pair of worlds W and W^* sharing an initial segment is fairly clear; roughly, it amounts to

---

[13] More radically, perhaps there are no such closest worlds at all; perhaps for any world including A, there is a closer that also includes it. See David Lewis, *Counterfactuals* (Blackwell, 1973), ch. 1, sect. 1.3. According to Lewis, a counterfactual $A \to B$ is true if and only if either A is impossible or some world W in which A and C hold is more similar to the actual world than any world in which A and C hold. In writing this section I have benefited from Lewis's analysis; I am grateful to him for a criticism that triggered substantial improvement in the argument of this chapter.

saying that the two worlds are the same up to a certain time t. And if there is no time t^* later than t such that $S_w^{-t^*}, = S_w^{-t^*}$, then at t W and W^* *branch*. Of course there will be a large class of worlds sharing S_w^{-t} with W and W^*; and if e is an event that takes place in W but not in W^*, there will be a class of worlds including S_w^{-t} in which e occurs and another class including it in which e does not.

Suppose we concede (or pretend) that we have this notion of an initial segment well in hand. It may then appear that we can construct a convincing argument for the conclusion that neither (7) nor (8) is true. For each of W and W^* are as similar to α, in the relevant respects, as any world including A. But if they share S_w^{-t} then are they not *equally* similar, in the appropriate ways, to α? Up to t things are just alike in these two worlds. What happens after t seems scarcely relevant to the question of what Curley would have done if offered the bribe. We should conclude, therefore, that W and W^* are equally similar to α; but these two worlds resemble α as much as any others; hence the closest worlds in which A is true do not speak with a single voice; hence neither (7) nor (8) is true.[14]

What about this argument? In the first place, it proves too much. It gains a specious plausibility from the case we are considering. We do not know, after all, whether Curley would have accepted the bribe—it is a fairly small one and perhaps his pride would have been injured. Let us ask instead whether he would have accepted a bribe of $36,000, everything else being as much as possible like the actual world. Here the answer seems fairly clear: indeed he would have. And this despite the fact that for any possible world W as close as you please to α in which Curley takes the bribe, there is a world W^* that shares the appropriate initial segment with W in which he manfully refuses it.

The argument suffers from another defect, however—one which is more instructive. Suppose we approach it by way of another example. Royal Robbins is climbing the Dihedral Wall of El Capitan. The usual method involving ropes and belays has lost its appeal; he is soloing the Wall unprotected. Just as he reaches Thanksgiving Ledge, some 2500 feet above the Valley floor, one of his hand holds breaks out. He teeters precariously on one foot, regains his balance, and leaps lightly on to the ledge, where he bivouacs; the next day he continues triumphantly to the top. Now suppose we consider

   (11) If Robbins had slipped and fallen at Thanksgiving Ledge, he would
         have been killed.

---

[14] This argument surfaced in discussion with David Kaplan.

No doubt we are initially inclined to accept this proposition. But should we? In the actual world Robbins did not fall at Thanksgiving Ledge; instead he nimbly climbed on to it and spent a comfortable night there. Now what happens in the closest worlds in which he falls? Well, there is at least one of these—call it W'—in which he falls at t just as he is reaching the Ledge; at the next moment $t+1$ (as close as you please to t) he shows up exactly where he is in α at $t+1$; and everything else goes just as it does in a. Would W' not be more similar to the actual world than any in which he hurtles down to the Valley floor, thus depriving American rockclimbing of its most eloquent spokesman? And if so, should we not rate (11) false?

The answer, of course, is that we are neglecting causal or natural *laws*. Our world α contains a number of these, and they are among its more impressive constituents. In particular, there are some implying (together with the relevant antecedent conditions) that anyone who falls unroped and unprotected from a ledge 2500 feet up a vertical cliff, moves with increasing rapidity towards the centre of the earth, finally arriving with considerable impact at its surface. Evidently not all of these laws are present in W', for the latter shares the relevant initial conditions with α but in it Robbins does not fall to the Valley floor—instead, after a brief feint in that direction, he reappears on the cliff. And once we note that these laws do not hold in W', so the claim goes, we shall no longer be tempted to think it very similar to α, where they do hold.

No doubt there is truth in this reply. But the relationship between causal laws and counterfactuals, like that between Guinevere and Sir Lancelot, is both intimate and notorious. A salient feature of the former, indeed, is that (unlike accidental generalizations) they are said to support or entail counter-factuals. So instead of denigrating W' on the grounds that its laws differ from α's, we might as well have complained, in view of the above con-nection, that W' lacks some of α's counterfactuals. One measure of similarity between worlds involves the question whether they share their counterfactuals.

We should be unduly hasty, I think, if we drew the conclusion that the possible worlds explanation of counterfactuals is viciously circular or of no theoretical interest or importance. But it does follow that we cannot as a rule *discover* the truth value of a counterfactual by asking whether its consequent holds in those worlds most similar to the actual in which its antecedent holds. For one feature determining the similarity of worlds is whether they share their counterfactuals.

And of course this is relevant to the argument we have been examining. As you recall, it went like this. There are worlds W and W^* that share S_w^{-t}; these worlds, therefore, are equally similar to α in the relevant respects. In W, however, Curley takes the bribe; in W^* he refuses. Accordingly, neither (7) nor (8) is such that its consequent is true in the closest worlds to α in which its antecedent is; hence neither (7) nor (8) is true. But now we see that this argument does not settle the matter. For from the fact that W and W^* share the appropriate initial segment, it does not follow that they are equally similar to α. Suppose that (7) *is* true; then W^* does not share that counterfactual with α, and is to that extent less similar to it than W. Here we have a relevant dissimilarity between the two worlds in virtue of which the one may indeed be more similar to the actual world than the other. Accordingly, the argument fails.

A second argument is sometimes given for the conclusion that we have no right to the assumption that either (7) or (8) is true: perhaps the fact is that

(12) If Curley had been offered a bribe of $20,000 and had believed that his decision would be headlined in the *Boston Globe*, he would have rejected the bribe.

If so, then (7) is false. But perhaps it is also true that

(13) If Curley had been offered a bribe of $20,000 and had believed that his venality would remain undetected, he would have accepted the bribe;

in which case (8) would be false. So if (12) and (13) are both true (as they might well be) then neither (7) nor (8) is.

This argument is in error. If we let '$\rightarrow$' represent the counterfactual connective, we see that the crucial inference here is of the form

$$\frac{A \rightarrow C}{\therefore A \,\&\, B \rightarrow C}$$

which is clearly fallacious (and invalid on both the Stalnaker and Lewis semantics for counterfactuals). No doubt it is true that

(14) If the Pope were a Protestant, he would be a dissembler;

it does not follow that

(15) If the Pope were a Protestant, had been born in Friesland and been a lifelong member of the Gereformeerde Kerk, he would be a dissembler.

Nor does it follow from (7) that, if Curley had been offered the bribe and had believed his decision would be headlined in the *Globe*, he would have accepted it.

Now of course the failure of these arguments does not guarantee that either (7) or (8) must be true. But suppose we think about a state of affairs that includes Curley's having been offered $20,000, all relevant conditions—Curley's financial situation, his general acquisitive tendencies, his venality—being the same as in fact, in the actual world. Our question is really whether there is something Curley would have done had this state of affairs been actual. Would an omniscient being know what Curley would have done—would he know, that is, either that Curley would have taken the bribe or that he would have rejected it?

The answer, I should think, is obvious and affirmative. There is something Curley would have done, had that state of affairs obtained. But I do not know how to produce a conclusive argument for this supposition, in case you are inclined to dispute it. I do think it is the natural view, the one we take in reflecting on our own moral failures and triumphs. Suppose I have applied for a National Science Foundation Fellowship and have asked you to write me a recommendation. I am eager to get the fellowship, but eminently unqualified to carry out the project I have proposed. Realizing that you know this, I act upon the maxim that every man has his price and offer you $500 to write a glowing, if inaccurate, report. You indignantly refuse, and add moral turpitude to any other disqualifications. Later we reflectively discuss what you would have done had you been offered a bribe of $50,000. One thing we would take for granted, I should think, is that there is a right answer here. We may not know what that answer is; but we would reject out of hand, I should think, the suggestion that there simply is none. Accordingly, I shall temporarily take it for granted, in what follows, that either (7) or (8) is true; as we shall see in Section 6 this assumption, harmless as it no doubt is, can be dispensed with.

6. LEIBNIZ'S LAPSE

Thus armed, let us return to the question that provoked this digression. Was it within God's power, supposing him omnipotent, to actualize just any possible world that includes his existence? No. In a nutshell, the reason is this. There is a possible world W where God strongly actualizes a totality T of states of affairs including Curley's being free with respect to taking the bribe, and where Curley takes the bribe. But there is another possible world W^* where God actualizes the very same states of affairs and where Curley *rejects* the bribe. Now suppose it is true as a matter of fact that if God had actualized T, Curley would have accepted the bribe: then God could not have actualized W. And if, on the other hand, Curley would have rejected the bribe, had God actualized T, then God could not have actualized W^*. So either way there are worlds God could not have actualized.

We can put this argument more fully as follows. Let C be the state of affairs consisting in Curley's being offered a bribe of \$20,000 and being free to accept or reject it; let A be Curley's accepting the bribe; and let GC be God's strongly actualizing C. Then by our assumption either

(16) $GC \rightarrow A$

or

(17) $GC \rightarrow \bar{A}$

is true. Suppose, first, that (16) is true. If so, then on the Stalnaker and Lewis semantics there is a possible world W such that GC and A hold in W, and such that A holds in any world as close where GC holds. No doubt in W God strongly actualizes many states of affairs in addition to C; let T be the state of affairs that includes each of these. That is, T is a state of affairs that God strongly actualizes in W; and T includes every state of affairs God strongly actualizes in W. It is evident that if God had strongly actualized T, then Curley would have accepted the bribe, i.e.,

(18) $GT \rightarrow A$.

For GT and A hold in W; by (16), in any world as close as W where GC holds, A holds; but GT includes GC; so, in any world as close as W where GT holds, A holds. Now there is no possible world in which God strongly actualizes A; for A is Curley's *freely* accepting the bribe. But then GT does not include A; for, if it did, any world where God actualizes T would be one where he actualizes A; there are no worlds where he actualizes A; and there are worlds—e.g. W—where he actualizes GT. So there is another possible world W^* where God actualizes the very same states of affairs as he does in W, and in which Curley rejects the bribe. W^* therefore includes GT and $\bar{A}$. That is, in W^* God strongly actualizes T but no state of affairs properly including T; and in W^* $\bar{A}$ holds. And now it is easy to see that God could not have actualized this world W^*.

For suppose he could have. Then there is a state of affairs C^* such that God could have strongly actualized C^* and such that, if he had, W^* would be actual. That is,

(19) $GC^* \rightarrow W^*$.

But W^* includes GT; so

(20) $GC^* \rightarrow GT$.

Now W^* either includes or precludes GC^*; if the latter, GC^* precludes W^*. But in view of (19) GC^* does not preclude W^* unless, contrary to our hypothesis, GC^* is impossible. So W^* includes GC^*. T, furthermore, is the largest state of affairs God actualizes in W^*; T, therefore, includes C^* and

GT includes GC^*. Hence the state of affairs $GT \& GC^*$ is or is equivalent to GT. By (18), $GT \to A$; hence

(21) $GC^* \& GT \to A$.

But from (20) and (21) it follows that

(22) $GC^* \to A$.[15]

But A precludes W^* and hence includes $\overline{W}^*$; so

(23) $GC^* \to \overline{W}^*$.

(19) and (23), however, are both true only if GC^* is impossible, in which case God could not have actualized C^*. Accordingly, there is no state of affairs C^* such that God could have strongly actualized C^* and such that if he had, W^* would have been actual. If (16) is true, therefore, there are possible worlds including his existence that God could not have actualized: those worlds, namely, where God actualizes T and Curley rejects the bribe. On the other hand, if

(17) $GC \to \bar{A}$

is true, then by precisely a similar argument there are other possible worlds God could not have actualized. As I have assumed, either (16) or (17) is true; so despite God's omnipotence there are worlds including his existence he could not have actualized.

Now the assumption that either (16) or (17) is true is fairly innocent; but it is also dispensable. For let W be a world where God exists, where Curley is free with respect to the action of taking a \$20,000 bribe, and where he accepts it; and as before, let T be the largest state of affairs God strongly actualizes in W. God's actualizing T (GT) includes neither Curley's accepting the bribe (A) nor his rejecting it ($\bar{A}$); so there is a world W^* where God strongly actualizes T and in which Curley rejects the bribe. Now

(24) $GT \to A$

is either true or false. If (24) is true, then by the previous argument God could not have actualized W^*.

On the other hand, if (24) is false, then God could not have actualized W. For suppose he could have; then (as before) there would be a state of affairs C such that God could have strongly actualized C and such that, if he had, W would have been actual. That is

---

[15] The argument form involved here is

$$\frac{\begin{array}{l} A \to B \\ A \& B \to C \end{array}}{\therefore A \to C.}$$

This form is intuitively valid and valid on both Stalnaker and Lewis semantics.

(25) $GC \rightarrow W$.

Now if (25) is true, then so is either

(26) $GC \text{ \& } GT \rightarrow W$

or

(27) $GC \text{ \& } \overline{GT} \rightarrow W$.[16]

Both (26) and (27), however, are false if (24) is. Consider (26): if (25) is true, then W includes GC (unless GC is impossible, in which case, contrary to the assumption, God could not have actualized it); but T is the largest state of affairs God strongly actualizes in W; hence GT includes GC. If so, however, $GC \text{ \& } GT$ is equivalent to GT. And, since (24) is false, the same goes for (26).

And now consider (27). Either GC includes GT or it does not. Suppose it does. As we have seen, if GC is possible and (25) is true, then W includes GC; but T includes C; so GT includes GC. So if GC includes GT, then GC and GT are equivalent. But (24) is false; hence so is (25), if GC includes GT. So GC does not include GT; hence $GC \text{ \& } \overline{GT}$ is a possible state of affairs. But W includes GT; hence $\overline{GT}$ includes $\overline{W}$; hence $GC \text{ \& } \overline{GT}$ includes $\overline{W}$; hence (since $GC \text{ \& } \overline{GT}$ is possible) (27) is false.

(24), therefore, is either true or false. And either way there are possible worlds including his existence that God could not have actualized. So there are possible worlds including his existence that God could not have actualized.

If we consider a world in which GT obtains and in which Curley freely rejects the bribe, we see that whether it was within God's power to actualize it depends in part upon what Curley would have done if God had strongly actualized T. Accordingly, there are possible worlds such that it is partly up to Curley whether or not God can actualize them. It is of course up to God whether or not to create Curley, and also up to God whether or not to make him free with respect to the action of taking the bribe at t. But if he creates him, and creates him free with respect to this action, then whether or not he takes it is up to Curley—not God.

Now we can return to the Free Will Defence and the problem of evil. The Free Will Defender, you recall, insists on the possibility that it is not within God's power to create a world containing moral good without creating one containing moral evil. His atheological opponent agrees with Leibniz in

---

[16] The form of argument involved here, namely

$$\frac{A \rightarrow B}{\therefore \ (A \text{ \& } C \rightarrow B) \lor (A \text{ \& } \check{C} \rightarrow B);}$$

is intuitively valid and valid on both Stalnaker and Lewis semantics.

claiming that *if* (as the theist holds) God is omnipotent, then *it follows* that he could have created just any possible world (or any such world including his existence) he pleased. We now see that this contention—call it *Leibniz's Lapse*—is a mistake. The atheologian is right in holding that there are many possible worlds containing moral good but no moral evil; his mistake lies in endorsing Leibniz's Lapse. So one of his central contentions—that God, if omnipotent, could have actualized just any world he pleased—is false.

7. TRANSWORLD DEPRAVITY

Now suppose we recapitulate the logic of the situation. The Free Will Defender claims that

> (28) God is omnipotent and it was not within his power to create a world containing moral good but no moral evil

is possible. By way of retort the atheologian insists that there are possible worlds containing moral good but no moral evil. He adds that an omnipotent being could have actualized just any possible world he chose. So if God is omnipotent, it follows that he could have actualized a world containing moral good but no moral evil; hence (28) is not possible. What we have seen so far is that his second premiss—Leibniz's Lapse—is false.

Of course this does not settle the issue in the Free Will Defender's favour. Leibniz's Lapse (appropriately enough for a lapse) is false; but this does not show that (28) is possible. To show this latter, we must demonstrate the possibility that among the worlds God could not have actualized are all the worlds containing moral good but no moral evil. How can we approach this question?

Let us return to Curley and his venality. The latter is unbounded; Curley's bribability is utter and absolute. We could put this more exactly as follows. Take any positive integer n. If (1) at t Curley had been offered n dollars by way of a bribe, and (2) he had been free with respect to the action of taking the bribe, and (3) conditions had otherwise been as much as possible like those that did in fact obtain, Curley would have accepted the bribe. But there is worse to come. Significant freedom, obviously, does not *entail* wrongdoing; so there are possible worlds in which God and Curley both exist and in which the latter is significantly free but never goes wrong. But consider W, any one of these worlds. There is a state of affairs T such that God strongly actualizes T in W and T includes every state of affairs God strongly actualizes in W. Furthermore, since Curley is significantly free in

W, there are some actions that are morally significant for him in W and with respect to which he is free in W. The sad truth, however, may be this: among these actions there is one—call it A—such that if God had actualized T, Curley would have gone wrong with respect to A. But then it follows (by the argument of Section 6) that God could not have actualized W. Now W was just any of the worlds in which Curley is significantly free but always does only what is right. It therefore follows that it was not within God's power to actualize a world in which Curley produces moral good but no moral evil. Every world God could have actualized is such that if Curley is significantly free in it, he takes at least one wrong action.

The intuitive idea underlying this argument can be put as follows. Of course God can create Curley in various states of affairs that include his being significantly free with respect to some action A. Furthermore, God knows in advance what Curley would do if created and placed in these states of affairs. Now take any one of these states of affairs S. Perhaps what God knows is that if he creates Curley, causes him to be free with respect to A, and brings it about that S is actual, then Curley will go wrong with respect to A. But perhaps the same is true for *any other* state of affairs in which God might create Curley and give him significant freedom; that is, perhaps what God knows in advance is that no matter *what* circumstances he places Curley in, so long as he leaves him significantly free, he will take at least one wrong action. And the present claim is not, of course, that Curley or anyone else is *in fact* like this, but only that this story about Curley is *possibly* true.

If it *is* true, however, Curley suffers from what I shall call *transworld depravity*.[17] By way of explicit definition:

(29) A person P *suffers from transworld depravity* if and only if for every world W such that P is significantly free in W and P does only what is right in W, there is a state of affairs T and an action A such that

   (1) God strongly actualizes T in W and W includes every state of affairs God strongly actualizes in W,

   (2) A is morally significant for P in W,

   and

   (3) if God had strongly actualized T, P would have gone wrong with respect to A.

What is important about the idea of transworld depravity is that if a person suffers from it, then it was not within God's power to actualize any

---

[17] I leave as homework the problem of comparing transworld depravity with what Calvinists call 'total depravity'.

world in which that person is significantly free but does no wrong—that is, a world in which he produces moral good but no moral evil. But clearly it is possible that everybody suffers from transworld depravity. If this possibility were actual, then God could not have created any of the possible worlds that include the existence and significant freedom of just the persons who do in fact exist, and also contain moral good but no moral evil. For to do so he would have had to create persons who were significantly free but suffered from transworld depravity. And the price for creating a world in which such persons produce moral good is creating one in which they also produce moral evil.

Now we might think this settles the question in favour of the Free Will Defender. But the fact is it does not. For suppose all the people that exist in α suffer from transworld depravity; it does not follow that God could not have created a world containing moral good without creating one containing moral evil. God could have created *other people*. Instead of creating us, he could have created a world containing people all right, but not containing any of us. And perhaps if he had done that, he could have created a world containing moral good but no moral evil.

Perhaps. But then again, perhaps not. Return to the notion of *essence* or *individual concept* as developed in Chapter V [of *The Nature of Necessity*]: an essence of Curley is a property he has in every world in which he exists and that is not exemplified in any world by any object distinct from Curley. An essence *simpliciter* is a property P such that there is a world W in which there exists an object x that has P essentially and is such that in no world W^* is there an object that has P and is distinct from x. More briefly, an essence is an encaptic property that is essentially exemplified in some world, where an encaptic property entails either P or $\bar{P}$, for every world-indexed property P.

And now recall that Curley suffers from transworld depravity. This fact implies something interesting about Curleyhood, Curley's essence. Take those worlds W such that *is significantly free in W and never does what is wrong in W* is entailed by Curley's essence. Each of these worlds has an important property, if Curley suffers from transworld depravity; each is such that God could not have actualized it. We can see this as follows. Suppose W^* is some world such that Curley's essence entails the property *is significantly free but never does what is wrong in W**. That is, W^* is a world in which Curley is significantly free but always does what is right. But of course Curley suffers from transworld depravity. This means (as we have already seen) that God could not have actualized W^*. So if Curley suffers from transworld depravity, then Curley's essence has this property: God could not have actualized any world W such that

Curleyhood contains the properties *is significantly free in W* and *always does what is right in W.*

We can use this connection between Curley's transworld depravity and his essence as the basis for a definition of transworld depravity as applied to essences rather than persons. We should note first that if E is a person's essence, then he is the instantiation of E; he is the thing that has (or exemplifies) every property in E. To instantiate an essence, God creates a person who has that essence; and in creating a person he instantiates an essence. Now we can say that

(30) An essence E *suffers from transworld depravity* if and only if for every world W such that E entails the properties *is significantly free in W* and *always does what is right in W*, there is a state of affairs T and an action A such that

(1) T is the largest state of affairs God strongly actualizes in W,

(2) A is morally significant for E's instantiation in W,

and

(3) if God had strongly actualized T, E's instantiation would have gone wrong with respect to A.

Note that transworld depravity is an accidental property of those essences and persons it afflicts. For suppose Curley suffers from transworld depravity: then so does his essence. There is a world, however, in which Curley is significantly free but always does what is right. If *that* world had been actual, then of course neither Curley nor his essence would have suffered from transworld depravity. So the latter is essential neither to those persons nor to those essences that exemplify it. But by now it is evident, I take it, that if an essence E *does* suffer from transworld depravity, then it was not within God's power to actualize a possible world W such that E contains the properties *is significantly free in W* and *always does what is right in W*. Hence it was not within God's power to create a world in which E's instantiation is significantly free but always does what is right.

Now the interesting fact here is this: it is possible that every creaturely essence[18] suffers from transworld depravity. But suppose this is true. God can create a world containing moral good only by creating significantly free persons. And, since every person is the instantiation of an essence, he can create significantly free persons only by instantiating some creaturely essences. But if every such essence suffers from transworld depravity, then no matter which essences God instantiated, the resulting persons, if free with respect to morally significant actions, would always perform at least

---

[18] i.e. every essence entailing *is created by God.*

some wrong actions. If every creaturely essence suffers from transworld depravity, then it was beyond the power of God himself to create a world containing moral good but no moral evil. He might have been able to create worlds in which moral evil is very considerably outweighed by moral good; but it was not within the power of omnipotence to create worlds containing moral good but no moral evil. Under these conditions God could have created a world containing no moral evil only by creating one without significantly free persons. But it is possible that every essence suffers from transworld depravity; so it is possible that God could not have created a world containing moral good but no moral evil.

8. THE FREE WILL DEFENCE TRIUMPHANT

Put formally, you remember, the Free Will Defender's project was to show that

(1) God is omniscient, omnipotent, and wholly good

is consistent with

(2) There is evil

by employing the truth that a pair of propositions p and q are jointly consistent if there is a proposition r whose conjunction with p is consistent and entails q. What we have just seen is that

(31) Every essence suffers from transworld depravity

is consistent with God's omnipotence. But then it is clearly consistent with (1). So we can use it to show that (1) is consistent with (2). For consider the conjunction of (1), (31), and

(32) God actualizes a world containing moral good.

This conjunction is evidently consistent. But it entails

(2) There is evil.

Accordingly (1) is consistent with (2); the Free Will Defence is successful.

Of course the conjunction of (31) with (32) is not the only proposition that can play the role of r in the Free Will Defence. Perhaps, for example, it was within the power of God to actualize a world including moral good but no moral evil, but not within his power to actualize one including no moral evil and including as much moral good as the actual world contains. So

(33) For any world W, if W contains no moral evil and W includes as much moral good as α contains, then God could not have actualized W

(which is weaker than (31)) could be used in conjunction with

(34) God actualizes a world containing as much moral good as α contains

to show that (1) and (2) are consistent. The essential point of the Free Will Defence is that the creation of a world containing moral good is a co-operative venture; it requires the uncoerced concurrence of significantly free creatures. But then the actualization of a world W containing moral good is not up to God alone; it also depends upon what the significantly free creatures of W would do if God created them and placed them in the situations W contains. Of course it is up to God whether to create free creatures at all; but if he aims to produce moral good, then he must create significantly free creatures upon whose co-operation he must depend. Thus is the power of an omnipotent God limited by the freedom he confers upon his creatures.[19]

9. GOD'S EXISTENCE AND THE *AMOUNT* OF MORAL EVIL

The world, after all, contains a *great deal* of moral evil; and what we have seen so far is only that God's existence is compatible with *some* evil. Perhaps the atheologian can regroup, arguing that at any rate God's existence is not consistent with the vast amount and variety of evil the universe actually contains. Of course we cannot measure moral evil—that is, we do not have units like volts or pounds or kilowatts so that we could say 'this situation contains about 35 turps of moral evil'. Still we can compare situations in terms of evil; we can see that some contain more moral evil than others. And perhaps the atheologian means to maintain that it is at any rate obvious that God, if omnipotent, could have created a *morally better* world—one containing a better mixture of moral good and evil than α—one, let us say, that contained as much moral good but less moral evil.

But is this really obvious? I do not think so. Possibly this was *not* within God's power, which is all the Free Will Defender needs. We can see this as follows. Of course there are many possible worlds containing as much moral good as α, but less moral evil. Let W^* be any such world. If W^* had been actual, there would have been as much moral good (past, present, and future) as in fact there was, is, and will be; and there would have been less moral evil in all. Now in W^* a certain set of S of essences is instantiated. So to actualize W^*, God would have had to create persons who were the instantiations of these essences. But perhaps one of these essences would have had an unco-operative instantiation. That is, possibly

[19] See William Wainwright, 'Freedom and Omnipotence', *Noûs*, 2 (1968), 293–301.

(35) There is a member E of S, a state of affairs T, and an action A such that

    (1) E's instantiation freely performs A in W^*,

    (2) T is the largest state of affairs God actualizes in W^*,

and

    (3) If God had strongly actualized T, E's instantiation would not have performed A.

I say it is possible that (35) is true; but clearly *if* it is, then for reasons by now familiar God could not have actualized W^*. And the fact is it is possible that every morally better world is like W in that God could not have actualized it. For it is possible that for every morally better world there is a member E of S, an action A, and a state of affairs T that meet the conditions laid down in (35). But if so, then (1) is compatible with the existence of as much evil as α does in fact contain.

10. GOD'S EXISTENCE AND *NATURAL* EVIL

But perhaps the atheologian can regroup once more. What about *natural* evil? Evil that cannot be ascribed to the free actions of human beings? Suffering due to earthquakes, disease, and the like? Is the existence of evil of *this sort* compatible with (1)? Here two lines of thought present themselves. Some people deal creatively with certain kinds of hardship or suffering, so acting that on balance the whole state of affairs is valuable. Perhaps their responses would have been less impressive and the total situations less valuable without the evil. Perhaps some natural evils and some persons are so related that the persons would have produced less moral good if the evils had been absent.[20] But another and more traditional line of thought is pursued by St. Augustine, who attributes much of the evil we find to *Satan*, or to Satan and his cohorts.[21] Satan, so the traditional doctrine goes, is a mighty non-human spirit who, along with many other angels, was created long before God created man. Unlike most of his colleagues, Satan rebelled against God and has since been wreaking whatever havoc he can. The result is natural evil. So the natural evil we find is due to free actions of non-human spirits.

---

[20] As in John Hick's *Soul-making* theodicy; see his *Evil and the God of Love* (London: Macmillan), 1966.

[21] See 'The Problem of Free Choice', in *Ancient Christian Writers*, xxii (New York: Paulist/ Newman Press), 71 ff.; and *Confessions and Enchiridion*, tr. and ed. Albert C. Outler (Philadelphia: Westminster Press), 341–6.

This is a *theodicy*, as opposed to a *defence*.[22] St. Augustine believes that natural evil (except for what can be attributed to God's punishment) is *in fact* to be ascribed to the activity of beings that are free and rational but non-human. The Free Will Defender, on the other hand, need not assert that this is *true*; he says only that it is *possible* (and consistent with (1)). He points to the possibility that natural evil is due to the actions of significantly free but non-human persons. We have noted the possibility that God could not have actualized a world with a better balance of moral good over moral evil than this one displays. Something similar holds here; possibly natural evil is due to the free activity of a set of non-human persons, and perhaps it was not within God's power to create a set of such persons whose free actions produced a greater balance of good over evil. That is to say, it is possible that

(36) All natural evil is due to the free activity of non-human persons; there is a balance of good over evil with respect to the actions of these non-human persons; and there is no world God could have created which contains a more favourable balance of good over evil with respect to the free activity of the non-human persons it contains.

Again, it must be emphasized that (36) is not required to be *true* for the success of the Free Will Defence; it need only be compatible with (1). And it certainly looks as if it is. If (36) *is* true, furthermore, then *natural* evil significantly resembles *moral* evil in that, like the latter, it is the result of the activity of significantly free persons. In fact both moral and natural evil would then be special cases of what we might call *broadly moral evil*—evil resulting from the free actions of personal beings, whether human or not. (Of course there is a correlative notion of broadly moral good.) To facilitate discussion, furthermore, let us stipulate that the *turp* is the basic unit of evil and that there are 10^{13} turps of evil in the actual world; the total amount of evil (past, present, and future) contained by α is 10^{13} turps. Given these ideas, we can combine (35) and (36) into one compendious statement:

(37) All the evil in the actual world is broadly moral evil; and every world that God could have actualized, and that contains as much broadly moral good as the actual world displays, contains at least 10^{13} turps of evil.

Now (37) appears to be consistent with (1) and

(38) God actualizes a world containing as much broadly moral good as the actual world contains.

<hr />

[22] I am indebted to Henry Schuurman for this use of these terms.

But (1), (37), and (38) together entail that there is a much evil as α contains; so (1) is consistent with the proposition that there is as much evil as α contains. I therefore conclude that the Free Will Defence successfully rebuts the charge of inconsistency brought against the theist. If evil is a problem for the believer, it is not that the existence of evil—moral or natural—is inconsistent with the existence of God.

VI

MIDDLE KNOWLEDGE AND THE PROBLEM OF EVIL

ROBERT MERRIHEW ADAMS

If President Kennedy had not been shot, would he have bombed North Vietnam? God only knows. Or does He? Does even He know what Kennedy would have done?

There is a little known but interesting literature on the general issue exemplified by this question. In the 1580s a fierce controversy erupted between the Jesuits and the Dominicans about the relation between God's grace and human free will. The Jesuits held, among other things, that many human actions are free in the sense that their agents are not logically or causally determined to do them. ('Free' will always be used in this sense in the present essay.) How then does God maintain control over human history? Not by causally determining human actions, as the Dominicans seemed to believe,[1] but by causing circumstances in which He knew that we would *freely* act in accordance with His plans. This answer was developed with great ingenuity by Luis de Molina, and defended by other Jesuit theologians, notably by Francisco Suarez. Their theory includes the thesis that God knows with certainty what every possible free creature would freely do in every situation in which that creature could possibly find himself. Such knowledge was called 'middle knowledge' by the Jesuits, because they thought it had a middle status between other kinds of knowledge—between God's knowledge of the merely possible and His knowledge of the actual; or between His knowledge of necessary truths, which all follow from the divine nature, and His knowledge of His own will and everything that is causally determined by His will.[2]

Robert Merrihew Adams, 'Middle Knowledge and the Problem of Evil', first published in *American Philosophical Quarterly*, 14 (1977), pp. 109–17. Used with permission.

[1] An acutely argued Dominican contribution to the debate is Diego (Didacus) Alvarez, OP, *De auxiliis divinae gratiae et humani arbitrii viribus, et libertate, ac legitima eius cum efficacia eorundem auxiliorum concordia* (Rome, 1590); see especially the seventh disputation.

[2] I believe Molina originated the term 'middle knowledge' (*scientia media*). I have given a very simplified account of his reasons for thinking it appropriate. See his *Liberi arbitrii cum gratiae*

This paper is about two questions. The first is whether middle knowledge is possible, even for God. I shall argue that it is not, on the ground that conditional propositions of the sort that are supposed to be known by middle knowledge cannot be true. I will examine (in section II) the attempts of Molina and Suarez to explain how God can have middle knowledge; and then (in section III) the account recently offered by Alvin Plantinga, who has reinvented the theory of middle knowledge. Two objections to my position will be discussed in section IV.

The idea of middle knowledge emerges in recent philosophical discussion chiefly because of its relevance to the second question that I shall discuss, which is whether God could have made free creatures who would always have freely done right. More precisely: Could God have brought it about that He had creatures who made free choices, but none of whom ever made wrong choices? The relevance of this question to the problem of evil is obvious and well known. If He could have, why didn't He? If He couldn't have, that's a good enough reason why He didn't. He could not have done it by causally determining the choices of creatures, for then their choices and acts would not have been free in the relevant sense. But it might seem that if God has middle knowledge, He could have secured creatures sinless but free by just creating those that He knew would not sin if allowed to act freely. In section V, therefore, we shall see what light the discussion of middle knowledge may shed on the question whether God could have arranged to have free creatures who were all sinless.

But first of all (in section I) I will try to explain why there seems to me to be a problem about the possibility of middle knowledge.

I

In the twenty-third chapter of the first book of Samuel it is written that after David had rescued the Jewish city of Keilah from the Philistines, and settled his men there, Saul made plans to besiege Keilah in order to capture David. When David heard of Saul's plans, he consulted God by means of an ephod, which apparently was an instrument of divination that yielded a yes-or-no answer to questions. David asked, 'Will Saul come down, as thy servant has heard?' The Lord answered affirmatively. Then David asked, 'Will the men of Keilah surrender me and my men into the hand of Saul?' And the Lord replied, 'They will surrender you.' Thereupon David evacuated his

donis, divina praescientia, providentia, praedestinatione et reprobatione concordia [hereafter abbreviated, *Concordia*], ed. John Rabeneck (Oña and Madrid, 1953), qu. 14, art. 13, disp. 52, nn. 9–10, and disp. 53, memb. 1, n. 6, and memb. 4, n. 4 (pp. 339 f., 360, 394).

men from Keilah, and hid out in the hills, with the result that Saul did not have the opportunity to besiege him in Keilah, and the men of Keilah did not have occasion to betray him to Saul (I Samuel 23: 1–14, RSV).

This passage was a favorite proof text for the Jesuit theologians. They took it to prove that God knew the following two propositions to be true:

(1) If David stayed in Keilah, Saul would besiege the city.
(2) If David stayed in Keilah and Saul besieged the city, the men of Keilah would surrender David to Saul.

This is a case of middle knowledge; for it is assumed that all the actions mentioned in (1) and (2) would have been *free*, in the relevant sense, if they had occurred.

If we suppose that God is omniscient we cannot consistently doubt that He had this middle knowledge unless we doubt that (1) and (2) were true. Therefore, as Suarez says, 'the whole controversy comes back to this, that we should see whether those conditionals have a knowable determinate truth'.[3]

But I do doubt that propositions (1) and (2) ever were, or ever will be, true. This is not because I am inclined to assert the truth of their opposites,

(3) If David stayed in Keilah, Saul would *not* besiege the city.
(4) If David stayed in Keilah and Saul besieged the city, the men of Keilah would *not* surrender David to Saul.

Suarez would say that (1) and (3), and (2) and (4), respectively, are pairs of contradictories, and therefore that one member of each pair must be true. He thus affirms what has been called the law of Conditional Excluded Middle. But this is a mistake. One does not obtain the contradictory of a conditional proposition by negating the consequent; one must negate the whole conditional, as was pointed out by Suarez's Dominican opponent, Diego Alvarez.[4] It is true that in everyday speech we might deny (1) by asserting (3), as we may deny a proposition by asserting any belief we hold that is obviously enough inconsistent with it. But we might also deny both of them by asserting, 'If David stayed in Keilah, Saul might or might not besiege the city.' I believe the case of what Saul would or might have done if David stayed in Keilah provides a plausible counterexample to the proposed law of Conditional Excluded Middle; and philosophers have found even more convincing counterexamples.[5]

[3] Suarez, *De gratia*, prol. 3, c. 7, n. 1, in his *Opera omnia* (Paris, 1856–78), vol. vii, p. 85. (All my page references to *De gratia* will be to this edition and volume.)
[4] Alvarez, *De auxiliis divinae gratiae et humani arbitrii viribus*, Bk. 2, disp. 7, n. 30 (p. 74). See Suarez, *De gratia*, prol. 2, c. 7, n. 24 (p. 95).
[5] David Lewis, *Counterfactuals* (Oxford, 1973), 79 f.; John H. Pollock, 'Four Kinds of Conditionals', *American Philosophical Quarterly*, 12 (1975), 53. The law of Conditional Excluded

I do not understand what it would be for any of propositions (1)–(4) to be true, given that the actions in question would have been free, and that David did not stay in Keilah. I will explain my incomprehension.

First we must note that middle knowledge is not simple *fore*knowledge. The answers that David got from the ephod—'He will come down', and 'They will surrender you'—are not understood by the theologians as categorical predictions. If they were categorical predictions, they would be false. Most philosophers (including Suarez but not Molina) have supposed that categorical predictions, even about contingent events, can be true by corresponding to the actual occurrence of the event that they predict. But propositions (1) and (2) are not true in this way. For there never was nor will be an actual besieging of Keilah by Saul, nor an actual betrayal of David to Saul by the men of Keilah, to which those propositions might correspond.[6]

Some other grounds that might be suggested for the truth of (1) and (2) are ruled out by the assumption that the actions of Saul and the men of Keilah are and would be free in the relevant sense. The suggestion that Saul's besieging Keilah follows by *logical* necessity from David's staying there is implausible in any case.[7] It would be more plausible to suggest that Saul's besieging Keilah follows by *causal* necessity from David's staying there, together with a number of other features of the situation which in fact obtained. But both of these suggestions are inconsistent with the assumption that Saul's action would have been free.

Since necessitation is incompatible with the relevant sort of free will, we might seek non-necessitating grounds for the truth of (1) and (2) in the actual intentions, desires, and character of Saul and the Keilahites. It does appear from the Biblical narrative that Saul actually intended to besiege David in Keilah if he could. Perhaps proposition (1) is true by virtue of its correspondence with Saul's intention. One might also suppose that (2) was true by virtue of correspondence with the desires and character of the leading men of Keilah, if not their fully formed intentions. Maybe they were cowardly, untrustworthy, and ungrateful. And I take it that neither the Jesuits nor Plantinga would say that Saul's intentions, or the desires and character of the Keilahites, necessitated their actions or interfered in any way with their freedom of will.

Middle was defended by Robert C. Stalnaker, in 'A Theory of Conditionals', *American Philosophical Quarterly Monograph Series*, no. 2, *Studies in Logical Theory*, ed. Nicholas Rescher (Oxford, 1968), 106 f.

[6] Suarez saw this point pretty clearly; see his 'De scientia Dei futurorum contingentium' [hereafter abbreviated, DSDFC], Bk. 2, c. 5, n. 6 (*Opera omnia*, vol. xi, p. 357).

[7] Suarez makes a similar point: DSDFC, Bk. 2, c. 5, n. 11 (p. 358).

But the basis thus offered for the truth of (1) and (2) is inadequate precisely because it is not necessitating. A free agent may act out of character, or change his intentions, or fail to act on them. Therefore the propositions which may be true by virtue of correspondence with the intentions, desires and character of Saul and the men of Keilah are not (1) and (2) but

    (5) If David stayed in Keilah, Saul would *probably* besiege the city.
    (6) If David stayed in Keilah and Saul besieged the city, the men of
        Keilah would *probably* surrender David to Saul.

(5) and (6) are enough for David to act on, if he is prudent; but they will not satisfy the partisans of middle knowledge. It is part of their theory that God knows infallibly what definitely would happen, and not just what would probably happen or what free creatures would be likely to do.[8]

II

I trust that it is clear by this point that there is reason to doubt the possibility of middle knowledge. Those who believe it possible have some explaining to do.

In Molina's explanation the superiority of God's cognitive powers bears the heaviest burden. He holds 'that the certainty of that middle knowledge comes from the depth and unlimited perfection of the divine intellect, by which [God] knows certainly what is in itself uncertain'.[9] This came to be known as the theory of 'supercomprehension'. According to it God's intellect so immensely surpasses, in its perfection, all created free will, that it 'supercomprehends' them—that is, it understands more about them than would be necessary merely to comprehend them.[10] But as Suarez pointed out in rejecting the theory of supercomprehension, to comprehend something is already to understand about it everything that is there to be understood, and it is absurd to suppose that anyone, even God, could understand more than that.[11] Molina seems to want to say that what free creatures would do under various possible conditions is not there, objectively, to be known, but that God's mind is so perfect that He knows it anyway. But that is impossible. The problem to be solved is how the relevant subjunctive conditionals can be true, and nothing that may be said about

---

[8] See Suarez, DSDFC, Bk. 2, c. 1, nn. 1–2, and c. 5, n. 9 (pp. 343 f., 357 f.).
[9] Molina, *Concordia*, qu. 14, art. 13, disp. 53, memb. 3, n. 10 (pp. 389 f.).
[10] Ibid., disp. 52, nn. 11, 17 (pp. 341, 345).
[11] Suarez, DSDFC, Bk. 2, c. 7, n. 6 (pp. 366 f.).

the excellence of God's cognitive powers contributes anything to the solution of that problem.

Suarez offers what seems to me the least clearly unsatisfactory type of explanation for the alleged possibility of middle knowledge. He appeals, in effect, to a primitive understanding, which needs no analysis, of what it is for the relevant subjunctive conditionals to be true. Consider a possible free creature, c, who may not ever exist, and a possible free action, a, which c may freely do or refrain from doing in a possible situation s. We are to consider c, not as actually existing, but as having 'possible being' in the cause (God) that is able to produce c. So considered, according to Suarez, c has a property (a *habitudo*, as Suarez puts it) which is either the property of being a possible agent who would in s freely do a, or the property of being a possible agent who would in s freely refrain from doing a. c has one of these properties, although there is nothing either internal or external to c, except the property itself, which would make or determine c to have one of these properties rather than the other. God has middle knowledge of what c would do in s, because God knows which of the two properties c has.[12]

Many philosophers would object to Suarez's ontology of merely possible entities, but perhaps one could develop a similar account of the relevant conditionals without such an ontology. God's *idea* of c, for example, is presumably an *existing* subject of properties. And one might ascribe to it, as a primitive property, the property of being an idea which, if it were satisfied by anything in s, would be satisfied by an agent that freely did a in s. This would have the disadvantage, however, of implying that whether c would do a in s depends, not on a property of c, but on a property of God's idea of c. That consequence might seem to compromise c's freedom of will.

My principal objection to Suarez's defense of the possibility of middle knowledge is not based on ontological considerations, however. I do not think I have any conception, primitive or otherwise, of the sort of *habitudo* or property that Suarez ascribes to possible agents with respect to their acts under possible conditions. Nor do I think that I have any other primitive understanding of what it would be for the relevant subjunctive conditionals to be true. My reason for saying that Suarez's defense is of the least clearly unsatisfactory type is that it is very difficult to refute someone who claims to have a primitive understanding which I seem not to have.

---

[12] I believe this is what Suarez's views come to, as they are found in *De gratia*, prol. 2, c. 7, nn. 21, 24, 25 (pp. 94–6).

III

In his several published discussions of the 'free will defense' to the problem of evil, Alvin Plantinga has assumed, in effect, that God can have middle knowledge; and in the most recent of these discussions he has defended this assumption.[13] Following Robert Stalnaker and David Lewis, Plantinga adopts what he calls 'the possible worlds explanation of counterfactuals'.[14] For proposition (1) to be true, according to Plantinga's theory, is for the following to be the case:

> (7) The actual world is more similar to some possible world in which David stays in Keilah and Saul besieges the city than to any possible world in which David stays in Keilah and Saul does not besiege the city.

There are two important reasons for denying that this analysis establishes the possibility of middle knowledge.

(A) To the extent that it is plausible, the possible worlds explanation does not really give us a new solution to our problem about the truth of the crucial conditionals. It merely offers us a new and up-to-date form for the expression of attempted solutions that we may already have considered and rejected. (In fairness it should be said that Plantinga does not claim otherwise.) Two points must be made here.

(i) If the explanation is to be plausible, the kinds of similarity among possible worlds that are allowed to be relevant to the truth and falsity of counterfactual conditionals must mirror the considerations that would in any case determine our judgment of their truth and falsity. Some similarities cannot plausibly be allowed any relevance at all. Among the possible worlds in which David stays in Keilah, for example, I suspect the most similar to the actual world is one in which Saul does not besiege Keilah, and in which the subsequent history of David, Saul, and of Israel and Judah goes very much as it did in the actual world. Perhaps in such a world Saul has a slightly different character, or acts out of character in a way that he

---

[13] The assumption passed unquestioned in Alvin Plantinga's *God and Other Minds* (Ithaca, 1967), ch. 6. In his *The Nature of Necessity* (Oxford, 1974), ch. 9, and less fully in 'Which Worlds Could God Have Created?' *The Journal of Philosophy*, 70 (1973), 539–52, it is defended. At the same time Plantinga has attempted (successfully, I think) to free a part of his larger argument from dependence on the assumption (*The Nature of Necessity*, pp. 182–4 [pp. 99–100 above]). Plantinga has not used the term 'middle knowledge', although it seems to me very apt for the expression of his views.

[14] *The Nature of Necessity*, p. 178 [p. 95 above]. See also Stalnaker, 'A Theory of Conditionals', and Lewis, *Counterfactuals*. In the present paper I shall disregard complications having to do with conditionals whose antecedents are impossible, as all the conditionals that will concern us have possible antecedents.

does not in the actual world; but I doubt that that is as great a dissimilarity as the dissimilarity between a world in which there is a siege of Keilah by Saul (and perhaps a killing of David by Saul) and a world in which there is not. I certainly would not conclude, however, that therefore Saul would not have besieged Keilah if David had stayed in the city.[15] That a world in which Saul besieges Keilah is in that respect unlike the actual world, is irrelevant to the question what Saul would have done if David stayed in Keilah. Some similarities between the actual world and other possible worlds are relevant to that question—for example, similarities and dissimilarities in causal laws and in people's characters. But we have already considered and rejected the idea of founding the truth of our crucial conditionals on causal laws or on people's characters.

(ii) Even the similarities that are allowed to be relevant to the truth of counterfactuals must not be given more decisiveness than we would otherwise accord to the considerations that they mirror. A world in which David stays in Keilah and Saul besieges the city is perhaps more similar to the actual world in respect of Saul's character than a world in which David stays in Keilah and Saul does not besiege the city. But we had better not conclude that therefore the former is more similar to the actual world than the latter for purposes of the possible worlds explanation, if we mean to adhere to the explanation. For this conclusion would give us more reason to reject the analysis in terms of similarity of possible worlds than to abandon our previous judgment that Saul *might* have acted out of character and so would only *probably*, not definitely, have laid siege to Keilah if David had stayed in the city. The issue here is a general one, and important. We have a well entrenched belief that under many counterfactual conditions many a person *might* have acted out of character, although he probably would not have. If the possible worlds explanation is to be plausible, it must not give such decisiveness to similarities of character and behavior as to be inconsistent with this belief.

(B) On the possible worlds theory, moreover, the truth of the crucial conditionals cannot be settled soon enough to be of use to God. The chief importance of middle knowledge, for Plantinga as well as Molina and Suarez, is that God is supposed to be guided by it in making decisions about the creation and providential governance of the world. And as Molina and Suarez insist, if God is to make such use of it, His middle knowledge must be prior, if not temporally, at least in the order of explanation (*prius ratione*, as Suarez puts it), to His decisions about what creatures to create.[16]

---

[15] Similar problems are discussed by Plantinga, *The Nature of Necessity*, pp. 174–9 [pp. 92–6 above], and Lewis, *Counterfactuals*, pp. 72–7, 91–5.

[16] See especially Suarez, DSDFC, Bk. 2, c. 4, n. 6, and c. 6, nn. 3, 6 (pp. 355, 361, 363).

For similar reasons the truth of the conditional propositions which are the object of middle knowledge must not depend on God's creative decisions. Ignoring angels (fallen or unfallen) for the sake of argument, let us suppose that Adam and Eve were the first free creatures that God made. We are to think of God as choosing from among many alternatives; among them were creating Adam and Eve, creating other free creatures instead of them, and making no free creatures at all. According to the theory of middle knowledge, God's decisions to make some free creatures, and Adam and Eve in particular, are to be explained in part by the truth of

> (8) If God created Adam and Eve, there would be more moral good than moral evil in the history of the world.[17]

This explanation would be viciously circular if the truth of (8) were later in the order of explanation than the decisions it is supposed to help explain.

Here we are dealing with a type of subjunctive conditionals that we may call *deliberative conditionals*. They ought not, in strictness, to be called *counterfactual*. For in asserting one of them one does not commit oneself to the falsity of its antecedent. That is because a deliberative conditional is asserted (or entertained) in a context of deliberation about whether to (try to) make its antecedent true or false. In asserting such a conditional one commits oneself rather to the view that its truth is independent of the truth or falsity of its antecedent.

There is a problem, which so far as I know has not been discussed in the literature, about applying to deliberative conditionals, as Plantinga does, the possible worlds explanation of counterfactuals.[18] Consider a deliberative conditional,

> (9) If I did *x, y* would happen.

Is (9) true? According to the possible worlds explanation, that depends on whether the actual world is more similar to some world in which I do *x* and *y* happens than to any world in which I do *x* and *y* does not happen. That in turn seems to depend on which world is the actual world. And which world is the actual world? That depends in part on whether I do *x*. Thus the truth of (9) seems to depend on the truth or falsity of its antecedent. Similarly the truth of (8) will depend on whether God creates Adam and Eve.

I think it may be possible for a possible worlds theory of deliberative

---

[17] I have simplified here, particularly in the antecedent. God is supposed to have known that there would be more moral good than moral evil in the world if He executed a long series of actions, beginning with the creation of Adam and Eve. Many of these actions would be occasioned in part by responses He supposedly knew creatures would freely make to earlier actions in the series.

[18] Stalnaker would apply it to deliberative conditionals too. Lewis might not; see his *Counterfactuals*, p. 4.

conditionals to overcome this difficulty in general, but not in such a way as to rescue the doctrine of middle knowledge. There is, I presume, a large class, K, of possible worlds that are more similar to some world in which I do x and y happens than to any world in which I do x and y does not happen. According to the possible worlds theory the truth of (9) depends on the actual world being some member of K, but not on *which* member of K it is. In asserting (9) in the context of deliberation I commit myself, in effect, to the view that the actual world is a member of K and that its membership in K does not depend on which I choose of the alternatives among which I am deliberating. This view may well be correct—if, for instance, x and y are linked by a strict causal law.

Similarly there is a class, K^*, of possible worlds that are more similar to some world in which God creates Adam and Eve and there is more moral good than moral evil in the history of the world than to any world in which God creates Adam and Eve and there is not more moral good than moral evil in the history of the world. The truth of (8) depends on the actual world being some member of K^*, according to the possible worlds theory. But how can the actual world's membership in K^* have been settled earlier in the order of explanation than God's decision whether to create Adam and Eve, or some other free creatures, or none? Here we face all the old difficulties about middle knowledge, and the possible worlds theory does nothing to help us answer this question. At most it explains why (8) is true, *given* that some member of K^* is actual.

Furthermore there is reason to believe that the actual world's membership in K^* cannot have been settled earlier in the order of explanation than God's decision. Let us say that one of God's alternatives is *represented in* K^* if and only if there is some world in K^* in which He chooses that alternative. If any of the alternatives among which God was choosing is not represented in K^*, then the actual world's membership in K^* depends on His rejecting that alternative, and therefore cannot be prior in the order of explanation to His decision. But I think at least one of God's alternatives is indeed unrepresented in K^*. For one alternative was to make no free creatures at all, and I do not see how a world in which there are no free creatures at all could be a member of K^*. Since it is free actions that are morally good and morally evil,[19] no possible world, w, will be a member of K^* unless there is some feature of w by virtue of which a difference in the free actions of free creatures in some worlds u and v would be a reason for counting u as more similar than v to w (in relevant respects). And any such feature of w must surely involve the existence in w of free creatures. If there

---

[19] Plantinga insists on this point (*The Nature of Necessity*, pp. 166 f. [p. 85 above]).

are no free creatures at all in *w*, what would make *w* more like a world in which most free creaturely decisions are good ones than like a world in which most free creaturely decisions are bad ones? I conclude that the actual world's membership in K^* cannot be earlier in the order of explanation than God's decision to make some free creatures. Therefore the truth of (8), on the possible worlds analysis, cannot be prior in order of explanation to that decision.

Perhaps it will be objected to me that the partisans of middle knowledge need not claim that the truth of (8) precedes God's creative choices in the order of explanation. It is enough for their explanations if God *believed* (8) prior to making the choices. My reply is that if God acted on a belief in (8) before it was settled that (8) is true, then the fact (if it is a fact) that there is more moral good than moral evil in the history of the world is due to God's good luck rather than His wisdom—whereas the chief motivation of the theological theory of middle knowledge has been the desire to maintain that such happy results of God's dealings with created freedom are due to His wisdom, and that He had no need at all of luck.

IV

Of the philosophical objections that may be raised against my critique of the theory of middle knowledge, two seem to me the most important.

(A) I have relied on the claim that in the circumstances assumed in our example about David and Saul at Keilah, what is true by virtue of Saul's intentions and character is not

·(1) If David stayed in Keilah, Saul would besiege the city,

but

(5) If David stayed in Keilah, Saul would *probably* besiege the city.

Suarez has an interesting objection to this claim. He argues, in effect, that (5) can only mean that (1) is probably true, and that in accepting (5) one commits oneself, albeit with some trepidation, to the truth of (1).[20] Certainly it would be pragmatically inconsistent to assert that (1) is probably true and deny (as I do) that there is any way in which (1) can be true.

In proposing (5) as an alternative to (1), however, I do not understand it as a claim that (1), or any other proposition, *is* probable. It is rather a claim that

(10) Saul will besiege Keilah

---

[20] Suarez, DSDFC, Bk. 2, c. 5, n. 9 (pp. 357 f.). I am simplifying here, but I think not in such a way as to make this argument less plausible.

would be probable, given facts that would (definitely, not just probably) obtain if David stayed in Keilah. While 'probably' is an epistemological term, moreover, it is used in (5) primarily to characterize dispositions or tendencies toward the truth of (10) that there would be if David stayed in Keilah. (5) does not imply that anyone would *know* the facts that would probabilify (10), but only that they would *obtain*, if David stayed in Keilah.

This view is consistent with treatment that (5) might receive under either of the two major types of theory of counterfactuals distinguished by Lewis. According to a *metalinguistic* theory, as Lewis puts it, 'a counterfactual is true, or assertable, if and only if its antecedent, together with suitable further premises, implies its consequent'.[21] Holding a theory of this type, we might say that (5) is true if and only if (10) would be probable on total evidence constituted by the antecedent of (5), together with suitable further premises. The suitable further premises in this case would be partly about Saul's intentions and character. Lewis has proposed for the *possible worlds* theory an essentially similar treatment of counterfactuals that involve probability in the way that (5) does.[22]

(B) Probably the most serious grounds for misgivings about my argument may be found in cases in which we seem to have confidence in what looks like a piece of middle knowledge. Suarez appeals to such confidence on the part of ordinary speakers,[23] and Plantinga endeavors to provide us with convincing examples of it.

In one of Plantinga's fictitious examples Curley Smith, a mayor of Boston, has accepted a bribe of $35,000 to drop his opposition to a proposed freeway route. In this case is the following true?

> (11) Smith would still have accepted a bribe to drop his opposition, if the bribe had been $36,000.

Plantinga thinks 'the answer seems fairly clear: indeed [Smith] would have' accepted the larger bribe;[24] and I agree.

But what makes (11) true? Let us note that it belongs to the class of subjunctive conditionals with antecedents assumed to be false and consequents assumed to be true, which have been called *semifactuals*. What makes (11) true, I think, is that its consequent is true and the truth of its antecedent would not have prevented, or made less likely, the event that makes the consequent true. My view here is in accord with Nelson Goodman's claim that 'in practice full counterfactuals affirm, while semifactuals deny,

[21] Lewis, *Counterfactuals*, p. 65.
[22] David Lewis, 'Counterfactuals and Comparative Probability', *Journal of Philosophical Logic*, 2 (1973), 437 f.
[23] Suarez, DSDFC, Bk. 2, c. 5, n. 8 (p. 357).
[24] Plantinga, *The Nature of Necessity*, p. 177 [p. 94 above].

that a certain connection obtains between antecedent and consequent'.[25] My account of what makes (11) true does not suggest a way in which (1) or (2) could be true, since they do not have true consequents to help make them true.

Furthermore, if my account is right, it was presumably not settled that (11) is true before (in the order of explanation) it was settled that Smith was going to be offered, and accept, $35,000, since his actual acceptance is part of what makes (11) true. I see no reason, therefore, to suppose that God could have known of the truth of (11) early enough in the order of explanation to make use of it as He is supposed to make use of middle knowledge.

Another type of case, not presented by Plantinga, perplexes me more. There does not normally seem to be any uncertainty at all about what a butcher, for example, would have done if I had asked him to sell me a pound of ground beef, although we suppose he would have had free will in the matter. We say he would certainly have sold me the meat, if he had it to sell. What makes us regard it as certain? Chiefly his character, habits, desires, and intentions, and the absence of countervailing dispositions. (He would have had no motive to refuse me.)

There are three alternative views one might take of this case. One might say that if I had asked the butcher to sell me the meat, (i) he would only probably have sold it to me, though we normally ignore the minute but real chance there would have been that he would refuse; *or* (ii) he would certainly have sold me the meat, because he would have been causally determined to do so by his character and dispositions; *or* (iii) his character and dispositions would not have causally determined his action, but they render it absolutely certain that he would have complied with my request.

I have rested an important part of my argument on the assumption that what a person's character and dispositions do not causally determine, they do not render absolutely certain. Alternative (iii) is inconsistent with this assumption. It still seems to me, however, that my assumption is sound and alternative (iii) is more implausible than (i) or (ii)—although I must admit that I am not altogether content with either of them. For what is the nature of the rendering certain in alternative (iii), if it is not causal determination? On some views—Humean views—of the nature of probability and causality, alternative (iii) is plainly impossible; and I do not know of any theory that would render it intelligible.

---

[25] Nelson Goodman, *Fact, Fiction, and Forecast* (London, 1954), 15.

V

Could God have arranged to have creatures who would perform free actions but only right ones? Let us consider the question first on the assumption that God has middle knowledge. In that case, we might think. He could have obtained sinless free creatures simply by making only those that He knew would always freely do right in those situations in which He would permit them to act freely.[26] Plantinga's response to this argument, a response which he develops with much greater elegance than I have space to reproduce here, is that God could not do this unless there are some possible free creatures who would in fact behave so well, and that perhaps none would. Plantinga proposes the hypothesis that all possible free creatures (or their essences) have *trans-world depravity*. Roughly speaking, a possible free creature (or its essence) has trans-world depravity, in Plantinga's sense, if and only if that creature *would* do some wrong if God created it and permitted it to act freely, no matter what else God did. If the hypothesis of universal trans-world depravity is true, God must have known it is true, if He had middle knowledge, and must therefore have known that some evil was the inescapable price of created freedom.

Plantinga does not claim that the hypothesis is true, or even that it is plausible.[27] He argues only that it is logically possible, because he is using it to defend the view that it is logically possible that both God and evil exist. I do not doubt that the latter is logically possible; but religious thought must seek an account of the relations between God and evil that is credible, as well as logically possible.

It is worth asking, therefore, whether the hypothesis of universal trans-world depravity is plausible, on the assumptions about truth of conditionals that Plantinga shares with the Jesuit theologians. I think Molina and Suarez would deny that any possible free creature (or any free creature's essence) has trans-world depravity; and they could support their denial with persuasive arguments. Suarez holds that 'it is alien to the common doctrine . . . and to the divine perfection and omnipotence, and is therefore of itself incredible enough, to say that God cannot predetermine [*praedefinire*] an honorable free act, in particular and with all [its] circumstances, by His absolute and effective will, the freedom of the created will still being preserved'.[28] God uses His middle knowledge to make such predeterminations effective,

---

[26] This argument is crisply stated by Nelson Pike, 'Plantinga on the Free Will Defense: A Reply', *The Journal of Philosophy*, 63 (1966), 93 f. 'Will' replaces 'would' in Pike's formulation, but it is clearly middle knowledge that is involved.

[27] Plantinga, *The Nature of Necessity*, cf. p. 165 with p. 189 [pp. 84 and 105 above].

[28] Suarez, DSDFC, Bk. 2, c. 4, n. 4 (p. 354).

choosing conditions and helps of grace that He knows will elicit a favorable response, and avoiding those under which He knows that the creature would not act according to the divine purpose. This presupposes, of course, that for every possible honorable free act of every possible free creature, in any possible outward circumstances, there are some incentives or helps of grace that God could supply, to which the creature would respond favorably though he could have responded unfavorably. But this is a very plausible presupposition if we assume, as Suarez does, that the theory of middle knowledge is correct, and that there is an infinite variety of natural and supernatural ways in which God can work on us inwardly, assisting our reasoning, affecting our feelings and perhaps our beliefs and desires, without causally determining our response.[29]

And if it is plausible to suppose that for every possible *particular* occasion of action there are possible divine operations that would elicit a favorable free response, is it not also plausible to suppose that for many possible free creatures, and even for whole worlds full of them, there are possible series of divine operations to which those creatures would respond by *always* freely doing right, never doing wrong? Molina held that both Jesus and Mary were preserved from all sin throughout their whole lives by God supplying them with gifts and aids that He knew would always elicit a favorable free response from them.[30] Presumably He could have done the same for others.

If the hypothesis of universal trans-world depravity is implausible, it might seem that I offer theodicy a better alternative. I deny the possibility of middle knowledge, because I deny that the relevant subjunctive conditionals are true. In particular, I deny that the following is true:

(12) If God had acted differently in certain ways, He would have had creatures who made free choices, but none of whom ever made wrong choices.

In other words, I deny that God could have made free creatures who *would* always have freely done right. The supposition that He could have done so is burdened with all the difficulties about truth of conditionals that afflict the theory of middle knowledge. Since (12) is not true, a reproach against God cannot rightly be based on its truth. And God cannot know that (12) is true, and cannot rightly be blamed for not using such knowledge.

My views about the truth of conditionals, however, do not tend to show that the following could not be true:

[29] Cf. ibid., n. 5 (p. 355).
[30] Molina, *Concordia*, qu. 14 art. 13, disp. 53, memb. 4, nn. 15–24 (pp. 399–405).

(13) If God had acted differently in certain ways, He would *probably* have had creatures who made free choices, but none of whom ever made wrong choices.

(14) If God had acted differently in certain ways, He would *probably* have had better behaved free creatures, on the whole, than He actually has.

In fact (13) seems to me rather implausible. Without middle knowledge God must take real risks if He makes free creatures (thousands, millions, or trillions of risks, if each free creature makes thousands of morally significant free choices). No matter how shrewdly God acted in running so many risks, His winning on *every* risk would not be antecedently probable. But I think (14) is very plausible. These judgments suggest that the necessity of permitting some evil in order to have free will in creatures may play a part in a theodicy but cannot bear the whole weight of it, even if the possibility of middle knowledge is rejected.

I am indebted to several, including David Kaplan, and especially David Lewis and Alvin Plantinga, for discussion and for comments on an earlier version of this paper, which was read to an American Philosophical Association symposium. An abstract of the earlier version, 'Middle Knowledge', appeared in *The Journal of Philosophy*, 70 (1973), 552–4. Work on the present version was supported by the US National Endowment for the Humanities.

VII

THE PROBLEM OF EVIL AND SOME VARIETIES OF ATHEISM

WILLIAM L. ROWE

This paper is concerned with three interrelated questions. The first is: Is there an argument for atheism based on the existence of evil that may rationally justify someone in being an atheist? To this first question I give an affirmative answer and try to support that answer by setting forth a strong argument for atheism based on the existence of evil.[1] The second question is: How can the theist best defend his position against the argument for atheism based on the existence of evil? In response to this question I try to describe what may be an adequate rational defense for theism against any argument for atheism based on the existence of evil. The final question is: What position should the informed atheist take concerning the rationality of theistic belief? Three different answers an atheist may give to this question serve to distinguish three varieties of atheism: unfriendly atheism, indifferent atheism, and friendly atheism. In the final part of the paper I discuss and defend the position of friendly atheism.

Before we consider the argument from evil, we need to distinguish a narrow and a broad sense of the terms 'theist', 'atheist', and 'agnostic'. By a 'theist' in the narrow sense I mean someone who believes in the existence of an omnipotent, omniscient, eternal, supremely good being who created the world. By a 'theist' in the broad sense I mean someone who believes in the existence of some sort of divine being or divine reality. To be a theist

William L. Rowe, 'The Problem of Evil and Some Varieties of Atheism', first published in *American Philosophical Quarterly*, 16 (1979), pp. 335–41. Used with permission.

[1] Some philosophers have contended that the existence of evil is *logically inconsistent* with the existence of the theistic God. No one, I think, has succeeded in establishing such an extravagant claim. Indeed, granted incompatibilism, there is a fairly compelling argument for the view that the existence of evil is logically consistent with the existence of the theistic God. (For a lucid statement of this argument see Alvin Plantinga, *God, Freedom, and Evil* (New York, 1974), 29–59.) There remains, however, what we may call the *evidential* form—as opposed to the *logical* form—of the problem of evil: the view that the variety and profusion of evil in our world, although perhaps not logically inconsistent with the existence of the theistic God, provides, nevertheless, *rational support* for atheism. In this paper I shall be concerned solely with the evidential form of the problem, the form of the problem which, I think, presents a rather severe difficulty for theism.

in the narrow sense is also to be a theist in the broad sense, but one may be a theist in the broad sense—as was Paul Tillich—without believing that there is a supremely good, omnipotent, omniscient, eternal being who created the world. Similar distinctions must be made between a narrow and a broad sense of the terms 'atheist' and 'agnostic'. To be an atheist in the broad sense is to deny the existence of any sort of divine being or divine reality. Tillich was not an atheist in the broad sense. But he was an atheist in the narrow sense, for he denied that there exists a divine being that is all-knowing, all-powerful and perfectly good. In this paper I will be using the terms 'theism', 'theist', 'atheism', 'atheist', 'agnosticism', and 'agnostic' in the narrow sense, not in the broad sense.

I

In developing the argument for atheism based on the existence of evil, it will be useful to focus on some particular evil that our world contains in considerable abundance. Intense human and animal suffering, for example, occurs daily and in great plentitude in our world. Such intense suffering is a clear case of evil. Of course, if the intense suffering leads to some greater good, a good we could not have obtained without undergoing the suffering in question, we might conclude that the suffering is justified, but it remains an evil nevertheless. For we must not confuse the intense suffering in and of itself with the good things to which it sometimes leads or of which it may be a necessary part. Intense human or animal suffering is in itself bad, an evil, even though it may sometimes be justified by virtue of being a part of, or leading to, some good which is unobtainable without it. What is evil in itself may sometimes be good as a means because it leads to something that is good in itself. In such a case, while remaining an evil in itself, the intense human or animal suffering is, nevertheless, an evil which someone might be morally justified in permitting.

Taking human and animal suffering as a clear instance of evil which occurs with great frequency in our world, the argument for atheism based on evil can be stated as follows:

1. There exist instances of intense suffering which an omnipotent, omniscient being could have prevented without thereby losing some greater good or permitting some evil equally bad or worse.[2]

___

[2] If there is some good, G, greater than any evil, (1) will be false for the trivial reason that no matter what evil, E, we pick the conjunctive good state of affairs consisting of G and E will outweigh E and be such that an omnipotent being could not obtain it without permitting E. (See Alvin Plantinga, *God and Other Minds* (Ithaca, 1967), 167.) To avoid this objection we may

2. An omniscient, wholly good being would prevent the occurrence of any intense suffering it could, unless it could not do so without thereby losing some greater good or permitting some evil equally bad or worse.

3. There does not exist an omnipotent, omniscient, wholly good being.

What are we to say about this argument for atheism, an argument based on the profusion of one sort of evil in our world? The argument is valid; therefore, if we have rational grounds for accepting its premises, to that extent we have rational grounds for accepting atheism. Do we, however, have rational grounds for accepting the premises of this argument?

Let's begin with the second premise. Let s_1 be an instance of intense human or animal suffering which an omniscient, wholly good being could prevent. We will also suppose that things are such that s_1 will occur unless prevented by the omniscient, wholly good (OG) being. We might be interested in determining what would be a *sufficient* condition of OG failing to prevent s_1. But, for our purpose here, we need only try to state a *necessary* condition for OG failing to prevent s_1. That condition, so it seems to me, is this:

Either   (i) there is some greater good, G, such that G is obtainable by OG only if OG permits s_1,[3]

or   (ii) there is some greater good, G, such that G is obtainable by OG only if OG permits either s_1 or some evil equally bad or worse,

or   (iii) s_1 is such that it is preventable by OG only if OG permits some evil equally bad or worse.

---

insert 'unreplaceable' into our premises (1) and (2) between 'some' and 'greater'. If E isn't required for G, and G is better than G plus E, then the good conjunctive state of affairs composed of G and E would be *replaceable* by the greater good of G alone. For the sake of simplicity, however, I will ignore this complication both in the formulation and discussion of premises (1) and (2).

[3] Three clarifying points need to be made in connection with (1). First, by 'good' I don't mean to exclude the fulfilment of certain moral principles. Perhaps preventing s_1 would preclude certain actions prescribed by the principles of justice. I shall allow that the satisfaction of certain principles of justice may be a good that outweighs the evil of s_1. Second, even though (1) may suggest it, I don't mean to limit the good in question to something that would *follow in time* the occurrence of s_1. And, finally, we should perhaps not fault OG if the good G, that would be loss were s_1 prevented, is not actually greater than s_1, but merely such that allowing s_1 and G, as opposed to preventing s_1 and thereby losing G, would not alter the balance between good and evil. For reasons of simplicity, I have left this point out in stating (i), with the result that (i) is perhaps a bit stronger than it should be.

It is important to recognize that (iii) is not included in (i). For losing a good greater than s_1 is not the same as permitting an evil greater than s_1. And this because the *absence* of a good state of affairs need not itself be an evil state of affairs. It is also important to recognize that s_1 might be such that it is preventable by OG *without* losing G (so condition (i) is not satisfied) but also such that if OG did prevent it, G would be lost *unless OG* permitted some evil equal to or worse than s_1. If this were so, it does not seem correct to require that OG prevent s_1. Thus, condition (ii) takes into account an important possibility not encompassed in condition (i).

Is it true that if an omniscient, wholly good being permits the occurrence of some intense suffering it could have prevented, then either (i) or (ii) or (iii) obtains? It seems to me that it is true. But if it is true then so is premise (2) of the argument for atheism. For that premise merely states in more compact form what we have suggested must be true if an omniscient, wholly good being fails to prevent some intense suffering it could prevent. Premise (2) says that an omniscient, wholly good being would prevent the occurrence of any intense suffering it could, unless it could not do so without thereby losing some greater good or permitting some evil equally bad or worse. This premise (or something not too distant from it) is, I think, held in common by many atheists and nontheists. Of course, there may be disagreement about whether something is good, and whether, if it is good, one would be morally justified in permitting some intense suffering to occur in order to obtain it. Someone might hold, for example, that no good is great enough to justify permitting an innocent child to suffer terribly.[4] Again, someone might hold that the mere fact that a given good outweighs some suffering and would be lost if the suffering were prevented, is not a morally sufficient reason for permitting the suffering. But to hold either of these views is not to deny (2). For (2) claims only that *if* an omniscient, wholly good being permits intense suffering *then* either there is some greater good that would have been lost, or some equally bad or worse evil that would have occurred, had the intense suffering been prevented. (2) does not purport to describe what might be a *sufficient* condition for an omniscient, wholly good being to permit intense suffering, only what is a *necessary* condition. So stated, (2) seems to express a belief that accords with our basic moral principles, principles shared by both theists and nontheists. If we are to fault the argument for atheism, therefore, it seems we must find some fault with its first premise.

Suppose in some distant forest lightning strikes a dead tree, resulting in a forest fire. In the fire a fawn is trapped, horribly burned, and lies in terrible

---

[4] See Ivan's speech in bk. v, ch. iv, of *The Brothers Karamazov*.

agony for several days before death relieves its suffering. So far as we can see, the fawn's intense suffering is pointless. For there does not appear to be any greater good such that the prevention of the fawn's suffering would require either the loss of that good or the occurrence of an evil equally bad or worse. Nor does there seem to be any equally bad or worse evil so connected to the fawn's suffering that it would have had to occur had the fawn's suffering been prevented. Could an omnipotent, omniscient being have prevented the fawn's apparently pointless suffering? The answer is obvious, as even the theist will insist. An omnipotent, omniscient being could have easily prevented the fawn from being horribly burned, or, given the burning, could have spared the fawn the intense suffering by quickly ending its life, rather than allowing the fawn to lie in terrible agony for several days. Since the fawn's intense suffering was preventable and, so far as we can see, pointless, doesn't it appear that premise (1) of the argument is true, that there do exist instances of intense suffering which an omnipotent, omniscient being could have prevented without thereby losing some greater good or permitting some evil equally bad or worse?

It must be acknowledged that the case of the fawn's apparently pointless suffering does not *prove* that (1) is true. For even though we cannot see how the fawn's suffering is required to obtain some greater good (or to prevent some equally bad or worse evil), it hardly follows that it is not so required. After all, we are often surprised by how things we thought to be unconnected turn out to be intimately connected. Perhaps, for all we know, there is some familiar good outweighing the fawn's suffering to which that suffering is connected in a way we do not see. Furthermore, there may well be unfamiliar goods, goods we haven't dreamed of, to which the fawn's suffering is inextricably connected. Indeed, it would seem to require something like omniscience on our part before we could lay claim to *knowing* that there is no greater good connected to the fawn's suffering in such a manner that an omnipotent, omniscient being could not have achieved that good without permitting that suffering or some evil equally bad or worse. So the case of the fawn's suffering surely does not enable us to *establish* the truth of (1).

The truth is that we are not in a position to prove that (1) is true. We cannot know with certainty that instances of suffering of the sort described in (1) do occur in our world. But it is one thing to *know* or *prove* that (1) is true and quite another thing to have *rational grounds* for believing (1) to be true. We are often in the position where in the light of our experience and knowledge it is rational to believe that a certain statement is true, even though we are not in a position to prove or to know with certainty that the statement is true. In the light of our past experience and knowledge it is, for example, very reasonable to believe that neither Goldwater nor McGovern will ever be elected President, but we are scarcely in the position of knowing with certainty that neither will ever be elected President. So, too, with (1), although we cannot know with certainty that it is true, it perhaps can be rationally supported, shown to be a rational belief.

Consider again the case of the fawn's suffering. Is it reasonable to believe that there is some greater good so intimately connected to that suffering that even an omnipotent, omniscient being could not have obtained that good without permitting that suffering or some evil at least as bad? It certainly does not appear reasonable to believe this. Nor does it seem reasonable to believe that there is some evil at least as bad as the fawn's suffering such that an omnipotent being simply could not have prevented it without permitting the fawn's suffering. But even if it should somehow be reasonable to believe either of these things of the fawn's suffering, we must then ask whether it is reasonable to believe either of these things of *all* the instances of seemingly pointless human and animal suffering that occur daily in our world. And surely the answer to this more general question must be no. It seems quite unlikely that *all* the instances of intense suffering occurring daily in our world are intimately related to the occurrence of greater goods or the prevention of evils at least as bad; and even more unlikely, should they somehow all be so related, that an omnipotent, omniscient being could not have achieved at least some of those goods (or prevented some of those evils) without permitting the instances of intense suffering that are supposedly related to them. In the light of our experience and knowledge of the variety and scale of human and animal suffering in our world, the idea that none of this suffering could have been prevented by an omnipotent being without thereby losing a greater good or permitting an evil at least as bad seems an extraordinary absurd idea, quite beyond our belief. It seems then that although we cannot *prove* that (1) is true, it is, nevertheless, altogether *reasonable* to believe that (1) is true, that (1) is a *rational* belief.[5]

[5] One might object that the conclusion of this paragraph is stronger than the reasons given warrant. For it is one thing to argue that it is unreasonable to think that (1) is false and another thing to conclude that we are therefore justified in accepting (1) as true. There are propositions such that believing them is much more reasonable than disbelieving them, and yet are such that *withholding judgment* about them is more reasonable than believing them. To take an example of Chisholm's: it is more reasonable to believe that the Pope will be in Rome (on some arbitrarily picked future date) than to believe that he won't; but it is perhaps more reasonable to suspend judgment on the question of the Pope's whereabouts on that particular date, than to believe that he will be in Rome. Thus it might be objected, that while we've shown that believing (1) is more reasonable than disbelieving (1), we haven't shown that believing (1) is more reasonable than withholding belief. My answer to this objection is that there are things we know which render (1) probable to the degree that it is more reasonable to believe (1) than to suspend judgment on (1). What are these things we know? First, I think, is the fact that there is an enormous variety and

Returning now to our argument for atheism, we've seen that the second premise expresses a basic belief common to many theists and nontheists. We've also seen that our experience and knowledge of the variety and profusion of suffering in our world provides *rational support* for the first premise. Seeing that the conclusion, 'There does not exist an omnipotent, omniscient, wholly good being' follows from these two premises, it does seem that we have *rational support* for atheism, that it is reasonable for us to believe that the theistic God does not exist.

II

Can theism be rationally defended against the argument for atheism we have just examined? If it can, how might the theist best respond to that argument? Since the argument from (1) and (2) to (3) is valid, and since the theist, no less than the nontheist, is more than likely committed to (2), it's clear that the theist can reject this atheistic argument only by rejecting its first premise, the premise that states that there are instances of intense suffering which an omnipotent, omniscient being could have prevented without thereby losing some greater good or permitting some evil equally bad or worse. How, then, can the theist best respond to this premise and the considerations advanced in its support?

There are basically three responses a theist can make. First, he might argue not that (1) is false or probably false, but only that the reasoning given in support of it is in some way *defective*. He may do this either by arguing that the reasons given in support of (1) are *in themselves* insufficient to justify accepting (1), or by arguing that there are other things we know which, when taken in conjunction with these reasons, do not justify us in accepting (1). I suppose some theists would be content with this rather modest response to the basic argument for atheism. But given the validity of the basic argument and the theist's likely acceptance of (2), he is thereby committed to the view that (1) is false, not just that we have no good reasons for accepting (1) as true. The second two responses are aimed at showing that it is reasonable to believe that (1) is false. Since the theist is committed to this view, I shall focus the discussion on these two attempts,

profusion of intense human and animal suffering in our world. Second, is the fact that much of this suffering seems quite unrelated to any greater goods (or the absence of equal or greater evils) that might justify it. And, finally, there is the fact that such suffering as is related to greater goods (or the absence of equal or greater evils) does not, in many cases, seem so intimately related as to require its permission by an omnipotent being bent on securing those goods (the absence of those evils). These facts, I am claiming, make it more reasonable to accept (1) than to withhold judgment on (1).

attempts which we can distinguish as 'the direct attack' and 'the indirect attack'.

By a direct attack, I mean an attempt to reject (1) by pointing out goods, for example, to which suffering may well be connected, goods which an omnipotent, omniscient being could not achieve without permitting suffering. It is doubtful, however, that the direct attack can succeed. The theist may point out that some suffering leads to moral and spiritual development impossible without suffering. But it's reasonably clear that suffering often occurs in a degree far beyond what is required for character development. The theist may say that some suffering results from free choices of human beings and might be preventable only by preventing some measure of human freedom. But, again, it's clear that much intense suffering occurs not as a result of human free choices. The general difficulty with this direct attack on premise (1) is twofold. First, it cannot succeed, for the theist does not know what greater goods might be served, or evils prevented, by each instance of intense human or animal suffering. Second, the theist's own religious tradition usually maintains that in this life it is not given to us to know God's purpose in allowing particular instances of suffering. Hence, the direct attack against premise (1) cannot succeed and violates basic beliefs associated with theism.

The best procedure for the theist to follow in rejecting premise (1) is the indirect procedure. This procedure I shall call 'the G. E. Moore shift', so-called in honor of the twentieth century philosopher, G. E. Moore, who used it to great effect in dealing with the arguments of the skeptics. Skeptical philosophers such as David Hume have advanced ingenious arguments to prove that no one can know of the existence of any material object. The premises of their arguments employ plausible principles, principles which many philosophers have tried to reject directly, but only with questionable success. Moore's procedure was altogether different. Instead of arguing directly against the premises of the skeptic's arguments, he simply noted that the premises implied, for example, that he (Moore) did not know of the existence of a pencil. Moore then proceeded indirectly against the skeptic's premises by arguing:

I do know that this pencil exists.
If the skeptic's principles are correct I cannot know of the existence of this pencil.

∴ The skeptic's principles (at least one) must be incorrect.

Moore then noted that his argument is just as valid as the skeptic's, that both of their arguments contain the premise 'If the skeptic's principles are correct Moore cannot know of the existence of this pencil', and concluded that the only way to choose between the two arguments (Moore's and the skeptic's) is by deciding which of the first premises it is more rational to believe—Moore's premise 'I do know that this pencil exists' or the skeptic's premise asserting that his skeptical principles are correct. Moore concluded that his own first premise was the more rational of the two.[6]

Before we see how the theist may apply the G. E. Moore shift to the basic argument of atheism, we should note the general strategy of the shift. We're given an argument: p, q, therefore, r. Instead of arguing directly against p, another argument is constructed—not-r, q, therefore, not-p—which begins with the denial of the conclusion of the first argument, keeps its second premise, and ends with the denial of the first premise as its conclusion. Compare, for example, these two:

$$\begin{array}{ll} \text{I. } p & \text{II. not-}r \\ \quad q & \quad q \\ \overline{} & \overline{} \\ \quad r & \quad \text{not-}p \end{array}$$

It is a truth of logic that if I is valid II must be valid as well. Since the arguments are the same so far as the second premise is concerned, any choice between them must concern their respective first premises. To argue against the first premise (p) by constructing the counter argument II is to employ the G. E. Moore shift.

Applying the G. E. Moore shift against the first premise of the basic argument for atheism, the theist can argue as follows:

not-3. There exists an omnipotent, omniscient, wholly good being.

2. An omniscient, wholly good being would prevent the occurrence of any intense suffering it could, unless it could not do so without thereby losing some greater good or permitting some evil equally bad or worse.

therefore,

not-1. It is not the case that there exist instances of intense suffering which an omnipotent, omniscient being could have prevented without thereby losing some greater good or permitting some evil equally bad or worse.

We now have two arguments: the basic argument for atheism from (1) and (2) to (3), and the theist's best response', the argument from (not-3) and (2) to (not-1). What the theist then says about (1) is that he has rational

[6] See, for example, the two chapters on Hume in G. E. Moore, *Some Main Problems of Philosophy* (London, 1953).

grounds for believing in the existence of the theistic God (not-3), accepts (2) as true, and sees that (not-1) follows from (not-3) and (2). He concludes, therefore, that he has rational grounds for rejecting (1). Having rational grounds for rejecting (1), the theist concludes that the basic argument for atheism is mistaken.

III

We've had a look at a forceful argument for atheism and what seems to be the theist's best response to that argument. If one is persuaded by the argument for atheism, as I find myself to be, how might one best view the position of the theist? Of course, he will view the theist as having a false belief, just as the theist will view the atheist as having a false belief. But what position should the atheist take concerning the *rationality* of the theist's belief? There are three major positions an atheist might take, positions which we may think of as some varieties of atheism. First, the atheist may believe that no one is rationally justified in believing that the theistic God exists. Let us call this position 'unfriendly atheism'. Second, the atheist may hold no belief concerning whether any theist is or isn't rationally justified in believing that the theistic God exists. Let us call this view 'indifferent atheism'. Finally, the atheist may believe that some theists are rationally justified in believing that the theistic God exists. This view we shall call 'friendly atheism'. In this final part of the paper I propose to discuss and defend the position of friendly atheism.

If no one can be rationally justified in believing a false proposition then friendly atheism is a paradoxical, if not incoherent position. But surely the truth of a belief is not a necessary condition of someone's being rationally justified in having that belief. So in holding that someone is rationally justified in believing that the theistic God exists, the friendly atheist is not committed to thinking that the theist has a true belief. What he is committed to is that the theist has rational grounds for his belief, a belief the atheist rejects and is convinced he is rationally justified in rejecting. But is this possible? Can someone, like our friendly atheist, hold a belief, be convinced that he is rationally justified in holding that belief, and yet believe that someone else is equally justified in believing the opposite? Surely this is possible. Suppose your friends see you off on a flight to Hawaii. Hours after take-off they learn that your plane has gone down at sea. After a twenty-four hour search, no survivors have been found. Under these circumstances they are rationally justified in believing that you have perished. But it is hardly rational for you to believe this, as you bob up and down in your life vest, wondering why the search planes have failed to spot you. Indeed, to amuse yourself while awaiting your fate, you might very well reflect on the fact that your friends are rationally justified in believing that you are now dead, a proposition you disbelieve and are rationally justified in disbelieving. So, too, perhaps an atheist may be rationally justified in his atheistic belief and yet hold that some theists are rationally justified in believing just the opposite of what he believes.

What sort of grounds might a theist have for believing that God exists? Well, he might endeavor to justify his belief by appealing to one or more of the traditional arguments: Ontological, Cosmological, Teleological, Moral, etc. Second, he might appeal to certain aspects of religious experience, perhaps even his own religious experience. Third, he might try to justify theism as a plausible theory in terms of which we can account for a variety of phenomena. Although an atheist must hold that the theistic God does not exist, can he not also believe, and be justified in so believing, that some of these 'justifications of theism' do actually rationally justify some theists in their belief that there exists a supremely good, omnipotent, omniscient being? It seems to me that he can.

If we think of the long history of theistic belief and the special situations in which people are sometimes placed, it is perhaps as absurd to think that no one was ever rationally justified in believing that the theistic God exists as it is to think that no one was ever justified in believing that human being would never walk on the moon. But in suggesting that friendly atheism is preferable to unfriendly atheism, I don't mean to rest the case on what some human beings might reasonably have believed in the eleventh or thirteenth century. The more interesting question is whether some people in modern society, people who are aware of the usual grounds for belief and disbelief and are acquainted to some degree with modern science, are yet rationally justified in accepting theism. Friendly atheism is a significant position only if it answers this question in the affirmative.

It is not difficult for an atheist to be friendly when he has reason to believe that the theist could not reasonably be expected to be acquainted with the grounds for disbelief that he (the atheist) possesses. For then the atheist may take the view that some theists are rationally justified in holding to theism, but would not be so were they to be acquainted with the grounds for disbelief—those grounds being sufficient to tip the scale in favor of atheism when balanced against the reasons the theist has in support of his belief.

Friendly atheism becomes paradoxical, however, when the atheist contemplates believing that the theist has all the grounds for atheism that he, the atheist, has, and yet is rationally justified in maintaining his theistic belief. But even so excessively friendly a view as this perhaps can be held by the atheist if he also has some reason to think that the grounds for theism are not as telling as the theist is justified in taking them to be.[7]

In this paper I've presented what I take to be a strong argument for atheism, pointed out what I think is the theist's best response to that argument, distinguished three positions an atheist might take concerning the rationality of theistic belief, and made some remarks in defense of the position called 'friendly atheism'. I'm aware that the central points of the paper are not likely to be warmly received by many philosophers. Philosophers who are atheists tend to be tough minded—holding that there are no good reasons for supposing that theism is true. And theists tend either to reject the view that the existence of evil provides rational grounds for atheism or to hold that religious belief has nothing to do with reason and evidence at all. But such is the way of philosophy.

---

[7] Suppose that I add a long sum of numbers three times and get result x. I inform you of this so that you have pretty much the same evidence I have for the claim that the sum of the numbers is x. You then use your calculator twice over and arrive at result y. You, then, are justified in believing that the sum of the numbers is *not* x. However, knowing that your calculator has been damaged and is therefore unreliable, and that you have no reason to think that it is damaged, I may reasonably believe not only that the sum of the numbers is x, but also that you are justified in believing that the sum is not x. Here is a case, then, where you have all of my evidence for p, and yet I can reasonably believe that you are justified in believing not-p—for I have reason to believe that your grounds for not-p are not as telling as you are justified in taking them to be.

I am indebted to my colleagues at Purdue University, particularly to Ted Ulrich and Lilly Russow, and to philosophers at The University of Nebraska, Indiana State University, and The University of Wisconsin at Milwaukee for helpful criticisms of earlier versions of this paper.

VIII

THE HUMEAN OBSTACLE TO EVIDENTIAL ARGUMENTS FROM SUFFERING: ON AVOIDING THE EVILS OF 'APPEARANCE'

STEPHEN J. WYKSTRA

Many of us—believers as well as nonbelievers, car mechanics as well as philosophers—have at some times in our lives felt instances of suffering in this world to be evidence against theism, according to which the universe is the creation of a wholly good Being who loves his creatures, and who lacks nothing in wisdom and power. If it has proven hard to turn this feeling into a good argument, it has, perhaps, proven just as hard to get rid of it. Indeed, the most logically sophisticated responses to the 'problem of evil' can leave one wondering whether our intuitive perplexities have not been lost in the gears of the formal machinery brought to bear on them. Maybe this is an unavoidable epiphenomenon of analysis; nevertheless, I want to try to mitigate it here.

For this reason (and a second forthcoming one), my springboard will be William Rowe's recent formulation of the case from suffering against theism.[1] Rowe exemplifies the recent turn away from 'logical' (or 'deductive', or 'demonstrative') formulations, construing the case instead as 'evidential' (or 'inductive', or 'probabilistic') in nature. The crux of his argument is that much suffering 'does not appear to serve any outweighing good'. This 'does not appear' defence is succinct and non-technical, affording considerable insight into our ordinary intuitions, but also making itself easy prey to misconstrual. I shall thus be amplifying Rowe's argument and defending it against specious criticisms, as well as—ultimately—rebutting it. This close

Stephen J. Wykstra, 'The Humean Obstacle to Evidential Arguments from Suffering: On Avoiding the Evils of Appearance', first published in *International Journal for Philosophy of Religion*, 16 (1984), pp. 73–93. Reprinted by permission of Kluwer Academic Publishers.

[1] William Rowe, 'The Problem of Evil and Some Varieties of Atheism', *American Philosophical Quarterly*, 16 (1979), 33–41 [Chapter VII above; bracketed page references are to the present collection].

attention to Rowe and his critics, however, is not an end-in-itself. It is a means of elucidating and vindicating a perspective from which we can see why a theist should, as Hume puts it, 'never retract his belief' on account of the suffering atheologians are inclined to adduce as evidence against theism. Vindicating this perspective requires coming to close grips with the most lucid atheological evidential case one can find—and this is my second reason for taking Rowe's work as a springboard.

I begin by giving an overview of Rowe's case, amplifying both its 'conceptual' and 'evidential' strands, and teasing out some difficulties in the construals given it by two critics, Bruce Reichenbach and Alvin Plantinga. Section 2 clarifies Rowe's crucial 'does not appear' claim and its role in his argument. Against Reichenbach, I argue that Rowe's reliance on this claim cannot be dismissed as an appeal to ignorance, for he is using 'appears' in what Chisholm calls its 'epistemic' sense, making his inference construable as a plausible application of 'the Principle of Credulity'. I then argue that Richard Swinburne is mistaken in building into this principle a restriction that would preclude the application Rowe tacitly gives it.

Having clarified Rowe's case by defending it against two specious criticisms, Section 3 diagnoses the real defect in Rowe's argument: his 'does not appear' claim contravenes a general condition that must be satisfied if we are to be entitled to this sort of claim. This condition—'the Condition of Reasonable Epistemic Access'—is explained, defended, and used to argue that the suffering in the world is not, as Rowe thinks, strong evidence against theism, and in fact isn't even weak evidence against it. The basic problem, I suggest, was identified by Hume as the main obstacle to any evidential case from suffering against 'theism'.

I conclude by giving an account of why we sometimes feel the credibility of theism weakened so much by cognizance of suffering and tragedy. For this feeling, if I am not mistaken, stems from a correct intuition about the bearing of suffering on theism; and we cannot understand why suffering does not really disconfirm theism unless we appreciate why, by an intuition not to be dismissed, it sometimes seems to.

1. ROWE'S CASE FOR ATHEISM

1.1. Deductive and Conceptual Aspects of Rowe's Case

Rowe's case has two stages, one 'evidential' and the other deductive. To bring the inductive stage into focus, we might best begin with the deductive argument Rowe gives [pp. 127–8] to logically (though not textually) culminate his case:

1. There exist instances of intense suffering which an omnipotent, omniscient being could have prevented without thereby losing some greater good or permitting some evil equally bad or worse.
2. An omniscient, wholly good being would prevent the occurrence of any intense suffering it could, unless it could not do so without thereby losing some greater good or permitting some evil equally bad or worse.
3. Therefore, there does not exist an omnipotent, omniscient, wholly good being.

The conclusion of this argument follows from the premises, but are the premises true? Rowe gives his 'evidential stage' to show it is reasonable to believe that premise 1 is true. But before turning to this, we should briefly attend to the rationale for premise 2. The heart of P2 is, I believe, a conceptual truth unpacking part of what it means to call any being—not just any omniscient being—morally good. The key idea is that a morally good being would allow an instance of suffering only if the being had an ulterior purpose justifying it in so doing, where such a justifying purpose must (conceptually 'must', in order to 'justify') involve:

> EITHER (A) the being's believing that there is some outweighing good that will obtain only if the being allows the suffering at issue or some comparable suffering;
> OR (B) the being's believing that there is some evil comparable to the suffering at issue that would obtain were the being to prevent this suffering.

To avoid tedious reiteration of (A) and (B), I shall for brevity's sake speak as though 'justifying purposes' consisted only of sort (A); and I shall refer to an instance of suffering as 'serving' an outweighing good which a being purposes in justifiedly allowing the suffering. In this shorthand, the key idea of Rowe's second premise is that a morally good being would allow[2] an instance of suffering only if the being believes that doing so serves some outweighing good. If this being is omniscient as well, his belief will of course be true; hence, in shorthand, premise 2: an omniscient and wholly good being will allow an instance of intense suffering only if doing so in fact

---

[2] By 'allow' I mean more than 'not prevent': one can allow something only if it is within one's power to prevent it. That I did not prevent the recent bad weather in California does not mean that I allowed it to occur.

serves some outweighing good. It should be carefully noted that to say a good is 'served' by God's allowing some instance of suffering is, on this definition, not merely to say that God uses the suffering to obtain the good: it is to say that his allowing of this (or some comparable) instance of suffering is the only way in which he can obtain the good.

Should we accept premise 2? In answering this we need to avoid three confusions. First, P2 claims only that if there is an omniscient and wholly good being, then there must *be* outweighing goods served by every instance of suffering he allows. This claim does not involve any presumption that we can know in any given case just *what* these goods are.

Second, 'serves' is not to be taken in a narrow 'means-to-an-end' sense, or in a sense that excludes deontological considerations. The theist may hold that some suffering results from the evil choices of morally free creatures, and that some other suffering is God's just punishment for such choices. In my shorthand, the theist is then holding: (1) that God allows the first sort of suffering because doing so 'serves' the great good of having a universe with morally free creatures in it; and (2) that the second sort 'serves' the great good of having a universe in which certain principles of justice, perhaps reflecting the holiness of God, are satisfied.

Third, one must note that by P2 it is, strictly speaking, God's *allowing* the suffering, and not the suffering itself, that must serve some outweighing good. P2 thus does *not* entail the notion that every instance of suffering is such that the world is 'really a better place' for having this suffering than it would be without it. The theist may rightly protest that such a notion fails to recognize that evil really is evil. But this is no reason to reject P2. To see this, consider what the import of P2 is—and is not—for suffering which, on a free will theodicy, is caused by the evil choices of morally free agents. The import of P2 is that God's prevention of all such suffering would not make the world a better place, for it would eliminate the good of moral freedom. But this does not mean that the suffering itself contributes, in the long run, to the world's being a good place: the world might well have been better if all this suffering had been prevented—not by God, but by those agents who through their choices caused it. Odd as it first seems, theists can (and I think should) insist that for some suffering, it is within our power but not within God's to prevent it without the loss of an outweighing good.

If we avoid these confusions, we can see the force of the claim that if God exists, there is some outweighing good related in the specified way to every instance of suffering he allows. For denying this is tantamount to saying that God could allow some intense suffering either because he enjoys the sight of occasional suffering for its own sake, or because he is indifferent to it. It is hard to see how such a being could be meaningfully praised as a *good*

God, worthy of our worship, our obedience, and—not least—our trust.[3] I take this to be a basic conceptual truth deserving assent by theists and nontheists alike; and though there may be technical difficulties in the way premise 2 formulates this truth, I shall assume that these can be remedied without affecting the validity of the argument.[4]

Granting this, and acknowledging that the argument is valid, atheism must be accepted if premise 1 is accepted. (By 'atheism' Rowe carefully means 'narrow atheism', i.e., the view that the omni-God of traditional theism does not exist: this of course does not rule out the existence of Apollo, the Ground of Being, the Force, or other objects of religious devotion or imagination.) The issue of concern—Rowe's, and mine here— is then whether there are reasons good enough to justify our acceptance of premise 1.

1.2. The Evidential Part of Rowe's Case

Premise 1 has, in effect two conjuncts: first, that there are instances of intense suffering; and second, that at least one of these instances has no 'God-justifying purpose' (as I shall put it)—i.e., serves no outweighing good that could justify an omniscient and omnipotent being in allowing the suffering. The first conjunct cannot reasonably be disputed. The second conjunct is the crucial and controversial one, and it is what I shall hereafter have in mind in referring to 'premise 1'.

Now Rowe's distinction between 'logical' and 'evidential' versions of the problem of evil betokens, I think, two ways of trying to support premise 1. Often it has been propounded on conceptual grounds alone—by arguing, for example, that if God is omnipotent, then by definition He must always be *able* to achieve any good he desires while still preventing all instances of intense suffering. But philosophical theologians from Aquinas to Plantinga have, Rowe owns, successfully defused this and other more sophisticated conceptual arguments for premise 1. So Rowe proposes to defend premise 1 in a different 'evidential' way, by appealing not only to conceptual truths, but also to broadly empirical knowledge of the scale and variety of human and animal suffering in our world. Such grounds do, Rowe claims, provide rational support for premise 1, and hence for atheism.

---

[3] There are of course those who would deny this on the grounds that there is no positive analogy at all between 'good' as applied to God and as applied to creaturely agents. I have neither space nor motivation to deal with this position here.

[4] These difficulties should not, however, be underestimated: see pp. 5–10 of Alvin Plantinga's 'The Probabilistic Argument from Evil', *Philosophical Studies* (1979), 1–53. Plantinga criticizes an earlier version of Rowe's argument than that considered here.

ON AVOIDING THE EVILS OF 'APPEARANCE'   143

Rowe's case for this has two phases. The first [pp. 129–31] focuses on a single instance of suffering: lightning starts a forest fire in which a fawn 'is trapped, horribly burned, and lies for several days in terrible agony before death relieves its suffering'. Rowe argues that the fawn's suffering is 'apparently pointless', for 'there does not appear to be any outweighing good such that the prevention of the fawn's suffering would require either the loss of that good or the occurrence of an evil equally bad or worse'. This does not, Rowe allows, prove that the fawn's suffering is pointless; but, he notes, the evidence often makes it reasonable to believe that a statement is true even though it does not allow us to prove or know with certainty that it is true. And in the case of the fawn's suffering, the evidence of 'apparent pointlessness' is such that 'it does not appear reasonable to believe' that there is a God-justifying purpose for it.

The second evidential phase adduces [pp. 131–2] the great number of instances of suffering which have this feature of apparent pointlessness. Even if we are by some chance mistaken about the fawn's suffering, is it reasonable to believe that *each* of these instances of seemingly pointless suffering is connected to an outweighing good in the way requisite to justify an omnipotent and omniscient being in allowing the suffering? The answer, says Rowe, 'surely must be no'. Given our knowledge of the scale and variety of suffering such a belief 'seems an extraordinary absurd idea, quite beyond our belief'. Rowe thus concludes that 'it seems that although we cannot prove that premise 1 is true, it is, nevertheless, altogether reasonable to believe it is true'. And since (taking premise 2 as true) atheism validly follows, 'it does seem that we have rational support for atheism, that it is reasonable for us to believe that the theistic God does not exist'.

1.3. 'Rational Support'

What does Rowe here mean by 'rational support'? Let us say that evidence e weakly supports (or confirms) claim c when e makes c to some degree more likely to be true than it would be on the antecedent evidence. And let us say that e strongly supports (or confirms) c when it increases the likelihood of c sufficiently to make c 'reasonable to believe' by a person who appreciates the evidence. (A parallel distinction can be drawn between a strong and weak sense of 'disconfirms.'[5]) Now in the passage cited above,

[5] Both senses of 'disconfirms' are dynamic, involving the degree to which the adduced evidence changes the likelihood of a claim from its likelihood on our background knowledge, and are thus to be distinguished from the 'static' sense (which Plantinga addresses) of the probability of a claim with respect to the adduced evidence alone. In probabilistic terms, claim c is weakly disconfirmed by e given background knowledge k whenever $P(c/k\&e) < P(c/k)$; and c is strongly

Rowe makes it clear that he is using 'support' in its strong sense: in a footnote [p. 132] he says he is claiming that certain facts about suffering 'make it more reasonable to accept premise 1 (and hence atheism) than to withhold judgement . . .'. And since atheism as we've defined it is just the negation of theism, evidence which strongly confirms atheism must, *ipso facto*, strongly disconfirm theism. Let us put this by saying that Rowe claims the facts of suffering provide a 'strong' evidential case for atheism (or—equivalently—against theism).

Now it is almost a truism of inductive logic, noted by both Reichenbach and Plantinga, that a proposition whose likelihood is low on (or reduced by) certain evidence e may yet be entirely reasonably believed; it may, for one thing, have a high likelihood on other evidence that overrides e. Reichenbach and Plantinga conclude from this that a 'strong' probabilistic case against theism must show that the likelihood of theism is low relative to some available body of 'total relevant evidence', not just that is low on (or reduced by) certain facts about suffering. Plantinga draws from this the further dictum that to make good such a case, the atheologian 'would be obliged to consider all the sorts of reasons natural theologians have invoked in favor of theistic belief', showing these do not outweigh whatever evidence is provided against theism by suffering.[6] And Reichenbach, with something like this in mind, construes Rowe as aiming 'to show that rational support for God's existence does not obtain'.[7]

But Rowe's case does not include any critical appraisal of the various arguments adduced by natural theologians. It thus seems odd to suggest he aims 'to show' that rational support for God's existence does not obtain. If, however, he is not aiming to show this, how can he—given the requirement of 'total relevant evidence'—claim to provide a strong probabilistic case against theism? Reichenbach's construal, taken together with Plantinga's dictum, would have us conclude that Rowe just forgets (or ignores) what he is obliged to do to achieve his aim.

There are, I suggest, two other ways to read Rowe, both more plausible than the construal just sketched. To see them we must note that the sentences using 'support' in its strong sense occur in the first section of Rowe's paper. In the second and third sections, Rowe considers what he

disconfirmed whenever, in addition, $P(c/k\&e) < R$, where R is some value—no doubt above .5—on which c becomes 'reasonable' to believe. I assume that given certain background knowledge k, the 'evidential import' of e on c is in some way 'objective'; and that if, given k, e makes it reasonable to believe c, then e makes it reasonable to disbelieve (believe to be false) the denial of c.

[6] Plantinga, 'The Probabilistic Argument from Evil', p. 3.
[7] Bruce Reichenbach, 'The Inductive Argument from Evil', *American Philosophical Quarterly*, 17 (1980), 223.

thinks is the theist's best response to the argument of the first section. That response—the 'G. E. Moore shift'—begins by pointing out that from the premise that God exists, and Rowe's second premise (P2), it follows that Rowe's first premise is false. The 'shift' is then to argue that it is reasonable to believe that God exists, and therefore is reasonable to believe that Rowe's first premise is false.

Rowe of course doesn't think that 'best strategy' succeeds, and he makes it clear that two things are involved in his thinking this: he 'finds himself persuaded' by the evidence for P1; and he doesn't think the evidence for the theist's first premise is sufficient to pull off the G. E. Moore shift. (Rowe does not here consider the issue, recently pressed by Plantinga, of why the reasonableness of theism requires that it be based on 'evidence'.[8] Neither shall I.) But Rowe doesn't make entirely clear what relation these two things have, and here lie two ways of reading his thought.

One possibility is that Rowe thinks the evidence of suffering makes his first premise worthy of acceptance because he judges, on independent grounds, that the various arguments for theism have weaknesses by vice of which they fail to outweigh the evidence from suffering against theism. His overall claim, on this construal, is that the evidence of suffering supports atheism in what we might call a 'qualifiedly strong' sense, viz., it strongly supports atheism *provided* that independent assessment of theistic arguments shows these to be as weak as Rowe, based on his independent study of them, gives us his word they are.

A second possibility is suggested by the strategy of G. E. Moore in executing the very 'shift' against David Hume to which Rowe refers. To justify a decision between his own first premise ('I know this pencil exists') and Hume's principles (which entail I don't know this), Moore thought it quite unnecessary to assess the reasons given by Hume for his principles. The best justification for rejecting Hume's principles, he argued, is just that I am justified in believing 'I know this pencil exists', from which it follows that Hume's principles (and any arguments for them) must be mistaken.[9] Similarly, perhaps Rowe means to claim that the evidence of suffering, just in making it unlikely that God exists, thereby shows it is unlikely that any theistic arguments hold water. This strategy may be compared to that of a scientist who argues that a certain body of evidence, because it massively disconfirms the flat-earth hypothesis, also shows it is unlikely that the arguments given for this hypothesis—by, say, members of the Flat Earth Society—are any good. When evidence e strongly disconfirms claim c in a

---

[8] See, for example, Plantinga's 'Reason and Belief in God', in Plantinga and Wolterstorff (eds.), *Faith and Rationality* (Notre Dame, 1983).

[9] See G. E. Moore, *Some Main Problems of Philosophy* (London, 1953), 136 ff.

way that makes it reasonable to believe, 'in advance' as it were, that none of the arguments for c are likely to counterbalance e, let us say e disconfirms c in a 'super strong' sense.

Plantinga seems not to envisage the possibility of probabilistic evidence which super-strongly disconfirms theism; there may indeed be incoherence in the very notion of such evidence (which does not rule out the possibility that it is the operative notion in Rowe's thinking). These are difficult issues. Fortunately, we need not settle them here. In what follows, I shall argue that the evidence of suffering, as Rowe adduces it, does not disconfirm theism (or confirm atheism) even in the weak sense. And since that weak sense is included in each of the stronger senses I have distinguished, my argument, if successful, will show that suffering doesn't disconfirm theism in any of these stronger senses either.

2. TWO MISCONSTRUALS OF ROWE

My critique in Section 3 shall focus on Rowe's claim, crucial to his case, that 'there does not appear to be any outweighing good' of a God-justifying sort served by (say) the fawn's suffering. To prepare the ground, I shall here clarify Rowe's use of 'appears' and its role in his argument by defending his case against two lines of criticism that seem to me mistaken.

2.1. Rowe's Use of 'Appears'

Though the term 'appears' is ubiquitous in his case, Rowe provides no explication of its meaning. I shall provide one, suggesting that he uses the term in something close to what Swinburne, following Chisholm, calls its 'epistemic' sense (as distinct from its 'comparative', 'phenomenal', and 'hedging' senses).[10] But the 'appears idiom' is a philosophical swamp with an enormous literature, most of it of dubious relevance to Rowe's use. To avoid getting bogged down in it, I propose the following as a paradigm of Rowe's use that will give us our initial bearings.

Imagine two teachers, Ken and Nick, discussing their young colleague Tom, whom Ken thinks has mentally snapped under the stress of job-seeking. Ken tells Nick of a recent incident: Tom had abruptly excused himself from an important departmental meeting, saying he had urgent personal business. As it was later learned, he spent the next hour out by the parking lot, digging up earthworms and making, of all things, a fat sandwich

---

[10] Richard Swinburne, *The Existence of God* (Oxford, 1979), 245 ff.

with them. 'So it appears', Ken says, 'that Tom has gone off the deep end.'
If Nick resists this conclusion, saying 'But perhaps Tom had some sane and
rational reason for needing a worm sandwich', Ken might adduce other
bizarre episodes of Tom's recent behavior. Of each he says 'Here again, it
does not appear that Tom had a rational and sane reason for so behaving';
and the instances together he puts forward as clinching a cumulative case:
'It is almost beyond belief that we could be mistaken about each of these
instances.'

Ken, like Rowe, uses 'appears' to register what he takes to be the
'evidential import' of the specific situations he adduces. This evidential
import may well be enthymematic, depending upon a complex web of
background beliefs: but typically, I think, a speaker using 'it appears that'
(or 'it does not appear that') in this way will regard these background beliefs
and their bearing as relatively unproblematic in the context of discussion.
In the above case, Ken would not think it behooved him to show, by a
detailed argument, that Tom's sandwich-making behavior evidences a
mental disorder. This conclusion of course rests upon some tacit inference;
but the evidential import of some things is more readily 'seen' than 'shown';
and the 'appears' idiom concerning us is characteristically used for just such
things.

There is, then, nothing inherently suspect about Rowe's appeal-without-
further-argument to the claim, of certain instances of intense suffering, that
they 'do not appear to serve any outweighing good'. He supposes that this is
something the thoughtful reader, contemplating such instances, will as it
were just see. The situations, when one attends to them unblinkered by
prejudice, exert their own pressure on one's beliefs, inclining one to
concur: 'No, that *doesn't* seem to serve any outweighing good of a God-
justifying sort.' The appears-claim can, Rowe takes it, provide a 'stopping
point' to his argument—and even philosophers must stop argument somewhere. Hear Hume on a different topic:

I know not whether the reader will readily apprehend this reasoning. I am afraid that,
should I multiply words about it or throw it into a greater variety of lights, it would
only become more obscure and intricate. In all abstract reasonings there is one point
of view which, if we can happily hit, we shall go further toward illustrating the subject
than by all the eloquence and copious expression in the world.[11]

All of this is not to say that 'appears' claims can't be disputed. Clearly
they can be, in at least two ways. One way is to admit that the adduced
situation does have the *prima facie* evidential import imputed to it (that
Tom's behavior, say, does *seem* schizophrenic), but to argue that there is

---

[11] David Hume, *Inquiry Concerning Human Understanding*, end of section VII.

other evidence that outweighs or defeats this *prima facie* evidence. The other way is to argue that the adduced situation does not even have the *prima facie* evidential import imputed to it by the 'appears' claim. My mode of argument will be the second and more radical of these.

2.2. *Reichenbach's Misconstrual*

Dismissing Rowe's case as 'an appeal to ignorance', Reichenbach writes:

the atheologian claims that instances of suffering which are seemingly or apparently pointless are in fact or likely pointless, for we do not know of any higher good to which they are a means. But this constitutes an appeal to ignorance; that we know of no higher good does not entail that there is no such good, or that one is unlikely.[12]

It is clear that Reichenbach takes the driving premise of Rowe's argument to be 'that we know of no higher good' of the requisite sort. But is this really the same as the claim that 'it does not appear that there is any outweighing good' of the requisite sort—which claim is, we have seen, the actual 'stopping point' of Rowe's case?

To answer this we must carefully note how the word 'not' functions in appears-locutions of this sort. In some locutions—believes-locutions, for example—the meaning of a sentence will depend on *where* the 'not' is located in it. Thus

'Rowe does not believe that Reagan has brown socks on'
and 'Rowe believes that Reagan does not have brown socks on'

express (to a philosopher at any rate) different propositions: the first, but not the second, is compatible with Rowe's having no beliefs at all about the color of Reagan's socks. But contrast this with the pair

(1) It does not appear to me that Mrs. Reichenbach is sane
and (2) It appears to me that Mrs. Reichenbach is not sane.

A philosopher might try to insist that, strictly speaking, (1) means just 'it is not the case that it appears to me that Mrs. Reichenbach is sane'; so let us call this the 'strict' sense of 'does not appear'. In this sense, if I have absolutely no acquaintance at all with Mrs. Reichenbach, it would be perfectly true for me to say 'it does not appear to me that Mrs. Reichenbach is sane'. But Mrs. Reichenbach might well feel she has a case for slander if I go around talking this way about her: for in ordinary usage, 'it doesn't appear to me that p' is almost always taken to mean 'it appears to me that not-p'. So let us call this the 'ordinary sense' of 'does not appear' locutions. The ordinary sense is, we may note, stronger than the strict sense.

---

[12] Reichenbach, 'The Inductive Argument from Evil', p. 226.

Reichenbach, we now can see, takes Rowe to be appealing to the premise 'there does not appear to be any outweighing good' in its *strict* sense: it isn't the case there appears to be any such good. And if this were all Rowe is appealing to, Reichenbach would surely be right in smelling an argument from ignorance. But *is* this all Rowe is appealing to?

That it *isn't* is all but given away by Reichenbach's own description of Rowe's argument. The argument, he tells us, is 'that instances of suffering which are seemingly or apparently pointless are in fact or likely pointless, for we do not know of any higher good to which they are a means'. Reichenbach thus has Rowe moving from

> 'We do not know of any higher good to which they (apparently pointless instances of suffering) are a means'

to

> 'Apparently pointless instances of suffering are in fact or likely pointless.'

This is curious, for the class of 'apparently pointless' instances of suffering is the class of instances which 'do not appear' to have a point in the ordinary (and stronger) sense: they are instances that appear to have no point. When Rowe concludes that it is reasonable to believe that instances of *this* class do not have a point, why suppose he is appealing to the weaker claim that we don't know of any good served by them?[13] Not only is there no textual basis for supposing this; there is no logical need for it in the argument. For if an instance of suffering appears not to have a point, *that* is a reason for thinking it has no point.

The form of Rowe's move, I am claiming, is not from

> 'It is not the case that it appears that p'
> (the strict sense of 'it doesn't appear . . .')

to

> 'It is reasonable to believe that not-p.'

This would indeed be an argument from ignorance. It is instead from

> 'It appears that not-p'
> (the ordinary sense of 'It doesn't appear that p')

---

[13] Of course, part of what grounds Rowe's claim about the fawn's suffering is that we don't see a point for it. But then, part of what grounds Ken's claim that Tom's behavior appears to have no sane purpose is that we don't see a sane purpose for it. It would be precipitous to charge from this that Ken's claim (or Rowe's) rests merely on an appeal to ignorance. To call a charge precipitous is not to say it is false; it is only to say that more work is needed before one can know whether it is true or false. In a sense, the remainder of my paper is not so much disagreement with Reichenbach as an effort to do the work he leaves undone.

to

'It is reasonable to believe that not-p.'

And *this* move is, on the face of it anyway, licensed by what many philosophers regard as a proper, indeed primary and indispensable, principle of justification: what Richard Swinburne calls 'the Principle of Credulity', or what might more descriptively be called 'the "seems so, is so" presumption'.[14] As Swinburne expounds it, the principle is that if something appears to be the case (in the epistemic sense of 'appears'), then this *prima facie* justifies one in believing it is the case. If we fail to distinguish the strict and ordinary senses of the 'does not appear' locution, we run the risk of failing—like Reichenbach—to see the real nerve of Rowe's argument.[15]

2.3. Swinburne's Slip

Commenting on the principle that 'how things seem to be is good grounds for a belief about how things are', Swinburne writes:

> Note that the principle is so phrased that how things seem postively to be is evidence of how they are, but how things seem not to be is not such evidence. If it seems to me there is present a table in the room, or a statue in the garden, then probably there is. But if it seems to me that there is no table in the room, then that is only reason for supposing that there is not, if there are good grounds for supposing that I have looked everywhere in the room, and . . . would have seen one if there was one there.[16]

So on Swinburne's account, the principle of credulity allows one to go from a 'positive seeming' like 'there seems to be a table in this room' to 'there probably is a table in this room'. But it does not entitle one to move from the 'negative seeming' (1) 'There seems to be no table in this room' to (2) 'There probably is no table in this room.' In order to move from (1) to (2) it must, says Swinburne, additionally be the case that (3) I have good grounds for believing that I would have seen a table if one were there. One needs (3) to get from (1) to (2) because (1) is a 'negative seeming': if it were instead a case of 'how things positively seem to be', one could go directly from (1) to (2) using the principle of credulity as one's inference ticket (subject, of course to the caveat that no defeating considerations are present).

The difficulty here is that the distinction between 'how things seem to be' and 'how they seem not to be' characteristically depends upon rather

---

[14] Swinburne, *The Existence of God*, pp. 254–71.

[15] It is worth noting that Rowe gives his qualified endorsement of the principle of credulity in his 'Religious Experience and the Principle of Credulity', *International Journal of the Philosophy of Religion*, 13 (1982), 85–92.

[16] Swinburne, *The Existence of God*, pp. 254–5.

arbitrary choices of formulation. Consider Swinburne's own example. Its seeming 'that no table is in the room' is formulated negatively. But suppose one were to say that it seems to one that the room is bare or empty? This seems to be a case of something's seeming positively to be the case—just as much so, at least, as if it seems to one that one's wife is bare; but then, this is a case of its seeming to one that no clothes are on one's wife, which makes it sound like a case of how something seems *not* to be—just as much so, at least, as its seeming to one that no articles of furniture are in the room. Since the distinction between positive and negative seemings depends so much upon formulation, it is hard to see how it can have the epistemic bite Swinburne gives it.

3. AVOIDING THE EVIL OF 'APPEARANCE'

3.1. CORNEA

If Swinburne's actual claim is mistaken, there may nevertheless be in its vicinity a sound intuition about 'does not appear' claims (in their ordinary and strong sense). Consider the use of such claims in the following three situations:

1) Searching for a table, you look through a doorway. The room is very large—say, the size of a Concorde hangar—and it is filled with bulldozers, dead elephants, Toyotas, and other vision-obstructing objects. Surveying this clutter from the doorway, and seeing no table, should you say: 'It does not appear that there is a table in the room'?

2) Your spouse asks you if the milk in the refrigerator is sour. Taking it out, opening it, and smelling it, you detect nothing of that characteristic odor of milk gone bad. You have a headcold which, as you know, almost entirely takes away your sense of smell. Should you inform your spouse: 'It does not appear that the milk is sour'?

3) A professor of ceramics, newly appointed as Dean of College, is deciding whether to award tenure to a young philosopher on the faculty. The Dean has never studied philosophy. Sitting in on a session of the philosopher's graduate seminar, he hears the philosopher speak many sentences which are Greek to him. (He's never studied any Greek either.) Of such a sentence, is he entitled to say 'it does not appear that this sentence has any meaning'?

In each of these situations, Swinburne's condition is not met: even if (in the first scenario) there were a table somewhere in the room, it is scarcely likely that you (lacking Superman's x-ray vision) would see it. But what precisely is the consequence of his condition's not being met? It is, one would think, that you are not entitled to make the 'does not appear' claim in question. If so, Swinburne's condition (or something close to it) is relevant in 'getting' to the belief that, say, no table is in the room (or that the milk is sour), but it is relevant: not, as Swinburne thinks, in order to reasonably move from 'It seems no table is present' to 'Probably no table is present'; but rather, in order to be entitled to the initial claim 'It seems no table is present.'

We are, I propose, here in the vicinity of a general condition—necessary rather than sufficient—for one's being entitled, on the basis of some cognized situation s, to claim 'it appears that p'. Since what is at issue is whether it is reasonable to think one has 'epistemic access' to the truth of p through s, let us call this 'the Condition Of Reasonable Epistemic Access', or—for short—CORNEA:

> On the basis of cognized situation s, human H is entitled to claim 'It appears that p' only if it is reasonable for H to believe that, given her cognitive faculties and the use she has made of them, if p were not the case, s would likely be different than it is in some way discernible by her.

CORNEA is, I think, made plausible by the examples I've given. It is desirable to undergird it with an epistemological rationale; but this is also difficult, requiring attention to numerous issues about Rowe's epistemic use of 'appears'. The following section (3.2) addresses some of these issues. I shall apply CORNEA to Rowe's case in 3.3.

3.2. CORNEA's Rationale

To explore the rationale for CORNEA, consider Swinburne's construal of the epistemic use of 'appears'. To say 'it appears (epistemically) that p' is, Swinburne stipulates, merely 'to describe what the subject is inclined to believe on the basis of his present sensory experience'. He thus explains:

If I say 'the ship appears to be moving', I am saying [1] that I am inclined to believe that the ship is moving, and [2] that it is my present sensory experience that leads me to have this inclination to belief.[17]

CORNEA presupposes a two-fold emendation of Swinburne's construal. The first is to add a third clause to the two conditions of Swinburne's construal. If Swinburne's [1] and [2] exhaust the meaning of the claim 'it appears that p', then CORNEA is false: for these two autobiographical

---

[17] Swinburne, *The Existence of God*, pp. 246.

claims can both be true even if the condition required by CORNEA is not satisfied. CORNEA presupposes the addition of the third clause:

[3] that I 'take' there to be an *evidential* connection between what I am inclined to believe and the cognized situation that inclines me to believe it. (Note that Swinburne's [2] involves only a *causal* connection between my experience and my belief-inclination.)

To illustrate the difference made by adding (3) to Swinburne's explication, imagine a man, Mort, who is inclined to believe 'this woman hates me' of any woman who, in conversing with him, does not constantly smile. Suppose further that Mort has, through psychoanalysis, become fully conscious that this belief-forming disposition is completely unreliable, and is the result of certain psychological traumas in his childhood. Now, talking with a normal woman (i.e., one who doesn't constantly smile), Mort once again feels in himself the familiar inclination to believe the woman hates him; but he also lucidly knows that this inclination is pathological, and is not due to the woman's behavior in any way 'evidencing' hatred of him. On Swinburne's explication of 'appears', it would be correct for Mort to assert 'This woman appears to hate me', for both of Swinburne's conditions are met. On my amended explication, the appears-claim would no longer be correct, for Mort no longer takes there to be an evidential connection between the woman's behavior and what he believes.

The example is intended to illustrate the difference made by my emendation, not to justify it. The epistemic use of 'appears' is a technical one, not arbitrable by appeal to ordinary usage; and fully justifying my proposal would require more chisholming[18] on this topic than space permits. The heart of the matter, however, is that since we want the epistemic sense of 'appears' to cover just those situations to which principles of epistemic justification (like Swinburne's principle of credulity) apply, those occasions will be ones which, though characterizable 'internally', nevertheless involve 'takings' of the sort that my third clause makes explicit. The case for this has been developed in several papers by Roderick Chisholm.[19]

The second revision we need to make is perhaps best seen, not as amending Swinburne's explication, but as defining a species of 'appears' that is different from the one Swinburne has in mind, though still belonging to the epistemic genus. Swinburne is concerned with that epistemic sense of

---

[18] To 'chisholm', according to *The Philosophers' Lexicon* (APA, 1978), is 'to make repeated small alterations in a definition or example'.

[19] *Perceiving: A Philosophical Study* (Ithaca, 1957), 75–7; 'On the Nature of Empirical Evidence', reprinted in Pappas and Swain (eds.), *Essays on Knowledge and Justification* (Ithaca, 1978), 269 ff., and ' "Appear", "Take", and "Evident" ' in Swartz (ed.), *Perceiving, Sensing, and Knowing* (Garden City, 1965).

'appears' covering what we might call 'sensory-epistemic appearing', i.e., belief-inclinations triggered by 'sensory experiences'. But we also often find ourselves with belief-inclinations produced when a broad (and perhaps largely tacit) range of considerations are brought to bear upon 'cognized situations'. Consider the following: a chess master finds himself strongly inclined to believe that White has a winning game after a novel pawn thrust on the 17th move of a complex Dragon line in the Sicilian Defence—and what 'triggers' this belief-inclination is his 'visualization' (in his imagination) of the situation after this move. (Many masters can play fine games of 'blindfold chess', having no need for sensory experience of the board.) If the master says 'It appears that this pawn thrust gives White a won game', he is using 'appears' in what we might call its 'cognitive-epistemic' sense. And this seems to be the way Rowe uses the term: in appealing to the fawn's suffering he is, after all, appealing not to a 'sensory experience', but to a 'cognized situation' (akin to the chess master's visualized board), which he takes to be uncontroversially instantiated in the real world, and which produces (*via* a range of other considerations) a strong inclination to believe a proposition about such suffering (viz., that it serves no God-justifying purpose).

Now it is perhaps not completely clear whether epistemic principles (like Swinburne's principle of credulity) have the same cogency when extended to cover cognitive-epistemic appearings. But let us grant Rowe such an extension. It remains true, I shall now argue, that appears-claims of the cognitive-epistemic sort are, like those of the sensory-epistemic sort, subject to CORNEA. Given the cognitive situation on the chess-board, our chess master is entitled to say 'It appears that White has a winning position' only if it is reasonable for him to believe that, given his cognitive faculties and the use he has made of them, if White did not have a winning position, the cognitive situation would be different than it is in some discernible features.

The rationale for CORNEA here derives from the 'taking' clause that is, as argued above, a third component of an epistemic appears-claim. If I say 'it appears that p', I am saying (among other things) that I take there to be an evidential connection between what I am inclined to believe (namely, that p) and the cognized situation that inclines me to believe it. If it is not reasonable for me to take this evidential connection to obtain, then I am not entitled to say 'it appears that p'. Now suppose that it is not reasonable for me to believe that if p were not the case, s would be different than it is in some discernible respect. That is (in shorthand): suppose it is not reasonable for me to believe that the 'epistemic access condition' is satisfied. In this event it can scarcely be reasonable for me to believe that an evidential connection obtains between what I am inclined to believe, and the cognized situation inclining me to believe it. Hence, if it is not reasonable for me to believe that the epistemic access condition is satisfied, then I am not entitled to say 'it appears that p'. So to be entitled (by cognizance of s) to say 'it appears that p', it must be reasonable for me to believe that if it were not the case that p, then s would likely be discernibly different than it is.

In here requiring that it be 'reasonable' for H to believe that the epistemic access condition is satisfied, I do not mean to require that H believe this in any conscious or occurrent way. I mean, roughly, only that should the matter be put to H, it would be reasonable for her to affirm that the condition is satisfied: that is, no norms of reasonable belief would be violated by her believing this. This need not always involve her having, or being able to produce, an evidential or inferential justification for so believing: in some cases, this might properly be believed in a 'basic' way. But even in these cases, if H has been made aware of good reasons for thinking the epistemic access condition is *not* satisfied, then it will not be reasonable for her to believe it is satisfied—unless she defeats these reasons with other considerations. And in now applying CORNEA to Rowe's case, I shall provide good reasons for thinking that the epistemic access condition is not satisfied for the appears-claim upon which his case rests.

3.3. CORNEA Applied

Return, then, to Rowe's fawn, suffering in a distant forest. Rowe's claim is that the suffering appears not to serve any God-justifying purpose. It is clear, I think, that the feature of the cognized situation crucial to Rowe's claim is that there is no outweighing good within our ken served by the fawn's suffering. CORNEA thus forces us to ask the following question: if there were an outweighing good of the sort at issue, connected in the requisite way to instances of suffering like this, how likely is it that this should be apparent to us?

We must note here, first, that the outweighing good at issue is of a special sort: one purposed by the Creator of all that is, whose vision and wisdom are therefore somewhat greater than ours. How much greater? A modest proposal might be that his wisdom is to ours, roughly as an adult human's is to a one-month old infant's. (You may adjust the ages and species to fit your own estimate of how close our knowledge is to omniscience.) If such goods as this exist, it might not be unlikely that we should discern some of them: even a one-month old infant can perhaps discern, in its inarticulate way, some of the purposes of his mother in her dealings with him. But if outweighing goods of the sort at issue exist in connection with instances of suffering, that we should discern most of them seems about as likely as that a one-month old should discern most of his parents' purposes for those pains they allow him to suffer—which is to say, it is not likely at all. So for any selected instance of intense suffering, there is good reason to think that if there is an outweighing good of the sort at issue connected to it, we would not have epistemic access to this: our cognized situation would be just as Rowe says it is with respect to (say) the fawn's suffering.

This doesn't quite mean that, by CORNEA, Rowe is not entitled to his does-not-appear claim: for CORNEA requires, not that the epistemic access condition be satisfied, but that it is reasonable for Rowe to believe it is satisfied. I have given reasons to think that such a belief would be false, but this doesn't show it is always unreasonable for anyone to have the belief: perhaps one couldn't rightly expect Rowe to have considered the reasons I've given. But if these reasons are good reasons, it seems fair to say that for anyone who (reading this paper) grasps them, it would be un- reasonable to believe that the epistemic access condition is satisfied. Unless the reasons I have given are defeated, the claim that a given instance of suffering 'does not appear (appears not) to serve any outweighing good' is comparable to the claim of the aforementioned ceramics teacher that a sentence of the philosopher does not appear to have any meaning. And it is evident that the case cannot be repaired merely by pointing out the number of instances of suffering which have no evident purpose—unless one has justification for believing that these instances belong to a class such that if Divinely purposed goods exist in connection with all known instances of suffering in this class, these goods would always or usually be within our ken.

In a footnote [p. 132], Rowe indicates that he attaches importance to the following consideration: for an outweighing good to provide a 'God- justifying purpose' (as I've called it) for an instance of suffering, the good and the suffering it serves must be connected in an especially intimate way—a way so intimate that even omnipotence cannot pry them apart. Let us call this 'the intimate-connection consideration'. If my appeal to CORNEA is correct, the relevance of this consideration turns upon whether it justifies one in concluding that the epistemic access condition is satisifed— viz., that if all instances of suffering are connected in this intimate way to outweighing goods, then when the suffering falls within our ken, so would the intimately-connected outweighing good by virtue of which God allows it. If the intimate-connection consideration could be shown to warrant this conclusion, Rowe's case would be vindicated *vis-à-vis* my critique.

But it is hard to see how the intimate-connection consideration can justify such a conclusion. And Rowe does not himself claim it provides such justification: indeed there is reason to think that he doesn't see his case as presupposing that the epistemic access condition is satisfied. He notes (p. 133) that one of 'the basic beliefs associated with theism' is that God's purposes for allowing suffering will generally be outside our ken, and he seems to concede the reasonableness of this—of, that is, the proposition that *if* theism is true, then the outweighing goods by virtue of which God allows suffering would generally be beyond our ken.

If CORNEA is correct, such a concession is fatal to Rowe's case: for by CORNEA, one is entitled to claim 'this suffering does not appear (i.e., appears not) to serve any Divinely-purposed outweighing good' only if it is reasonable to believe that if such a Divinely-purposed good exists, it would be within our ken. So to vindicate Rowe's case from the CORNEA-critique, one must show the reasonableness of believing that if theism is true, then a basic belief long regarded as a logical extension of theism is probably false. The prospects of doing this do not seem especially bright.[20]

3.4. Philo's Reluctant Concession

The basic point underlying my critique of Rowe's case is broadened by Philo, the closet atheist of Hume's *Dialogues*. In Section XI, Philo is pressed by Cleanthes on whether the misery in the world is significant evidence against the existence of a beneficent and supremely powerful Creator. In answer, Philo distinguishes two issues: (1) whether suffering constitutes *negative* evidence against Cleanthes' theism; and (2) whether this suffering makes it more difficult to develop, from our knowledge of nature, positive arguments for theism. To the first of these issues—the one concerning us—Philo concedes that the answer is 'No'. Philo's reason should have a familiar ring: a person, brought into the universe with the assurance that it was the creation of such a being

... might, perhaps, be surprised at the disappointment, but would never retract his former belief, if founded on any very solid argument; since such a limited intelligence must be sensible of his own blindness and ignorance, and must allow, that there may be many solutions of those phenomena, which will forever escape his comprehension.[21]

The intense suffering in the world fails to strongly disconfirm theism, Philo thus concedes, because of the limited cognitive access we can presume to have to 'solutions of those phenomena'.

---

[20] Some issues related to my line of argument are discussed by F. J. Fitzpatrick in 'The Onus of Proof in Arguments about the Problem of Evil', *Religious Studies*, 17 (1981), 19–38, and by David O'Conner in 'Theism, Evil, and the Onus of Proof: Reply to F. J. Fitzpatrick', *Religious Studies*, 19 (1983), 241–7.

[21] David Hume, *Dialogues Concerning Natural Religion*, second paragraph of pt. XI.

Arguably because of an oversight that we today have no excuse for repeating, Hume fails to see, or at least to show, the full import of Philo's concession. It is only 'theism' *of the sort proposed by Cleanthes* that Philo concedes is not disconfirmed by suffering: *traditional* theism, he in contrast avers, is not merely disconfirmed by suffering, it is decisively disproven by it. For traditional theism (which Rowe has in mind) asserts that God is omnipotent, and this—thinks Philo—entails that he is able to achieve any good he desires without allowing any suffering at all, so that there can be no 'justifying purpose' for his allowing any suffering. Cleanthes, acceding to this 'disproof', proposes to save theism by allowing that God, though 'supremely powerful', falls short of being omnipotent (or 'infinite' in power). Deliberately or not, Hume here keeps both Philo and Cleanthes (not to mention poor Demea) in ignorance of the case (made among others by Aquinas) that even an omnipotent God is subject to logical constraints, not being able to make married bachelors and similar non-things, for example. In our day the work of Plantinga and others has made much clearer the import of such broadly logical constraints, making this talk by Philo (or, only a few decades ago, by Mackie) of 'decisive disproof' look like naive bluster. Acknowledging that 'no one has succeeded in establishing such an extravagant claim', Rowe (like others) thus retreats to the more modest 'evidential' approach. But the very insights (about the logical constraints on omnipotence) that lead us to see Hume's claim as 'extravagant' also collapse his distinction between the 'supremely powerful' God of Cleanthes and the 'omnipotent' God of traditional theism. Hence, if Hume is right in having Philo concede that suffering fails to strongly disconfirm Cleanthes' theism, then Hume has also placed an obstacle in the way of a retreat to an evidential case from suffering against traditional theism. By amplifying Philo's insight and applying it to Rowe's case, my aim has been to show that the obstacle is a considerable one indeed.

4. ETIOLOGY OF AN ERROR

My critique of Rowe may seem to show too much. Can it really be that the vast suffering in our world serving no goods within our ken does not even *appear* to serve no God-justifying purpose, and hence does not even *weakly* disconfirm theism? Is it not more sensible to allow, as Basil Mitchell does, that

The theologian surely would not deny that the fact of pain counts against the assertion that God loves men. This very incompatibility generates the most intractable

ON AVOIDING THE EVILS OF 'APPEARANCE' 159

of theological problems—the problem of evil. So the theologian *does* recognize the fact of pain as counting against Christian doctrine. But . . . he will not allow it—or anything—to count decisively against it . . .[22]

Perhaps Mitchell's *argument* here is less than compelling: for what theologians may generally have found intractable is the project of theodicy—of giving an *account* of the goods by virtue of which God allows pain; and if they go on to take *this* as evidence against theism—well, even theologians are not exempt from conceptual confusions. Nevertheless, it is—among believers as well as non-believers—a persistent intuition that the inscrutable suffering in our world in some sense disconfirms theism. And a convincing critique of Rowe should show why such suffering should strike so many as disconfirming evidence if, as I have argued, it is not. One factor may be failure to distinguish the strict from the ordinary sense of 'does not appear', making it easy to slide from the weak claim that it isn't the case that some suffering appears to serve as a God-justifying purpose, to the stronger claim that some suffering appears not to serve such a purpose. But there is, I shall in conclusion suggest, a deeper source of confusion.

Rowe, I have allowed, is right in claiming that a wholly good God must be 'against' suffering in this sense: such a being would allow suffering only if there were an outweighing good served by so doing. Rowe is also correct in seeing that such goods are, in a great many cases, nowhere within our ken. The linchpin of my critique has been that if theism is true, this is just what one would expect: for if we think carefully about the sort of being theism proposes for our belief, it is entirely expectable—given what we know of our cognitive limits—that the goods by virtue of which this Being allows known suffering should very often be beyond our ken. Since this state of affairs is just what one should expect if theism were true, how can its obtaining be evidence *against* theism?

But suppose one has not thought (in the light of our evident cognitive limitations) about the sort of Being theism proposes, and so has not realized what is 'contained' in the theistic proposal. Reflection on instances of tragic suffering, forcing one to 'postulate' hidden outweighing goods, will then seem to increase what must be believed to believe theism. And with its content so 'increased', theism may then seem more top-heavy than it did, relative to whatever evidential base one takes it to have. And this might well reduce one's confidence that it is true, or increase one's confidence that it is false.

What, then, is wrong with saying that such instances of suffering are disconfirming evidence against theism? Is not the situation parallel to, say,

[22] Basil Mitchell, 'Theology and Falsification' (response to Flew), in Flew and MacIntyre (eds.), *New Essays in Philosophical Theology* (Macmillan, 1955).

the initial disconfirmation of Copernicus's theory by the absence of observable stellar parallax? (To preserve his theory in the face of this, Copernicus was led to say that the stars were immensely more distant than anyone had any good reason to believe.) The difference is this. The absence of observed stellar parallax required Copernicus to *add* a postulate to his theory. The observed sufferings in the world do require us to say that there are outweighing goods connected to them that are entirely outside our ken, but this is not an *additional* postulate: it was implicit in theism (taken with a little realism about our cognitive powers) all along. If we have realized the magnitude of the theistic proposal, cognizance of suffering thus should not in the least reduce our confidence that it is true. When cognizance of suffering does have this effect, it is perhaps because we had not understood the sort of being theism proposes for belief in the first place.

The main arguments of this paper have benefited from discussions in William Rowe's NEH Summer Seminar in 1982, and in the weekly philosophy colloquia at Calvin College during May, 1983. I am especially indebted to Del Ratzsch, William Alston, William Rowe, and Alvin Plantinga for criticisms, suggestions, and encouragement; and to a 1983 NEH Summer Research Grant for related research.

IX

EVIL AND THE THEISTIC HYPOTHESIS: A RESPONSE TO WYKSTRA

WILLIAM L. ROWE

Wykstra's paper, 'The Humean Obstacle to Evidential Arguments from Suffering' [Chapter VIII in this collection], is both conceptually rich and an important advance to our understanding of the evidential argument from evil. Its conceptual richness lies in its analysis of the epistemic notion of 'appears' and its advancement of a necessary condition (CORNEA) for being entitled to make the claim: 'It appears that p (not-p).' Its advance in our understanding of the evidential argument from evil consists in his application of CORNEA to the very starting point in the *justification* of the first premise of the deductive argument against theism I presented in the article of which his essay is a critique. My response will assume the conceptual contribution Wykstra has made, focussing mainly on the question of whether he has shown that CORNEA is in fact not satisfied when we make claims such as, 'It appears that there are instances of suffering that do not serve outweighing goods otherwise unobtainable by an omnipotent, omniscient being.' To this end it is important to begin with a distinction that will play a crucial role in my discussion.

Let's call *standard theism* any view which holds that there exists an omnipotent, omniscient, omnigood being who created the world. Letting 'O' abbreviate 'an omnipotent, omniscient, omnigood being', standard theism is any view which holds that O exists. Within standard theism, we can distinguish *restricted* theism and *expanded* theism. Expanded theism is the view that O exists, conjoined with certain other significant religious claims, claims about sin, redemption, a future life, a last judgment, and the like. (Orthodox Christian theism is a version of expanded theism.) Restricted theism is the view that O exists, unaccompanied by other, independent religious claims. I will return to this distinction, but at the outset I want to focus on restricted standard theism—the view that O exists.

William L. Rowe, 'Evil and the Theistic Hypothesis: A Response to Wykstra', first published in *International Journal for Philosophy of Religion*, 16 (1984), pp. 95–100. Reprinted by permission of Kluwer Academic Publishers.

Consider the following proposition:

1. There exist instances of intense suffering which an omnipotent, omniscient being could have prevented without thereby losing some greater good or permitting some evil equally bad or worse.

In the paper Wykstra criticizes, I argued that to the extent that we have rational grounds for accepting (1), to that extent we have rational grounds for rejecting the claim that O exists. Furthermore, I argued that we do have rational grounds for accepting (1). What grounds? I there claimed that (1) is a rational belief given three things: first, our knowledge of the vast amount of intense human and animal suffering that occurs daily in our world; second, our understanding of the goods that do exist and that we can imagine coming into existence; and third, our reasonable judgments as to what an omnipotent being can do. (To these three I now would add a fourth: our reasonable judgments of what an all-wise omnigood being would endeavor to accomplish with respect to human (and animal) good and evil in the universe.) To illustrate this claim, I set forth an example of intense suffering (the fawn's suffering) and observed that as far as we can determine it serves no greater good at all, let alone one that is otherwise unobtainable by an omnipotent being. Recognizing, however, that, appearances to the contrary, it might nevertheless serve such an outweighing good, I then claimed that it seems quite incredible that all the instances of suffering which serve no greater good we know or can think of, should, nevertheless, be such that none could have been prevented by an omnipotent being without loss of greater good.

These claims about what it is that rationally justifies us in accepting (1) have been challenged by several philosophers; but no one, in my judgment, has raised such an important point (and clarifications) as has Wykstra. So let's now turn to consider his basic objection.

In my earlier paper I made ample use of the phrase 'it appears that' and its substitutes; and since Wykstra's objection is couched in such phrases, it will be best to retain them in discussing our disagreement. Suppose then that we are simply unable to think of any good that exists or might come into existence that both outweighs the fawn's suffering and couldn't be obtained by an omnipotent, omniscient being without permitting that suffering. We might then claim that

2. It appears that the fawn's suffering is pointless—i.e., it appears that the fawn's suffering does not serve an outweighing good otherwise unobtainable by an omnipotent, omniscient being.

We can now understand Wykstra's central objection, based as it is on his view of the importance of CORNEA in our being entitled to make claims such as (2). Put in its simplest terms it comes to this. If someone claims that it appears that S is not P, that person is entitled to that claim only if she has no reason to think that if S were P things would strike us pretty much the same. Thus on detecting no sour odor, the person with the cold is not entitled to the claim that it appears that the milk is not sour because he presumably has a reason (the cold) to think that if the milk were sour things would strike him pretty much the same—he would still detect no odor of sourness. Now let's return to (2). Wykstra believes that we are not entitled to affirm (2) because, in his judgment, we have good reason to think that were the fawn's suffering actually to serve an outweighing good, otherwise unobtainable by O, things would strike us in pretty much the same way— we would still be in the position of not being able to think of any good that exists or might come into existence that both outweighs the fawn's suffering and couldn't be otherwise obtained by an omnipotent, omniscient being. The reason he gives is that were O to exist, it would be likely that the outweighing good in relation to which O must permit the fawn's suffering would be a good quite beyond our ken. And if such good were beyond our ken, then we would still be in the position of not being able to see what good is served by the fawn's suffering. Thus Wykstra concludes that were O to exist, the fawn's suffering would likely have just the feature I claim it to have—of serving no outweighing good we know to exist or can think of which is otherwise unobtainable by an omnipotent, omniscient being.

It's helpful, I think, to view Wykstra's objection as having two steps. The first step is the claim that in the situation described we are entitled to affirm proposition (2) only if the following proposition is true:

3. We have no reason to think that were O to exist things would strike us in pretty much the same way concerning the fawn's suffering.

The second step in Wykstra's objection is the claim that (3) is false. For were O to exist, Wykstra thinks it likely that the outweighing good in relation to which O must permit the fawn's suffering would be a good beyond our ken.

My response to Wykstra will focus entirely on the second step in his objection: the step which claims that were O to exist things would strike us in pretty much the way they do so far as instances of human and animal suffering are concerned.

Before criticizing this step, however, it's important to note that Wykstra *could* hold that in the situation described we are entitled to affirm proposition (2) only if (3') is true.

3'. We have reason to think that were O to exist things would strike us differently concerning the fawn's suffering.

He might then argue that (3′) is false and that, therefore, it is *not* reasonable to believe that were the fawn's suffering actually to serve an outweighing good, otherwise unobtainable by an omnipotent being, things would likely strike us differently concerning the fawn's suffering. In the discussion that follows I have taken Wykstra to be arguing that (3) is false and that, therefore, his condition CORNEA is not satisfied. (A careful reading of pages 87–9 [pp. 155–7 above] makes it clear that it is (3), not (3′), that he holds must be true if we are entitled to affirm (2).) My comments, therefore, concern only his attempt to show that (3) is false. It would be another matter to determine whether (3′) is also necessary for being entitled to claim (2), and another matter yet to determine whether (3′) is true or false.

Given the history of humans and animals, and the sorry tale of their sufferings through the ages, and given our inability to discover among the goods we know or can imagine, goods that both outweigh these sufferings and are unobtainable by omnipotence unless these sufferings are permitted, why should we think, as Wykstra does, that this is just how things would likely be, if O exists? It's true, as Wykstra observes, that O's mind can grasp goods that are beyond our ken. The idea, then, is that since O grasps goods beyond our ken, we've reason to think it likely that the goods in relation to which O permits many sufferings that occur would be *unknown* to us. Let's look at Wykstra's reasoning here. He starts with

4. O's mind grasps goods beyond our ken.

moves to

5. It is likely that the goods in relation to which O permits many sufferings are beyond our ken.

and concludes with

6. It is likely that many of the sufferings in our world do not appear to have a point—we can't see what goods justify O in permitting them.

The difficulty with this reasoning is that the move from (4) to (5) presupposes that the goods in question *have not occurred*, or, at the very least, that if they have occurred they, nevertheless, remain quite unknown to us (in themselves or in their connections with the sufferings in our world). And, so far as I can see, the mere assumption that O exists gives us no reason to think that either of these is true. If O exists it is indeed likely, if not certain, that O's mind grasps many good states of affairs that do not obtain and which, *prior to their obtaining*, are such that we are simply unable to think of or imagine them. That much is reasonably clear. But the mere assumption that O exists gives us no reason whatever to suppose *either* that the greater goods in virtue of which he permits most sufferings are goods that come into existence far in the future of the sufferings we are aware of, *or* that once they do obtain we continue to be ignorant of them and their relation to the sufferings.

The fact that O's mind can apprehend non-actual good states of affairs that we are not able to think of gives us reason to assent to the following proposition:

> 7. If O exists then the outweighing goods in relation to which some sufferings are permitted by O are, *antecedent to their obtaining*, beyond our ken.

But this proposition is insufficient to justify the claim that if O were to exist the sufferings in our world would appear to us as they in fact do. I conclude, therefore, that Wykstra has provided no adequate justification for the second step in his objection. And without that step, the objection fails.

Earlier, I distinguished restrictive standard theism from expanded standard theism. I now want to bring this distinction to bear on our problem. Standard theism implies (roughly) that the sufferings that occur are permitted by O by virtue of outweighing goods otherwise unobtainable by O. Restricted standard theism gives us *no* reason to think that these goods, once they occur, remain beyond our ken. Nor does restricted standard theism give us any reason to think that the occurrence of the goods in question lies in the distant future of the occurrence of the sufferings that O must permit to obtain them. So I conclude, contrary to Wykstra, that the mere hypothesis of O's existence gives us no good reason to think that things would appear to us just as they do so far as the sufferings of animals and humans in our world are concerned. I conclude, therefore, that we've been given no convincing reason to reject my view that the items mentioned at the outset give us reason to believe that (1) is true and, therefore, that O does not exist.

But what about expanded theism? Suppose, for example, that we add to the hypothesis that O exists the claim made by Saint Paul in his letter to the Church at Rome: 'For I reckon that the sufferings we now endure bear no comparison with the splendor, as yet unrevealed, which is in store for us.' Playing fast and loose with biblical hermeneutics, suppose we set forth the Pauline doctrine as follows:

> 8. The goods for the sake of which O must permit vast amounts of human and animal suffering will be realized only at the end of the world.

We now have a version of expanded standard theism, a version consisting of the conjunction of the proposition that O exists and proposition (8). Let's call this particular expansion of standard theism EST (expanded standard theism). EST is not rendered unlikely by the items that render RST (restricted standard theism) unlikely. And this, for precisely the reason Wykstra so clearly and carefully sets forth. Given EST we have some reason to think that the fawn's suffering might well appear to us just the way it does appear. So the fact that it appears to us as it does in no way renders EST more unlikely than it otherwise is.

Since the facts about suffering do not tell against EST, if RST implied EST (or something close to it) then Wykstra's objection would be decisive against my claim that the facts about suffering render RST unlikely. But it is clear, I believe, that RST does not imply EST. It is not so clear, however, that Wykstra would accept this point. He seems to think that the theistic hypothesis somehow 'contains' the claim that the goods for the sake of which O permits the sufferings in the world are, to a large extent, quite beyond our ken. On p. 89 [p. 157] he speaks of this claim as a 'logical extension of theism'. On p. 91 [p. 160] he says that the claim is not an 'additional postulate', but instead was 'implicit' in theism all along. But this is a mistake. What is 'implicit' in theism (RST) is that O's mind grasps goods that are beyond our ken (proposition (4) above). And, as we've seen, (4) is significantly different from the proposition that Wykstra claims to be a part of the theistic hypothesis. My own best judgment is that the crucial proposition Wykstra claims to be implicit in theism is in fact an added postulate that produces a version of expanded theism, a version that is not rendered unlikely by the facts about suffering that I claim to render restricted standard theism unlikely.

Wykstra notes that among believers as well as nonbelievers there is a 'persistent intuition that the inscrutable suffering in our world in some sense disconfirms theism'. I would say that there are two distinct intuitions at work concerning suffering and theism. First, there is the intuition that the magnitude and intensity of human and animal suffering disconfirms theism. It is hard to see that suffering of this magnitude and intensity is just what we should expect on the hypothesis that O exists. Second, there is the intuition that the existence of so much suffering for which we are unable to see any point at all disconfirms theism. It is hard to see that the existence of so much suffering for which we can see no point whatever is just what we should expect on the hypothesis that O exists. Both of these intuitions are, I believe, essentially correct. Given our cognitive limitations and O's omni-science and omnipotence, Wykstra has argued that a good deal of the suffering in our world can be expected to have the characteristic of being inscrutable to us. He concludes that our second intuition is based on a failure to see what is really contained in the theistic hypothesis. But, if I am right, what Wykstra has done is 'read into' the theistic hypothesis a proposition that is part of the story of traditional theism, thus creating a version of expanded theism. He has, unwittingly, changed the question. The crucial question is whether the facts about suffering in our world tend to disconfirm the hypothesis that O exists. That question cannot be shown to deserve a negative answer merely by showing that we can supplement the hypothesis that O exists with other propositions such that the supplemented result is not disconfirmed by the facts that are claimed to disconfirm the hypothesis that O exists. Wykstra, I believe, would agree with this last point. What he would disagree with me about is whether he has really supplemented the theistic hypothesis in the way I have suggested he has done. If he has not, then he has found a fundamental error in my original paper. And even if he has unwittingly supplemented the hypothesis that O exists in the way I have suggested, his paper remains an important contribution to our understanding of the basic issues involved in evaluating the evidential argument from evil.

X

SOUL-MAKING AND SUFFERING

JOHN HICK

[CHAPTER XII. THE STARTING-POINT]

THE 'VALE OF SOUL-MAKING' THEODICY

[. . .] In the light of modern anthropological knowledge some form of two-stage conception of the creation of man has become an almost unavoidable Christian tenet. At the very least we must acknowledge as two distinguishable stages the fashioning of *homo sapiens* as a product of the long evolutionary process, and his sudden or gradual spiritualization as a child of God. But we may well extend the first stage to include the development of man as a rational and responsible person capable of personal relationship with the personal Infinite who has created him. This first stage of the creative process was, to our anthropomorphic imaginations, easy for divine omnipotence. By an exercise of creative power God caused the physical universe to exist, and in the course of countless ages to bring forth within it organic life, and finally to produce out of organic life personal life; and when man had thus emerged out of the evolution of the forms of organic life, a creature had been made who has the possibility of existing in conscious fellowship with God. But the second stage of the creative process is of a different kind altogether. It cannot be performed by omnipotent power as such. For personal life is essentially free and self-directing. It cannot be perfected by divine fiat, but only through the uncompelled responses and willing co-operation of human individuals in their actions and reactions in the world in which God has placed them. Men may eventually become the perfected persons whom the New Testament calls 'children of God', but they cannot be created ready-made as this.

The value-judgement that is implicitly being invoked here is that one who has attained to goodness by meeting and eventually mastering temptations, and thus by rightly making responsible choices in concrete situations, is

John Hick, 'Soul-Making and Suffering', pp. 255–61 and 318–36 from *Evil and the God of Love* by John Hick (rev. edn., 1978). Copyright © 1966, 1977 by John Hick. Reprinted by permission of Harper & Row Publishers, Inc. and the author.

good in a richer and more valuable sense than would be one created *ab initio* in a state either of innocence or of virtue. In the former case, which is that of the actual moral achievements of mankind, the individual's goodness has within it the strength of temptations overcome, a stability based upon an accumulation of right choices, and a positive and responsible character that comes from the investment of costly personal effort. I suggest, then, that it is an ethically reasonable judgement, even though in the nature of the case not one that is capable of demonstrative proof, that human goodness slowly built up through personal histories of moral effort has a value in the eyes of the Creator which justifies even the long travail of the soul-making process.

The picture with which we are working is thus developmental and teleological. Man is in process of becoming the perfected being whom God is seeking to create. However, this is not taking place—it is important to add—by a natural and inevitable evolution, but through a hazardous adventure in individual freedom. Because this is a pilgrimage within the life of each individual, rather than a racial evolution, the progressive fulfilment of God's purpose does not entail any corresponding progressive improvement in the moral state of the world. There is no doubt a development in man's ethical situation from generation to generation through the building of individual choices into public institutions, but this involves an accumulation of evil as well as of good.[1] It is thus probable that human life was lived on much the same moral plane two thousand years ago or four thousand years ago as it is today. But nevertheless during this period uncounted millions of souls have been through the experience of earthly life, and God's purpose has gradually moved towards its fulfilment within each one of them, rather than within a human aggregate composed of different units in different generations.

If, then, God's aim in making the world is 'the bringing of many sons to glory',[2] that aim will naturally determine the kind of world that He has created. Antitheistic writers almost invariably assume a conception of the divine purpose which is contrary to the Christian conception. They assume that the purpose of a loving God must be to create a hedonistic paradise; and therefore to the extent that the world is other than this, it proves to them that God is either not loving enough or not powerful enough to create such a world. They think of God's relation to the earth on the model of a human being building a cage for a pet animal to dwell in. If he is humane he

---

[1] This fact is symbolized in early Christian literature both by the figure of the Antichrist, who continually opposes God's purposes in history, and by the expectation of cataclysmic calamity and strife in the last days before the end of the present world order.

[2] Hebrews 2: 10.

will naturally make his pet's quarters as pleasant and healthful as he can. Any respect in which the cage falls short of the veterinarian's ideal, and contains possibilities of accident or disease, is evidence of either limited benevolence or limited means, or both. Those who use the problem of evil as an argument against belief in God almost invariably think of the world in this kind of way. David Hume, for example, speaks of an architect who is trying to plan a house that is to be as comfortable and convenient as possible. If we find that 'the windows, doors, fires, passages, stairs, and the whole economy of the building were the source of noise, confusion, fatigue, darkness, and the extremes of heat and cold' we should have no hesitation in blaming the architect. It would be in vain for him to prove that if this or that defect were corrected greater ills would result: 'still you would assert in general, that, if the architect had had skill and good intentions, he might have formed such a plan of the whole, and might have adjusted the parts in such a manner, as would have remedied all or most of these inconveniences'.[3]

But if we are right in supposing that God's purpose for man is to lead him from human *Bios*, or the biological life of man, to that quality of *Zoe*, or the personal life of eternal worth, which we see in Christ, then the question that we have to ask is not, Is this the kind of world that an all-powerful and infinitely loving being would create as an environment for his human pets? or, Is the architecture of the world the most pleasant and convenient possible? The question that we have to ask is rather, Is this the kind of world that God might make as an environment in which moral beings may be fashioned, through their own free insights and responses, into 'children of God'?

Such critics as Hume are confusing what heaven ought to be, as an environment for perfected finite beings, with what this world ought to be, as an environment for beings who are in process of becoming perfected. For if our general conception of God's purpose is correct the world is not intended to be a paradise, but rather the scene of a history in which human personality may be formed towards the pattern of Christ. Men are not to be thought of on the analogy of animal pets, whose life is to be made as agreeable as possible, but rather on the analogy of human children, who are to grow to adulthood in an environment whose primary and overriding purpose is not immediate pleasure but the realizing of the most valuable potentialities of human personality.

Needless to say, this characterization of God as the heavenly Father is not a merely random illustration but an analogy that lies at the heart of the Christian faith. Jesus treated the likeness between the attitude of God to

[3] *Dialogues Concerning Natural Religion*, pt. xi. Kemp-Smith's ed. (Oxford: Clarendon Press, 1935), 251.

man, and the attitude of human parents at their best towards their children, as providing the most adequate way for us to think about God. And so it is altogether relevant to a Christian understanding of this world to ask, How does the best parental love express itself in its influence upon the environment in which children are to grow up? I think it is clear that a parent who loves his children, and wants them to become the best human beings that they are capable of becoming, does not treat pleasure as the sole and supreme value. Certainly we seek pleasure for our children, and take great delight in obtaining it for them; but we do not desire for them unalloyed pleasure at the expense of their growth in such even greater values as moral integrity, unselfishness, compassion, courage, humour, reverence for the truth, and perhaps above all the capacity for love. We do not act on the premise that pleasure is the supreme end of life; and if the development of these other values sometimes clashes with the provision of pleasure, then we are willing to have our children miss a certain amount of this, rather than fail to come to possess and to be possessed by the finer and more precious qualities that are possible to the human personality. A child brought up on the principle that the only or the supreme value is pleasure would not be likely to become an ethically mature adult or an attractive or happy personality. And to most parents it seems more important to try to foster quality and strength of character in their children than to fill their lives at all times with the utmost possible degree of pleasure. If, then, there is any true analogy between God's purpose for his human creatures, and the purpose of loving and wise parents for their children, we have to recognize that the presence of pleasure and the absence of pain cannot be the supreme and overriding end for which the world exists. Rather, this world must be a place of soul-making. And its value is to be judged, not primarily by the quantity of pleasure and pain occurring in it at any particular moment, but by its fitness for its primary purpose, the purpose of soul-making.[4]

In all this we have been speaking about the nature of the world considered simply as the God-given environment of man's life. For it is mainly in this connection that the world has been regarded in Irenaean and in Protestant thought.[5] But such a way of thinking involves a danger of anthropocentrism

[4] The phrase 'the vale of Soul-making' was coined by the poet John Keats in a letter written to his brother and sister in April 1819. He says, 'The common cognomen of this world among the misguided and superstitious is "a vale of tears" from which we are to be redeemed by a certain arbitrary interposition of God and taken to Heaven—What a little circumscribed straightened notion! Call the world if you Please "The vale of Soul-making".' In this letter he sketches a teleological theodicy. 'Do you not see', he asks, 'how necessary a World of Pains and troubles is to school an Intelligence and make it a Soul?' (*The Letters of John Keats*, ed. M. B. Forman. London: Oxford University Press, 4th ed., 1952, pp. 334–5.)

[5] Thus Irenaeus said that 'the creation is suited to [the wants of] man; for man was not made for its sake, but creation for the sake of man' (*AH* v xxix. 1), and Calvin said that 'because we

from which the Augustinian and Catholic tradition has generally been protected by its sense of the relative insignificance of man within the totality of the created universe. Man was dwarfed within the medieval world-view by the innumerable hosts of angels and archangels above him—unfallen rational natures which rejoice in the immediate presence of God, reflecting His glory in the untarnished mirror of their worship. However, this higher creation has in our modern world lost its hold upon the imagination. Its place has been taken, as the minimizer of men, by the immensities of outer space and by the material universe's unlimited complexity transcending our present knowledge. As the spiritual environment envisaged by Western man has shrunk, his physical horizons have correspondingly expanded. Where the human creature was formerly seen as an insignificant appendage to the angelic world, he is now seen as an equally insignificant organic excrescence, enjoying a fleeting moment of consciousness on the surface of one of the planets of a minor star. Thus the truth that was symbolized for former ages by the existence of the angelic hosts is today impressed upon us by the vastness of the physical universe, countering the egoism of our species by making us feel that this immense prodigality of existence can hardly all exist for the sake of man—though, on the other hand, the very realization that it is not all for the sake of man may itself be salutary and beneficial to man!

However, instead of opposing man and nature as rival objects of God's interest, we should perhaps rather stress man's solidarity as an embodied being with the whole natural order in which he is embedded. For man is organic to the world; all his acts and thoughts and imaginations are conditioned by space and time; and in abstraction from nature he would cease to be human. We may, then, say that the beauties and sublimities and powers, the microscopic intricacies and macroscopic vastnesses, the wonders and the terrors of the natural world and of the life that pulses through it, are willed and valued by their Maker in a creative act that embraces man together with nature. By means of matter and living flesh God both builds a path and weaves a veil between Himself and the creature made in His image. Nature thus has permanent significance; for God has set man in a creaturely environment, and the final fulfilment of our nature in relation to God will accordingly take the form of an embodied life within 'a new heaven and a new earth'.[6] And as in the present age man moves slowly towards that fulfilment through the pilgrimage of his earthly life, so also

know that the universe was established especially for the sake of mankind, we ought to look for this purpose in his governance also'. (*Inst.* 1. xvi. 6.)

[6] Revelation 21: 1.

'the whole creation' is 'groaning in travail', waiting for the time when it will be 'set free from its bondage to decay'.[7]

And yet however fully we thus acknowledge the permanent significance and value of the natural order, we must still insist upon man's special character as a personal creature made in the image of God; and our theodicy must still centre upon the soul-making process that we believe to be taking place within human life.

This, then, is the starting-point from which we propose to try to relate the realities of sin and suffering to the perfect love of an omnipotent Creator. And as will become increasingly apparent, a theodicy that starts in this way must be eschatological in its ultimate bearings. That is to say, instead of looking to the past for its clue to the mystery of evil, it looks to the future, and indeed to that ultimate future to which only faith can look. Given the conception of a divine intention working in and through human time towards a fulfilment that lies in its completeness beyond human time, our theodicy must find the meaning of evil in the part that it is made to play in the eventual outworking of that purpose; and must find the justification of the whole process in the magnitude of the good to which it leads. The good that outshines all ill is not a paradise long since lost but a kingdom which is yet to come in its full glory and permanence.

From this point of view we must speak about moral evil; about pain, including that of the lower animals; about the higher and more distinctively human forms of suffering; and about the relation between all this and the will of God as it has been revealed in Jesus Christ.

*　　*　　*

[CHAPTER XV. SUFFERING]

1. SUFFERING AS A FUNCTION OF MEANING

We shall, I believe, be using the words to mark an important distinction within human experience if we differentiate between pain on the one hand and suffering, misery, or anguish (three terms that I shall use synonymously) on the other. Pain is, as we have seen in the previous chapter [of *Evil and the God of Love*], a specific physical sensation.[8] Suffering, however, is a mental state which may be as complex as human life itself. The endurance of pain is sometimes, but not always or even usually, an ingredient of suffering.

[7] Romans 8: 21–2.　　　[8] See [*Evil and the God of Love*], pp. 292 f.

Anguish is a quality of experience whose nature could not be communicated by description to someone who had never undergone it; and we can in fact conceive of personal creatures who have always been entirely free from it. However, we human beings are not of such a breed, and have no great difficulty in communicating with one another about the forms of human misery. Attempting, then, to define an all-too-common dimension of our experience, I would suggest that by suffering we mean that state of mind in which we wish violently or obsessively that our situation were otherwise. Such a state of mind involves memory and anticipation, the capacity to imagine alternatives, and (in man) a moral conscience. For the characteristic elements of human suffering are such relatively complex and high-level modes of consciousness as regret and remorse; anxiety and despair;[9] guilt, shame, and embarrassment; the loss of someone loved,[10] the sense of rejection, of frustrated wishes, and of failure. These all differ from physical pain in that they refer beyond the present moment. To be miserable is to be aware of a larger context of existence than one's immediate physical sensations, and to be overcome by the anguished wish that this wider situation were other than it is.

Suffering, so characterized, is a function of sin. Our human experience can become an experience of suffering to us because we engage in it self-centredly. But in themselves our finitude, weakness, and mortality do not constitute situations from which we should violently wish to escape; if we were fully conscious of God and of His universal purpose of good we should be able to accept our life in its entirety as God's gift and be free from anguish on account of it.

It should be added that suffering can be either self-regarding or other-regarding. My violent and obsessive wish that the situation in which I am involved were different may have in view my own interest or the interest of others. It may spring from self-concern or from sympathy. This distinction is relevant to the theological question as to whether Christ, as one who was sinless, can have experienced suffering. The answer, I suggest, is as follows. In general our human sufferings are self-regarding; we wish *for our own sake* that our situation were otherwise. Christ's suffering, on the other hand—as when he wept in sorrow over Jerusalem—was an other-regarding anguish; he grieved, not for himself, but on account of others. We may say, then, not that Christ, as God incarnate, did not suffer, but that he did not suffer egoistically, as we do.

[9] *Constructive Aspects of Anxiety*, ed. Seward Hiltner and Karl Menninger (New York: Abingdon Press, 1963), contains valuable psychological and theological discussions of anxiety.
[10] For a deeply moving diary of meditation upon a bereavement, see *A Grief Observed*, by N. W. Clerk (C. S. Lewis) (London: Faber & Faber, 1961).

2. PAIN AS A CAUSE OF SUFFERING

As a limiting case, very intense pain may so dominate consciousness as for the time being to shut out the wider context of our existence and itself constitute a situation of suffering—a situation that we violently desire to escape from. But more often pain occurs in interplay with other factors. We saw in the previous chapter [of *Evil and the God of Love*] that a situation within which we feel pain can sometimes be such as to render the pain itself endurable, or even such as to make the situation as a whole one which we welcome—as in the case of the soldiers at the bloody Anzio beach-head, to whom a wound meant release from intolerable strain and danger, and offered the prospect of 'peace with honour', rest, comfort, and home.[11] Again, the explorer, the member of a scientific expedition in rough country, the mountain climber, the yachtsman, may put up with considerable amounts of discomfort and even pain without these destroying the positive quality of his situation as a whole as one in which he is happy rather than miserable. The excitement of adventure, the zest of new experiences, the joy of discovery and achievement, the pride of triumphing over difficulties, may be able to absorb a good deal of pain from minor injuries, hunger and thirst, heat and cold, tired limbs and aching muscles, and the other hazards and hardships of the climb of the hunt or the voyage or expedition. If this were not so, adventurous people would not climb the world's greatest mountains, or sail solo across the Atlantic, or explore the polar regions and the parched deserts, or undertake any of the thousand and one great and small designs that are attempted every day for the sake of the sheer adventure of the attempt and the special satisfaction of the accomplishment.

But the greater part of human misery transcends physical pain. What makes illness, for example, an experience of suffering is very often not pain as such but other elements in the situation: fear of permanent disability or of death; anxiety about one's family, or finances, or career; the frustration of one's plans; or the humiliation of helplessness and of dependence upon others. And what often renders miserable the hard existence of the peasant scratching a bare subsistence from the soil must be a constant nagging anxiety about the future, with its ever-impending threat of starvation. And what darkens the lives of so many in the richly affluent societies of the United States and Europe, and causes them to be desperately unhappy amid abundance—so that the richest nations in the world have the highest

---

[11] See [*Evil and the God of Love*], p. 296.

rates of suicide, drug addiction, alcoholism, divorce, and juvenile delin-
quency[12]—is not material lack but a morally paralysing sense of meaninglessness in life as a whole. And again, it is not usually sheer unendurable
physical pain that drives men to take their own lives, but such more
complex spiritual causes as anxiety, fear, remorse, failure in personal
relationships, or a terrible, engulfing inner emptiness and despair. Hume
was right in emphasizing the sufferings of the soul as much as the threats of
surrounding nature. 'The disorders of the mind,' he said, 'though more
secret, are not perhaps less dismal and vexatious. Remorse, shame,
anguish, rage, disappointment, anxiety, fear, dejection, despair; who has
ever passed through life without cruel inroads from these tormentors? How
many have scarcely ever felt any better sensations? Labour and poverty, so
abborred by everyone, are the certain lot of the far greater number: And
those few privileged persons who enjoy ease and opulence, never reach
contentment or true felicity.' So far Hume speaks the truth; but he turns
away from the truth when he continues, 'All the goods of life united would
not make a very happy man, but all the ills united would make a wretch
indeed; and any one of them almost (and who can be free from every one?),
nay, often the absence of one good (and who can possess all?) is sufficient to
render life ineligible.'[13] It is certainly a great mistake to underestimate the
extent of human suffering, which indeed exceeds the wide scope of our
imagination. But it is also a great mistake to underestimate the extent of
human contentment and happiness and hope. Life can be grey and grim;
but it can also contain great and wide pockets of light and happiness, of
beauty and charm. There are many joys within the world of persons—love
and courting, parenthood, the fun of family life, friendship and loyalty, the
service of stirring human causes. There is the world around us, the trees
and clouds, mountains and lakes and valleys and seas and flowers and grass
and animals; and the kind of day that is so saturated with warmth and
beauty that, as Emerson said, 'To have lived through all its sunny hours,

[12] For a number of reasons, precise comparative figures for the statistics indicating human
misery are difficult to obtain. Nevertheless a general correlation is evident between high
standards of living and a high incidence of the symptoms of unhappiness mentioned above. For
example, the highest divorce figures for 1948 (number of divorces per 1,000 marriages in the
preceding decade) were: USA, 248.1; France, 207.2; Denmark, 193.3; England and Wales,
138.5; Sweden, 115.2. (Woytinsky, W. S. and E. S., *World Population and Production*, New
York: The Twentieth Century Fund, 1953, pp. 187 f.) The other statistics are likewise very high
for the wealthiest communities. For example, according to the *Encyclopaedia Britannica Year
Book*, 1963 (p. 671), 'Benjamin Pasamanick's study of an urban population has indicated that
one person in eight at a single point in time suffers from a psychiatric disorder.' In another field,
the *New York Times* reported on 30 November 1964, that in highly affluent Westchester County
in New York State there were 23,000 alcoholics under treatment.

[13] *Dialogues*, pt. x, Kemp-Smith's ed., pp. 240–1.

seems longevity enough.'[14] There are the adventures of the mind in science and philosophy and the joy of creativity in the arts. There is the sense of God's presence and purpose in this gross earth and fleshly life. There are all kinds of deep satisfactions and fulfilments that can make one thankful to be alive in the world as it is. If we must compare two virtual infinites, we can only say that the sum of contentment and happiness is greater than the sum of misery, since otherwise mankind would long since have destroyed itself. Men have to be very miserable indeed to reject life as not worth having, for even amid deep pain and distress they can usually relate the present moment to a wider situation within which there is the hope of a better future. However, the thought that human contentment outweighs human misery offers no solution to the problem of evil, for the basic problem of theodicy would arise even if the sum of man's suffering were only half or a quarter as considerable as it now is.

3. A PARADISE WITHOUT SUFFERING?

Seeking to relate the sad facts of human misery to the problem of theodicy, we have to ask ourselves whether a world from which suffering was excluded would serve what we are supposing to be the divine purpose of soul-making. Having been created through the long evolutionary process as a personal creature made in the 'image' of God, would man be able to grow without suffering towards the finite 'likeness' of God?

So far as human nature itself is concerned, the question concerns man's liability to bring suffering upon himself and upon his fellows by his own selfishness, greed, cruelty, and lovelessness. This aspect of the human situation was considered in Chapter XIII [of *Evil and the God of Love*]. We concluded that in order for man to be endowed with the freedom in relation to God that is essential if he is to come to his Creator in uncompelled faith and love, he must be initially set at an epistemic 'distance' from that Creator. This entails his immersion in an apparently autonomous environment which presents itself to him *etsi deus non daretur*, 'as if there were no God'. We further saw that when man is so circumstanced, it is not only possible for him to centre his life upon himself rather than upon God, but that it is virtually inevitable that he will do so. Man's 'fallenness' is thus the price paid for his freedom as a personal being in relation to the personal Infinite. God is so overwhelmingly great that the children in His heavenly

---

[14] 'Nature', *Basic Selections from Emerson*, ed. Eduard C. Lindeman (New York: Mentor Books, 1954), 11.

family must be prodigal children who have voluntarily come to their Father from a far country, prompted by their own need and drawn by His love. This means that the sinfulness from which man is being redeemed, and the human suffering which flows from that sinfulness, have in their own paradoxical way a place within the divine providence. Their place, however, is not that of something that ought to exist but of something that ought to be abolished. The contribution which sin and its attendant suffering make to God's plan does not consist in any value intrinsic to themselves but, on the contrary, in the activities whereby they are overcome, namely redemption from sin, and men's mutual service amid suffering.

Given, then, that man must be free—free to centre his life upon himself and so to bring suffering upon both himself and others—what does this imply concerning the nature of our environment? We have already seen, in discussing the possibility of a world without pain, that such an anaesthetic existence would lack the stimuli to hunting, agriculture, building and social organization, and to the development of the sciences and technologies, which have been essential foci of human civilization and culture. If we now expand further the notion of a painless world into one in which there is no suffering of any kind, we shall find that the integral character of the present order entails that more would be lost even than civilization and culture.

We may again follow David Hume as our guide to a world devoid of pain and suffering, and continue the discussion arising out of his second complaint concerning the universe. He makes here two suggestions, one more and one less radical. The more radical one is this: 'Might not the Deity exterminate all ill, wherever it were to be found; and produce all good, without any preparation or long progress of causes and effects?'[15] In other words, might not God directly intervene in the workings of nature to prevent any occasion of suffering and to produce a maximum of pleasure and happiness?

The initial answer is of course that God, being omnipotent, could do this. But let us imagine Hume's suggested policy being carried out, noting in particular its consequences for man's status as a moral being. It would mean that no wrong action could ever have bad effects, and that no piece of carelessness or ill judgement in dealing with the world could ever lead to harmful consequences. If a thief were to steal a million pounds from a bank, instead of anyone being made poorer thereby, another million pounds would appear from nowhere to replenish the robbed safe; and this, moreover, without causing any inflationary consequences. If one man tried to

---

[15] *Dialogues*, pt. xi, Kemp-Smith's ed., p. 253.

murder another, his bullet would melt innocuously into thin air, or the blade of his knife turn to paper. Fraud, deceit, conspiracy, and treason would somehow always leave the fabric of society undamaged. Anyone driving at breakneck speed along a narrow road and hitting a pedestrian would leave his victim miraculously unharmed; or if one slipped and fell through a fifth-floor window, gravity would be partially suspended and he would float gently to the ground. And so on. We can at least begin to imagine a world custom-made for the avoidance of all suffering. But the daunting fact that emerges is that in such a world moral qualities would no longer have any point or value. There would be nothing wrong with stealing, because no one could ever lose anything by it; there would be no such crime as murder, because no one could ever be killed; and in short none of the terms connoting modes of injury—such as cruelty, treachery, deceit, neglect, assault, injustice, unfaithfulness—would retain its meaning. If to act wrongly means, basically, to harm someone, there would no longer be any such thing as morally wrong action. And for the same reason there would no longer be any such thing as morally right action. Not only would there be no way in which anyone could injure anyone else, but there would also be no way in which anyone could benefit anyone else, since there would be no possibility of any lack or danger. It would be a world without need for the virtues of self-sacrifice, care for others, devotion to the public good, courage, perseverance, skill, or honesty. It would indeed be a world in which such qualities, having no function to perform, would never come into existence. Unselfishness would never be evoked in a situation in which no one was ever in real need or danger. Honesty, good faith, commitment to the right would never be evoked in circumstances in which no one could ever suffer any harm, so that there were no bad consequences of dishonesty, bad faith, or moral vacillation. Courage would never be evoked in an environment devoid of all dangers; determination and persistence would never be evoked in the absence of any challenges and obstacles. Truthfulness would never be evoked in a world in which to tell a lie never had any ill effects. And so on. Perhaps most important of all, the capacity to love would never be developed, except in a very limited sense of the word, in a world in which there was no such thing as suffering. The most mature and valuable form of love in human life is the love between a man and a woman upon which the family is built. This love is not a merely physical or a purely romantic enjoyment of each other, although that is where it begins and that should always be an element within it. But it can grow into something more than this, namely a joint facing of the task of creating a home together and the bearing of one another's burdens through all the length of a lifetime. Such love perhaps expresses itself most fully in mutual giving and helping and sharing in times of difficulty.[16] And it is hard to see how such love could ever be developed in human life, in this its deepest and most valuable form of mutual caring and sharing, except in an environment that has much in common with our own world. It is, in particular, difficult to see how it could ever grow to any extent in a paradise that excluded all suffering. For such love presupposes a 'real life' in which there are obstacles to be overcome, tasks to be performed, goals to be achieved, setbacks to be endured, problems to be solved, dangers to be met; and if the world did not contain the particular obstacles, difficulties, problems, and dangers that it does contain, then it would have to contain others instead. The same is true in relation to the virtues of compassion, unselfishness, courage, and determination—these all presuppose for their emergence and for their development something like the world in which we live. They are values of personal existence that would have no point, and therefore no place, in a ready-made Utopia. And therefore, if the purpose for which this world exists (so far as that purpose concerns mankind) is to be a sphere within which such personal qualities are born, to purge it of all suffering would be a sterile reform.

At the same time, it is to be noted that we have, in all this, discerned only a very general connection between the kind of world in which we are living and the development of so many of the more desirable qualities of human personality. We have seen that, from our human point of view, this is a world with rough edges, a place in which man can live only by the sweat of his brow, and which continually presents him with challenges, uncertainties, and dangers; and yet that just these features of the world seem, paradoxically, to underlie the emergence of virtually the whole range of the more valuable human characteristics.

4. EXCESSIVE OR DYSTELEOLOGICAL SUFFERING

But we have now to consider the all-important question of the *amount* of suffering in the world. The less radical form of Hume's second suggestion is

---

[16] As James Hinton argued in his classic meditation on the mystery of pain, 'We could never have felt the joy, never had had even the idea, of love, if sacrifice had been impossible to us.' (*The Mystery of Pain*, 1866, London: Hodder & Stoughton, 1911, p. 51). Cf. Josiah Royce: 'Even love shows its glory as love only by its conquest over the doubts and estrangements, the absences and the misunderstandings, the griefs and the loneliness, that love glorifies with its light amidst all their tragedy.' (*The World and the Individual*, New York: The Macmillan Co., 1901, vol. ii, p. 409.) Royce presented his own idealist theodicy here and in 'The Problem of Job' (*Studies in Good and Evil*, 1898, reprinted in Walter Kaufmann (ed.), *Religion From Tolstoy to Camus*, New York: Harper & Row, 1961).

that God should not interfere in the workings of nature to such an extent that no objective order remains, but should interfere only secretly and on special occasions to prevent exceptional and excessive evils. 'A fleet, whose purposes were salutary to society, might always meet with a fair wind. Good princes enjoy sound health and long life: Persons born to power and authority, be framed with good tempers and virtuous dispositions.'[17] This suggestion seems more plausible than the previous one. But nevertheless it is not free from difficulty. For evils are exceptional only in relation to other evils which are routine. And therefore unless God eliminated all evils whatsoever there would always be relatively outstanding ones of which it would be said that He should have secretly prevented them. If, for example, divine providence had eliminated Hitler in his infancy we might now point instead to Mussolini as an example of a human monster whom God ought secretly to have excised from the human race; and if there were no Mussolini we should point to someone else. Or again, if God had secretly prevented the bombing of Hiroshima we might complain instead that He could have avoided the razing of Rotterdam. Or again, if He had secretly prevented the Second World War, then what about the First World War, or the American Civil War, or the Napoleonic wars, and so through all the major wars of history to its secondary wars, about which exactly the same questions would then be in order? There would be nowhere to stop, short of a divinely arranged paradise in which human freedom would be narrowly circumscribed, moral responsibility largely eliminated, and in which the drama of man's story would be reduced to the level of a television serial. We always know that the rugged hero who upholds law and order is going to win the climactic gun fight. And if every time a tyrant set out to trample upon human freedom we could be sure in advance that some apparent accident would providentially remove him from the scene it would no longer be true that the price of liberty is eternal vigilance; and indeed vigilance, and the willingness to make sacrifices for human liberty, would no longer be virtues and would no longer be evoked in mankind. If we knew in advance that no really serious threat to them could ever arise, the struggle for righteousness and human dignity would become unreal. Once again, then, we are confronted by the integral character of the existing order of things such that bane and blessing are intimately bound together within it, and such that not even an unfettered imagination can see how to remove the possibility of the one without at the same time forfeiting the possibility of the other.

There is more to be said about excessive suffering in the world, and a

---

[17] *Dialogues*, pt. xi, Kemp-Smith's ed., p. 254.

more serious difficulty to be faced, when we turn in Hume's fourth complaint from social to natural evils. But first we may note his third complaint, which is that man is too sparsely endowed with powers and in particular with the capacity for perseverance.

In order to cure most of the ills of human life [he says], I require not that man should have the wings of the eagle, the swiftness of the stag, the force of the ox, the arms of the lion, the scales of the crocodile or rhinoceros; much less do I demand the sagacity of an angel or cherubim. I am contented to take an increase in one single power or faculty of his soul. Let him be endowed with a greater propensity to industry and labour; a more vigorous spring and activity of mind; a more constant bent to business and application. . . . Almost all the moral, as well as natural evils of human life arise from idleness; and were our species, by the original constitution of their frame, exempt from this vice or infirmity, the perfect cultivation of land, the improvement of arts and manufactures, the exact execution of every office and duty, immediately follow; and men at once may fully reach that state of society, which is so imperfectly attained by the best-regulated government.[18]

Once again, this seems at first sight to be an enlightened and constructive proposal. And yet its flaw is not far to seek. If all men were endowed with, let us say, twice as much industry and perseverance as at present, this would mean not only that good men would work twice as hard for good ends but also that evil men would work twice as hard for evil ends. And the resulting state of the world would be proportionately the same. Criminals would be twice as industrious, but the police twice as active to frustrate them. In our contemporary political mythology, the children of darkness—whether 'red' or 'imperialist'—would arm themselves twice as quickly, and the children of light would follow suit; and as a result the world would be in an even more dangerous state than it is now.

But it is Hume's fourth and last complaint that raises the really insoluble problems. This concerns the way in which various elements of the world order which are in themselves good, such as wind, rain, and heat, the 'humours and juices of the body' and the passions of the mind, often exceed, as he says, 'those bounds in which their utility consists'. For example, 'the winds are requisite to convey the vapours along the surface of the globe, and to assist men in navigation: But how often, rising up to tempests and hurricanes, do they become pernicious? Rains are necessary to nourish all the plants and animals of the earth; But how often are they defective? how often excessive? Heat is requisite to all life and vegetation; but is not always found in the due proportion. On the mixture and secretion of the humours and juices of the body depend the health and prosperity of the animal: But the parts perform not regularly their proper function. . . .'[19]

[18] *Dialogues*, pt. xi, Kemp-Smith's ed., pp. 256–7.
[19] *Dialogues*, pt. xi, Kemp-Smith's ed., pp. 256–7.

Hume's point could be elaborated indefinitely. Let the hypothesis of a divine purpose of soul-making be adopted, and let it be further granted that an environment which is to serve this purpose cannot be a permanent hedonistic paradise but must offer to man real tasks, challenges, and problems. Still the question must be asked: Need the world contain the more extreme and crushing evils which it in fact contains? Are not life's challenges often so severe as to be self-defeating when considered as soul-making influences? Man must (let us suppose) cultivate the soil so as to win his bread by the sweat of his brow; but need there be the gigantic famines, for example in China, from which millions have so miserably perished? Man must (let us suppose) labour on the earth's surface to make roads, and dig beneath it to extract its coals and minerals; but need there be volcanic irruptions burying whole cities, and earthquakes killing thousands of terrified people in a single night? Man must (let us suppose) face harsh bodily consequences of over-indulgence; but need there also be such fearful diseases as typhoid, polio, cancer, angina? These reach far beyond any constructive function of character training. Their effect seems to be sheerly dysteleological and destructive. They can break their victim's spirit and cause him to curse whatever gods there are. When a child dies of cerebral meningitis, his little personality undeveloped and his life unfulfilled, leaving only an unquenchable aching void in his parents' lives; or when a charming, lively, and intelligent woman suffers from a shrinking of the brain which destroys her personality and leaves her in an asylum, barely able to recognize her nearest relatives, until death comes in middle life as a baneful blessing; or when a child is born so deformed and defective that he can never live a properly human life, but must always be an object of pity to some and revulsion to others . . . when such things happen we can see no gain to the soul, whether of the victim or of others, but on the contrary only a ruthlessly destructive process which is utterly inimical to human values. It seems as though 'As flies to wanton boys, are we to the gods, They kill us for their sport'.[20]

It is true that sometimes—no one can know how often or how seldom—there are sown or there come to flower even in the direst calamity graces of character that seem to make even that calamity itself worth while. A selfish spirit may be moved to compassion, a thoughtless person discover life's depths and be deepened thereby, a proud spirit learn patience and humility, a soft, self-indulgent character be made strong in the fires of adversity. All this may happen, and has happened. But it may also fail to happen, and instead of gain there may be sheer loss. Instead of ennobling, affliction may

[20] Shakespeare, *King Lear*, iv. i. 38–9.

crush the character and wrest from it whatever virtues it possessed. Can anything be said, from the point of view of Christian theodicy, in face of this cosmic handling of man, which seems at best to be utterly indifferent and at worst implacably malevolent towards him?

5. THE TRADITIONAL ANSWER: NATURE PERVERTED BY FALLEN ANGELS

The notion of a pre-mundane fall, whether of human souls (as was taught by Origen, and again in modern times by Julius Müller) or of a life-force that had not yet become individualized (as N. P. Williams suggested), has been rejected above as a speculation which conceals rather than solves the problem of the origin of moral evil.[21] There is, however, another related conception of a pre-mundane fall which differs from these in that it has some basis, however slight, in Scripture; and it has been invoked by several writers as solving in principle our present problem concerning the apparently malevolent aspects of nature. This is the idea of a fall of angelic beings preceding and accounting for both the fall of man and the disordered and dysteleological features of the natural world.[22] It might be suggested that these angels are in charge of the world, perhaps different angels being concerned with different aspects of nature, like the gods of the old Greek pantheon, and that when they fell from grace their apostasy was reflected in distortions of nature and in perverted biological developments of various kinds. That the animal species prey upon one another, that there are microbes and bacteria which cause disease in animal bodies, that there are weaknesses in the earth's crust producing volcanoes and tornadoes, that there are violent extremes of temperature, uninhabitable climates, droughts and blights, may all be due to the malevolence or heedlessness of higher beings who were appointed as nature's guardians but who have become enemies of nature's God.

In support of such a theory it might be claimed that in the New Testament miracles we see the power of God at work reversing nature's tragic departure from the course intended for it in the original divine plan. When

---

[21] See [*Evil and the God of Love*], pp. 251 f.

[22] This is to be found in a number of writers; for example, C. C. J. Webb, *Problems in the Relations of God and Man* (Oxford: Clarendon Press, 1915), 269–71; C. S. Lewis, *The Problem of Pain* (London: Centenary Press, 1940), 122 f.; Dom Bruno Webb, *Why Does God Permit Evil?* (London: Burns, Oates & Washbourne, Ltd., 1941), Leonard Hodgson, *For Faith and Freedom* (Oxford: Basil Blackwell, 1956–7), i. 213 f.; Dom Illtyd Trethowan, *An Essay in Christian Philosophy* (London: Longmans, Green & Co., 1954), 128; E. L. Mascall, *Christian Theology and Natural Science* (London: Longmans, Green & Co., 1956), 301 f.

Jesus healed the sick and stilled the storm he was overturning the work of fallen spirits who still exercise control over this world. This, it might be added, was a contemporary Jewish understanding of disease which seems also to have been shared by Jesus himself.

Such a speculation has its attractions. It would allow us to recognize unequivocally the inimical character of disease, accident, and decay, even to the extent of seeing a malevolent activity behind them. But, on the other hand, it would revive the fundamental contradiction that lies at the heart of the traditional Augustinian theodicy. It would trace all evil back to a common source in the incomprehensible rebellion of finitely perfect beings who were enjoying the full happiness of God's presence. This would be a return to the unintelligible notion of the self-creation of evil *ex nihilo*, against which I have argued at length above. It must also be objected against this speculation that it would lead to a gnostic rejection of the natural order as evil. If the world is ruled by 'obscure, unfeeling and unloving powers', as Sigmund Freud also believed,[23] we ought to regard it with horror as the sphere of something malevolent and fearful. But for the most part mankind has found it to be otherwise and our minstrels, the poets of all ages, have celebrated the goodness of the earth, the bountifulness of nature, and the infinite delights and ever-changing beauties of earth's seasons. Both Jewish and Christian poets have been in the forefront of this celebration, directing it upwards in gratitude to God. Are we, then, to split the seamless coat of nature and say that the lilies of the field, together with rich harvests and beautiful sunsets, are ruled by good spirits, whilst diseases, earthquakes and storms are produced by evil spirits? This would indeed be a desperate expedient. For all that the sciences teach us about the workings of nature tends to emphasize its unity as a single system of cause and effect exhibiting the same laws throughout.

There are reasons, then, to proceed along a different path which, whilst not being obliged to reject the traditional doctrine of the pre-human fall of the angels, does not try to make use of it to solve the problems of theodicy.

6. SOUL-MAKING AND MYSTERY

The problem of suffering remains, then, in its full force. If what has been said in this and the previous chapter (of *Evil and the God of Love*] is valid the problem does not consist in the occurrence of pain and suffering as such; for we can see that a world in which these exist in at least a moderate degree

---

[23] *New Introductory Lectures on Psycho-Analysis*, Standard Edition of Complete Psychological Works, vol. xxii (London: Hogarth Press, 1964), 167 and 173.

may well be a better environment for the development of moral personalities than would be a sphere that was sterilized of all challenges. The problem consists rather in the fact that instead of serving a constructive purpose pain and misery seem to be distributed in random and meaningless ways, with the result that suffering is often undeserved and often falls upon men in amounts exceeding anything that could be rationally intended.

Further, I have argued that we ought to reject the traditional theories that would rationalize the incidence of misery: the theory that each individual's sufferings represent a just punishment for his own sins, whether committed in this life or in some pre-natal realm; and the theory that the world is in the grip of evil powers, so that the dysteleological surplus of human misery is an achievement of demonic malevolence. Moreover, I do not now have an alternative theory to offer that would explain in any rational or ethical way why men suffer as they do. The only appeal left is to mystery. This is not, however, merely an appeal to the negative fact that we cannot discern any rationale of human suffering. It may be that the very mysteriousness of this life is an important aspect of its character as a sphere of soul-making. Perhaps, as the Cambridge Platonist Ralph Cudworth thought, 'it is in itself fit, that there should be somewhere a doubtful and cloudy state of things, for the better exercise of virtue and faith'.[24]

To test this possibility let us employ once again the method of counter-factual hypothesis, and try to imagine a world which, although not entirely free from pain and suffering, nevertheless contained no unjust and un-deserved or excessive and apparently dysteleological misery. Although there would be sufficient hardships and dangers and problems to give spice to life, there would be no utterly destructive and apparently vindictive evil. On the contrary, men's sufferings would always be seen either to be justly deserved punishments or else to serve a constructive purpose of moral training.

In such a world human misery would not evoke deep personal sympathy or call forth organized relief and sacrificial help and service. For it is presupposed in these compassionate reactions both that the suffering is not deserved and that it is *bad* for the sufferer. We do not acknowledge a moral call to sacrificial measures to save a criminal from receiving his just punishment or a patient from receiving the painful treatment that is to cure him. But men and women often act in true compassion and massive generosity and self-giving in the face of unmerited suffering, especially when it comes in such dramatic forms as an earthquake or a mining disaster. It seems, then, that in a world that is to be the scene of compassionate love

---

[24] *The True Intellectual System of the Universe* (1678), trans. by J. Harrison (London: Thomas Tegg, 1845), vol. III, ch. v, sect. 5, p. 477.

and self-giving for others, suffering must fall upon mankind with something of the haphazardness and inequity that we now experience. It must be apparently unmerited, pointless, and incapable of being morally rationalized. For it is precisely this feature of our common human lot that creates sympathy between man and man and evokes the unselfish kindness and goodwill which are among the highest values of personal life. No undeserved need would mean no uncalculating outpouring to meet that need.

Further, the systematic elimination of unjust suffering, and the consequent apportioning of suffering to desert, would entail that there would be ·no doing of the right simply *because* it is right and without any expectation of reward. For the alternative to the present apparently random incidence of misfortune would be that happiness should be the predictable result of virtue, and misery the predictable outcome of wickedness. Under such a régime virtuous action would be immediately rewarded with happiness, and wicked action with misery. What Kant called the good will, which does the right simply and solely because it is right, and of which he said that this is the only intrinsically good thing in the world or out of it,[25] would be excluded. For whilst the possibility of the good will by no means precludes that right action shall in fact eventually lead to happiness, and wrong action to misery, it does preclude this happening so certainly, instantly, and manifestly that virtue cannot be separated in experience and thought from its reward, or vice from its punishment. Accordingly a world in which the sinner was promptly struck down by divine vengeance and in which the upright were the immediate recipients of divine reward would be incompatible with that divine purpose of soul-making that we are supposing to lie behind the arrangement of our present world.

Our 'solution', then, to this baffling problem of excessive and undeserved suffering is a frank appeal to the positive value of mystery. Such suffering remains unjust and inexplicable, haphazard and cruelly excessive. The mystery of dysteleological suffering is a real mystery, impenetrable to the rationalizing human mind. It challenges Christian faith with its utterly baffling, alien, destructive meaninglessness. And yet at the same time, detached theological reflection can note that this very irrationality and this lack of ethical meaning contribute to the character of the world as a place in which true human goodness can occur and in which loving sympathy and compassionate self-sacrifice can take place. 'Thus, paradoxically,' as H. H. Farmer says, 'the failure of theism to solve all mysteries becomes part of its case!'[26]

[25] Immanuel Kant, *Fundamental Principles of the Metaphysic of Morals*, sect. 1, *ab init*. Cf. *Critique of Practical Reason*, Bk. II, ch. II, sect. IX.
[26] *Towards Belief in God* (London: SCM Press, 1942), 234.

My general conclusion, then, is that this world, with all its unjust and apparently wasted suffering, may nevertheless be what the Irenaean strand of Christian thought affirms that it is, namely a divinely created sphere of soul-making. But if this is so, yet further difficult questions now arise. A vale of soul-making that successfully makes persons of the desired quality may perhaps be justified by this result. But if the soul-making purpose fails, there can surely be no justification for 'the heavy and the weary weight of all this unintelligible world'.[27] And yet, so far as we can see, the soul-making process does in fact fail in our own world at least as often as it succeeds.

At this point a further, eschatological, dimension of Christian belief becomes importantly relevant, and must be brought into the discussion in the next chapter [of *Evil and the God of Love*].

[27] Wordsworth, 'Lines composed a few miles above Tintern Abbey'.

XI

NATURAL EVIL AND THE LOVE OF GOD

DIOGENES ALLEN

There is some important data which has not as yet found its way into philosophic discussions on the problem of evil. Some religious people report that suffering, instead of being contrary to the love of God, is actually a medium in and through which his love can be experienced. This looks highly paradoxical, but it will be our purpose to show that it is intelligible and that it has important consequences for philosophical discussions of the problem of evil.

My procedure will be to deal primarily with the suffering caused by the natural world. I will argue that when a person performs certain specific *actions*, it becomes possible for that person to conceive of God's love and to experience it in and through suffering. Investigations of the problem of evil are often conducted in ignorance of these actions and the data rendered accessible by such actions.

I will begin by an examination of Epictetus' claim that 'from everything that happens in the universe it is easy for a man to find occasion to praise providence',[1] and will specify the first action a person must perform to find this plausible. I will then draw upon an autobiographical letter of Simone Weil and her essay, 'The Love of God and Affliction' to specify two other acts. I will show the relevance of all this for philosophic discussions of the problem of evil, both at various junctures in the article and at the end.

I

Epictetus claims that 'from everything that happens in the universe it is easy for a man to find occasion to praise providence'. In the first instance this refers to the teleological order of nature. Just as a sword is fitted to a

Diogenes Allen, 'Natural Evil and the Love of God', first published in *Religious Studies*, 16 (1980), pp. 439–56. Reprinted by permission of the author and Cambridge University Press. The substance of the article was incorporated into Professor Allen's book, *Traces of God*, Cowley Publications, Cambridge, Mass. 1981.

[1] *Arrian's Discourses of Epictetus*, trans. W. A. Oldfather, 2 vols. (London: Heinemann and New York: G. P. Putnam's Sons, 1928), I. vi. 1.

scabbard and a scabbard to a sword, so too are coloured objects and light
fitted to our vision and our vision to them (I. vi. 4–8). Everything in nature
has some purpose, and so each item helps to make our universe a cosmos—
a harmonious whole. Each creature fulfils its purpose by acting in accordance
with its nature; human beings, because they have reason, have the task of
discerning these purposes and rendering praise for the glory of the ordered
whole (I. vi. 18–22 and I. xvi, especially 16–21).

But all does not go well for human beings. Epictetus responds to this fact
by asserting that we can make use of whatever befalls us (I. vi. 23–43). The
goodness of the cosmos is not that everything goes according to our will,
with each of our desires catered for; but if we take a comprehensive view of
the entire order of the universe, we will see that we are but one item among
many in a vast interconnected whole. Many pleasant and unpleasant things
occur to individuals because of the interconnections, but in every instance
we have the ability to bear whatever happens to us 'without being degraded
or crushed thereby' (I. vi. 40–1). We can wipe our noses because we have
hands; we can accept being lame as a small sacrifice toward the rest of the
universe; we can even endure an unavoidable death from the hands of
either nature or the social order without degradation.

This is achieved by recognizing 'necessity' and by exercising the only real
freedom we have. Our position in the physical and the social world is that of
but one reality among many in a system of interconnected events, most of
which are utterly beyond our control. What is beyond an individual's
control can sometimes injure his wealth, his social position, his body, and
even bring utter destruction. In such circumstances an individual's only real
freedom is the manner in which he responds to untoward events beyond his
control. He can complain about his misfortune; or he can bear whatever
comes, even death, without degradation by seeing its necessity and yielding
to it courageously and magnanimously.

One thus makes *use* of whatever befalls, by using it to bring out these
qualities of character. A person can thus be grateful to providence,
whatever happens to him, for providing him with the capacity to recognize
the universe as an ordered whole and for the capacity to yield to the
adversity it brings—even death—with courage and dignity. Thus Epictetus
can exclaim:

Bring now, O Zeus, what difficulty Thou wilt; for I have an equipment given to me by
Thee, and resources wherewith to distinguish myself by making use of the things that
come to pass. (I. vi. 37–8)

But we might ask Epictetus: It may indeed be possible to make use of
everything that happens to us and thus have reason to praise providence,

but could not things have been better arranged than they are? If we try to follow up that question, two things result. (1) We find that we can never get it resolved. (2) We fail to learn from suffering.

We can never get this question resolved because things in the world are so connected that we do not know what consequences the alteration of any one factor might have for the rest of the universe. Hume's Philo, for example, considers some possible changes that would *apparently* greatly improve the world. All animate creatures could be motivated solely by pleasure or the abatement of pleasure, instead of also by pain. People might have been endowed with more diligence, and hence provide for their needs more adequately. But then he declines to pronounce with definiteness on the matter. 'This decision seems too presumptuous for creatures so blind and ignorant.'[2]

Although we do not know whether the universe could have been better arranged, Hume's Philo claims that the world-order fails to cater sufficiently to our well-being and to that of animals for it to merit our praise for its goodness.

Look round this universe. What an immense profusion of beings, animated and organized, sensible and active! You admire this prodigious variety and fecundity. But inspect a little more narrowly these living existences, the only beings worth regarding. How hostile and destructive to each other! How insufficient all of them for their own happiness! How contemptible or odious to the spectator! The whole presents nothing but the idea of a blind nature, impregnated by a great vivifying principle, and pouring fourth from her lap, without discernment or parental care, her maimed and abortive children.[3]

Hume in this part of his *Dialogues* is concerned with showing that the world's order is such that it does not allow us to infer that its source is *good*. In this context he is not disputing whether its order makes it most likely that it has an intelligent designer. It is strictly a matter of the goodness of its source. That point is to be determined on the basis of the goodness of the cosmos. So we are asking: Is the cosmos praiseworthy and thus a basis for praising the goodness of its source (should it have one)? The world's goodness is judged in terms of how well it provides for the well-being of human beings and other living creatures. On this basis his character Philo is very negative, as we have seen.

How hostile and destructive to each other! How insufficient all of them for their own happiness! How contemptible or odious to the spectator!

[2] David Hume, *Dialogues Concerning National Religion*, ed. N. K. Smith (Indianapolis: Bobbs-Merrill, 1947), 210.
[3] Ibid. 211.

But Epictetus believes that a world-order is achieved by each thing following its nature, which involves, for example, being eaten and used. 'Each of the animals God constitutes, one to be eaten, another to serve in farming, another to produce cheese . . .' (I. vi. 15–16). Each fulfils its purpose by being itself. 'For them it is sufficient to eat and drink and rest and procreate, and whatever else of these things within their own province the animals severally do . . .' (I. vi. 15–16). Human beings also perform actions of this type, but we also have as our purpose the use of our understanding to discern the way things fit together and serve each other.

God has brought man into the world to be a spectator of Himself and His works, and not merely a spectator, but also an interpreter. Wherefore it is shameful for a man to begin and end just where irrational animals do . . . (I. vi. 19–20).

We are to render praise because of the abilities given to us. 'Great is God that he hath given us hands, and power to swallow, and a belly and power to grow unconsciously, and to breathe while asleep' (I. xvi. 17–18). We are also to render praise, as we have seen, for the ability to withstand whatever befalls us, without being crushed or degraded thereby. We follow our nature and fulfil our purpose, then, by our discernment of the orderliness of nature and by rendering praise.

If, indeed, I were a nightingale, I should be singing as a nightingale; if a swan, as a swan. But as it is I am a rational being, therefore I must be singing hymns of praise to God (I. xvi. 20–1).

What is the significance of the disagreement between Hume's Philo and Epictetus over the goodness of nature? It is granted that we cannot settle the question of whether nature could have been better arranged than it is, but the reason the question is raised is because one of them is dissatisfied with its actual arrangement. One of them is dissatisfied because he expects that everything that lives ought to be better looked after and ought not to suffer so much. Naturally the world-order will then fail to provide such a person with a basis to praise the goodness of its designer (should it have one).

But to approach nature with the expectation that we ought to be better looked after, makes it unlikely that we will learn from suffering. Suffering can teach us that we are a very small part of the universe and that we are not to expect as much as we do from its workings. When this is learned, we can then see more soberly and accurately what it does provide for us. What it does provide gives us ample reason to be grateful, in spite of the tragedies its workings produce, whether for us or for others. Indeed in our humbled and more realistic condition we can see the glory of the entire world-order and be grateful for our capacity to yield ourselves to it courageously and magnanimously even when we are caught in its workings. Let us examine this claim in some detail.

II

Most of our thoughts and actions are self-serving in various degrees. We stand at the centre, with all other people and events in orbit around ourselves. Everything is seen from our perspective and is evaluated, understood, and thought about in such a way as to enhance or protect ourselves. But sometimes we rise above our egotism. However rarely, we do at times restrain our self-concern, even though perhaps not perfectly.

One way this can occur is in relation to the fact that we are material beings. We are part of the natural physical order, subject to its laws, subject to microbes and viruses, subject to ageing and decay, subject to death. We encounter here certain realities that are not completely avoidable. We can mitigate them, as we ought to whenever possible, but we cannot completely avoid them.

How do we react to the fact that we are material beings, subject to wear and tear? How do we react to illness, to accident, to decay, to death? Do we respond egotistically? Most of the time we do. But sometimes people do not; they transcend their egotism. This is done when people recognize their vulnerability, recognize it as part of the human condition, part of being a piece of matter.

But egotism is common. 'Why did this happen to me? What did I ever do wrong?' This is often said or felt with a sense of indignation, of outrage, of offence, or self-pity. At other times when we feel that we suffer adversity unfairly, we become mute with depression. These are just samples from a host of quite automatic and normal reactions to adversity.

But these automatic responses can be the occasion for *reflection*. They can be an occasion to ask oneself: 'Why did I think that I was immune to such misfortune? Why did I think that good and evil are parcelled out according to some scheme of merit?' Such reflection can lead us to recognize more fully something we already know: we are material, and as a piece of matter we are vulnerable to injury, illness, and decay. To realize this is to realize our status, our place—to realize what we are. It is to come to terms with a hard fact.

But it is also to transcend the psyche's egocentric mechanism. Egocentricity seeks to expand, to get its own way, to go as far as it can. But when the flow of our self-regard is painfully interrupted, reflection can lead to a new awareness of our limitations, and it may lead to *an act of acceptance* of such limitations. To accept to any degree our status as a piece of matter is, paradoxically, to transcend to that extent being merely a piece of matter. Any degree of humility means that one has performed an action which a piece of non-living matter or nonhuman living matter does not perform.

Thus our automatic self-centred responses to suffering, which on reflection yield to a more realistic recognition of what we are (vulnerable piece of matter), paradoxically enable us to recognize that we have by that very act transcended being *merely* a piece of matter; for we are not encompassed completely by the principles that govern the rest of matter. In this sense, we are spiritual beings. Our spirituality is found and is affirmed precisely in and with the fact that we are material—subject to the grinding wear and tear of matter. In facing the material facts of illness, accident, decay, and death we can rise above our egotism and discover that we are spiritual beings.

Here is an example of such a response to the unavoidable price of being a piece of matter:

> Waiting for a lab report,
> Dependent on mysterious authorities,
> Gazing at my daughter in hospital,
> Her mother and I sharing a hard fellowship,
> I know a timeless, tribeless circumstance;
> I drive to the hospital in an eternal procession,
> I eat in the snack bar among the whole human race;
> My tears began 100,000 years ago
> And will never stop.[4]

The person in this poem moves from a mere concern for his child to join the human race. He sees her illness as part and parcel of humanity's vulner-ability, and his tears as part of the tears of people throughout the ages. His drive to the hospital is not just his own journey, but part of an eternal procession; in the snack bar he eats among the whole human race. The title is 'Common Life'—not a title that refers solely to his daughter's illness. He has transcended the mechanism of the self-centred psyche.

The fact of our material vulnerability can be the occasion to move us off centre, to melt the illusion that we are immensely significant, and to show us that we are dust and ashes, formed of the clay of the earth. That is part of the truth about us. But in that very recognition, in the very act of being humbled, we can recognize that we are spiritual beings. To say, in the face of hard realities, 'Yes, it is so' is to break out of the fetters of egocentricity and to exhibit a capacity not found in the rest of matter.

Epictetus stressed the attainment of this kind of humility. He regarded people, and himself specifically, as part of the cosmos with no special

---

[4] Ray Lindquist, 'Common Life'.

privileges beyond the ability to perceive its order, to give thanks for its positive benefits and for the ability to endure whatever happens to us without being crushed or degraded thereby. Only with such humility—a humility that is achieved by one's response to adversity—is it possible for a person to look at this world and to find it gloriously ordered and praiseworthy. Without such humility we do not perceive its goodness because its order often brings adversity to us.

Philosophic discussions of the problem of evil often treat suffering only as evidence that runs counter to a theistic world view. If we regard suffering only as counter-evidence, as did Hume, then we are unlikely to learn from suffering. Our egocentricity will remain intact. We then will judge the world without humility and thus be unable to see that it is praiseworthy despite the adversity it brings to us and other creatures.

It is perfectly proper to consider the implications of suffering as Hume and others have. That is, to trace out the implications of the suffering caused by the workings of nature when looked at with one kind of expectation. But this should not blind one to a recognition of the effects our vulnerability to suffering can have on our egocentricity, if suffering is reflected on along the lines we have suggested. Nor should we ignore how this can enable a person, as it did Epictetus, to see that that order of nature is glorious, not odious, and that we have ample reason to be grateful for it, even when pressed by extreme adversity, since we have the capacity to endure all things without being crushed or degraded. Nature is not good enough to warrant the gratitude and praise of a person who lacks such humility, that is to say, who lacks a realistic view of himself as but a small part of nature.

III

It might be objected: the world-order may be good enough for a stoic, but a stoic is not a theist. For a stoic the cosmos is ordered by an immanent principle, but there is no transcendent creator and ruler of nature. Are not people much more important in various theistic schemes than has been so far granted? In fact, in Christianity they are said to be the object of a perfect love. Their vulnerability to accident, disease, and tragic death from natural forces does not seem to cohere with the picture of a loving Father who cares for people more than he does for the birds of the air and the lilies of the field.

Actually *belief* in a loving Father is precisely what enables a person to perform, in the face of adversity, a second act. It is that action which enables a person to *experience* God's love in the midst of suffering. It can be performed only by a person who believes in a loving God and who also has the humility of the stoic. The first act is a necessary condition for the performance of the second. Those who have found themselves not to be encompassed completely by the principles that operate in all matter, by yielding to nature's might, can yield themselves to its might *as a reality that obeys God*. We have been told that when we do this, we find ourselves experiencing God's love. Sister Basilea Schlink claims, 'When you are in suffering say, "Yes, Father," and strength will flow into your heart.'[5] She offers this not as a theory but as what actually happens when you so act. There are others who make the same claim: a gracious presence is experienced.[6]

Such a gracious presence cannot be known *theoretically*. It comes only by the *act* of affirming God's rule and way of ruling. For a Christian, nature operates as it does—following its intrinsic principles—not merely of its own accord, but because it is so created and presently sustained by God. In saying 'Yes, Father' to the *unavoidable* effects of nature on us, we submit to nature's might as something that obeys another, and not to it merely as a senseless destructive force. Through this act it is claimed that the gracious presence of God is known; it flows into one and gives a felicity that is beyond the calculation of the pluses and minuses of the pleasant and unpleasant things of this life. The goodness of God is not understood solely in terms of the health and well-being that is enjoyed, and then set over against the untoward things that have happened or may happen to us. God is himself good, a unique good, whose value cannot be compared to the creaturely goods and evils we know. And it is God's own goodness, his Spirit, it is claimed, that comes more fully into a person, and comes precisely through the untowardness of material things and a person's own response to their untowardness.

The act by which one says 'Yes, Father'—yielding to nature's might as something that obeys God—is not necessarily a self-conscious act. It seems

---

[5] Sister Basilea Schlink founded soon after World War II a Protestant order of nuns, the *Marienschwestern*, with its home base near Darmstadt, West Germany. She has a series of such aphorisms printed on individual cards, as well as several books on the spiritual life, including accounts of the specific benefits of illness.

[6] See Simone Weil, *The Need for Roots* (New York: Harper & Row, 1971), 283–302. Also see Edith Barfoot, 'The Joyful Vocation to Suffering', reprinted in *The Witness of Edith Barfoot* (Oxford: Basil Blackwell, 1977). Edith Barfoot spent seventy of her eighty-seven years in suffering: rheumatoid arthritis successively deprived her of movement, eyesight, and ultimately hearing.

In order to prevent a possible serious misunderstanding, it should be noted that those we are citing were (are) not quietists. Schlink is, and Weil was, extremely active in seeking to alleviate and prevent suffering, and to improve human life and social institutions.

to have been done by Simone Weil when she was suffering from intense headaches and reciting George Herbert's poem 'Love'. She says she did not realize it but she was actually praying, and—

Christ himself came down and took possession of me . . . I had never foreseen the possibility of that, of real contact, person to person, here below, between a human being and God . . . Moreover, in this sudden possession of me by Christ, neither my senses nor my imagination had any part; I only felt in the midst of my suffering the presence of a love.[7]

One would like to know more about this experience, especially how Simone Weil knew that it was Christ who was present. Nonetheless, it does illustrate that this act of consent to God in suffering does not have to be a self-conscious act.

Not only was the act which she describes not self-conscious, but there had been a long preparation for this reception of God's love—again not self-consciously. Part of that preparation was her learning—bit by bit—the lesson of our material vulnerability—the first action described above. But in no case is the act whereby one yields to nature's might *as something which obeys God* simply a matter of reading an article such as this and then saying on the next occasion of an illness, 'Yes, Father'. One must first learn to see that nature is an orderly whole, with each part operating as it does without any regard for any other part. One must face one's vulnerability to its workings, and not think that this essential vulnerability can be avoided by prayer,[8] any more than Jesus could escape destruction by his prayers in the garden of Gethsemane. Only when one has had one's egocentricity pierced by the workings of nature, and when the fact of vulnerability has formed part of the substance of one's character, is one perhaps ready actually to yield oneself to nature as a reality that obeys the Father—to yield not with one's lips but with one's entire self. That 'Yes, Father' is what people such as Schlink, Barfoot, and Weil claim leads to a reception of a gracious love in the midst of suffering.

Of course we cannot accept at face value the claim of these women that *God* is experienced by yielding to the workings of nature as forces obedient to God. To believe in God and to act on that belief in the face of adversity *might* make a person feel marvellous whether there is a God or not; at least that seems a reasonable assumption to make. So we cannot tell without further investigation whether it is reasonable to say that God's presence is or is not being experienced by them. But there is no reason to doubt that a felicity is experienced which transcends the normal pluses and minuses of life. That data does exist.

[7] Simone Weil, *Waiting on God* (Glasgow: Collins, 1959), 35–6.
[8] Weil, *Need for Roots*, pp. 282–3.

Our purpose here is to get that data introduced into philosophic discussions of the problem of evil and to show its relevance for those discussions. Suffering is almost always discussed primarily as counter-evidence to a theistic world view. It is thought that unless its existence is explained, the presumption is against theism.[9] It is not noticed, however, that suffering may be a route to humility and hence a route to finding nature praiseworthy, as well as a route to experiencing God's love. We do not therefore have to have a satisfactory account of why suffering exists and so remove an apparently crippling objection to theism before we can have a rational faith. Without such an explanation, a humble person finds nature good in spite of the serious adversities it brings; and a humble person can find God's love precisely by yielding to suffering as his will.

This does not render pointless the kind of investigation normally pursued in the philosophy of religion concerning suffering. But it does seriously modify any estimate of the reasonableness of affirming the existence of a God in view of the suffering caused by the natural world.

IV

If what has been said so far is sound, we could stop at this point with our case apparently made. But one of the people we have relied upon to supply us with data concerning what happens when one responds appropriately to suffering, supplies us with some additional data that cannot be accommodated within the specified framework. Simone Weil describes a type of suffering which she calls *malheur*, or 'affliction' as it is usually translated in English editions of her writings. It is a type of suffering that does crush or degrade us.

We can here give only an approximate sketch of her brilliant and complex analysis of the nature of affliction, drawing primarily upon only one of her essays.[10] Affliction is not primarily physical suffering: it can be caused by physical suffering, if that is very prolonged or frequent, and it has physical effects, such as when one has difficulty breathing at the news of the death of a beloved person. If there is a complete absence of physical pain, there is no

---

[9] See E. H. Madden and P. H. Hare, *Evil and the Concept of God* (Springfield, Ill.: Charles C. Thomas, 1968), especially pp. 3–4, 12–17. They argue this point of view very well. Cf. my article, 'Motives, Rationales, and Religious Beliefs', *American Philosophical Quarterly* (Apr. 1966), 111–27, which anticipates and replies to this position.

[10] Simone Weil, 'The Love of God and Affliction', in *On Science, Necessity, and the Love of God* (London: Oxford University Press, 1968). The first half of this essay can also be found in *Waiting on God*. For a presentation and discussion of the relevant texts see Claude Borocco, 'Le Malheur chez Simone Weil', *Cahiers Simone Weil* (Sept. 1978), 18–29.

affliction, because our thought automatically flees from affliction. For there to be affliction, there must be some event or events that uproot a life and affect it physically, socially, and psychologically. Physical distress keeps the mind fastened on one's affliction; but the source of affliction is primarily social. A person is uprooted from the fabric of social relations, so that he no longer counts for anything. There is social degradation, or at least fear of it.

Even more horrible, psychologically the afflicted person inwardly feels the contempt and disgust which others express toward one who is socially of no account. An afflicted person feels self-contempt and disgust, and even guilt and defilement in proportion to his innocence!

When dealing with affliction, we are moving out of the range of suffering caused simply by the operations of the natural world. But we are forced to go beyond natural evil for four reasons: (1) Physical suffering is essential to affliction. (2) Affliction can be brought on by prolonged or frequent physical suffering. (3) Affliction breaks the framework we have so far used to deal with suffering caused by the natural world. (4) As we will see, Weil's account of how we may find the love of God in affliction enables us to relate physical suffering brought on by nature to the love of God in a new way. So far we have only claimed that we can experience God's love *through* suffering; now we will see how we may experience the love of God *in* suffering itself.

Weil does not argue for the goodness of the cosmos on the basis of such a simple teleology as that of Epictetus, with such analogies as the fit of a sword and a scabbard. She employs a more sophisticated understanding of nature as a system of relations that can often be expressed mathematically. Nonetheless, she shares with Epictetus the essential idea that the cosmos is a gloriously ordered whole, and that it is our function to perceive the goodness of its order and to praise God for it. As she puts it:

It is our function in this world to consent to the existence of the universe. God is not satisfied with finding his creation good; he wants it also to find itself good. That is the purpose of the souls which are attached to minute fragments of this world . . . ('The Love of God and Affliction', p. 193).

She also shares Epictetus' outlook concerning suffering brought on by things over which we have no control and which result from the order of the universe. As she puts it:

The world's beauty gives us an intimation of its claim to a place in our heart. In the beauty of the world harsh necessity becomes an object of love. What is more beautiful than the effect of gravity on sea-waves as they flow in ever-changing folds, or the almost eternal folds of the mountains?

The sea is not less beautiful in our eyes because we know that ships are sometimes wrecked. On the contrary this adds to its beauty. If it altered the movement of its waves to spare a ship it would be a creature gifted with discernment and choice, and not this fluid perfectly obedient to every external pressure. It is this obedience which makes the sea's beauty (p. 178).

So, like Epictetus, she can face lameness or even death and yet praise the cosmos whose order causes them.

But there is one phenomenon which Epictetus did not consider or apparently know about: affliction. Epictetus' final refuge against adversity is that no matter how severe an adversity we face, it need not degrade us or crush us. No matter what happens to us, we can give thanks for the order of the universe, our power to perceive its order, and our power to yield even our lives to it. Although it takes great courage and nobility to bear our own destruction, it is that very capacity which gives us dignity. So we have reason to render praise for the order of events which gives us the occasion to actualize or exercise our powers. A person can find reason to praise the goodness of the cosmos and all its events because there is this final refuge of dignity.

But in Weil we find that this final refuge is not impregnable; for the condition of affliction is one in which we *are* crushed or degraded. Affliction fills us with self-contempt, disgust, and a sense of guilt and defilement. If we are unprepared for affliction, we are overwhelmed by it; it crushes us. There is nothing of us intact whereby we could nobly yield to it. 'That is why those who plunge men into affliction before they are prepared to receive it are killers of souls' (p. 173). But even if we are prepared for it, there is no question of acquiring nobility by consenting to self-disgust and a sense of defilement! So there is no way to encounter affliction and to keep from either being crushed or degraded in our own eyes. Simone Weil therefore writes:

The great enigma of human life is not suffering but affliction. It is not surprising that the innocent are killed, tortured, driven from their country, made destitute or reduced to slavery, put into concentration camps or prison cells, since they are criminals who perform such actions. It is not surprising either that disease is the cause of long sufferings, which paralyse life and make it into an image of death, since nature is at the mercy of the blind play of mechanical necessities. But it *is* surprising that God should have given affliction the power to seize the very soul of the innocent and to possess them as sovereign master (pp. 171–2).

That such events should lead the innocent *victim* of them to feel self-contempt, disgust, and even guilt and a sense of defilment, instead of the *criminal*, is an arrangement that baffles her. What purpose is served by having persons not only battered, outraged, and uprooted, but having them regard *themselves* with loathing and a sense of defilement?

We now come to the heart of the matter. Weil claims that in affliction we have the most perfect contact with the love of God that is possible for a human being in this life. Contact with his love through the medium of the world is pleasant when nature's effect on us is pleasant. Contact with his love can be joyous even in the midst of suffering; for we can receive his gracious presence in the midst of our distress. Finally, it is possible after such a presence is known for a person to be in distress and to recognize the very distress to be itself a contact with the love of God. This is not simply to recognize a gracious presence *through* yielding to suffering; it is to find the distress itself as the touch of his love.

She illustrates her claim in this fashion. We should think of a friend who has been away for a long time and who, upon returning, grips us very hard. It hurts, but that grip is his love. It feels just as painful as when it is the grip of someone who wants to hurt us, but in this case it is an effect of one who loves us and wants contact with us. Sometimes through the universe of matter God grips us very hard. That grip, though painful, is an *indirect* contact with his love: his love is on the other side of nature, pressing on us through nature, just as much when it hurts us as when the same workings of nature bring us great joy, as for example in the beauty of the world.

The idea that in suffering itself we can be in contact with God's love is conceivable to Simone Weil because of Christ's affliction on the Cross. To understand her claim we need to give a summary of some of her fundamental theological views. These kinds of ideas rarely, if ever, find their way into philosophic discussions on the problem of evil. But if we are patient enough to allow them to be sketched, their relevance to philosophic discussions of suffering caused by the natural world's operations can be made clear.

First, the Son and the Father are one God through their love for one another before the foundation of the world. The Son, when he became incarnate, became separated by a distance from the Father. 'Distance' is a metaphor. Its concrete meaning is to designate what is subject to the forces of nature in contrast to what is not. The incarnate Son is subject to natural forces and so is in the world; the Father is not subject to them.[11] So the Father and the Son are separated by the 'distance' of the created world.

Second, many of the events produced by the working of nature and by human actions are pleasant to us; some of them are not. Severely adverse events can make us suffer greatly. 'Affliction' is understood by her as the

---

[11] Through the Father, Jesus can command nature as, for example, when he stilled the stormy sea and walked on water. But of himself, in the New Testament accounts he is subject to the forces of gravity, to the need to eat, and to death.

most serious suffering of all, involving physical pain, social humiliation, and psychological despair.

Third, Christ is described in the New Testament as one who was afflicted. He can be said to have been driven to the greatest possible distance from the Father, for Paul says, 'he became sin for us'. Holiness and sin are infinitely 'distant' from one another. So Weil takes it that Christ, in suffering the crucifixion, is the farthest removed from the Father's presence it is possible to be.

Fourth, the distance between the Father and the Son is also thought of as an exact measure of their love. The Son is afflicted by the Father for our sakes: he enters the world and is subject to it and he is crucified to establish contact between what is and what is not subject to nature and to destructive egocentricity (sin). This happened because of the Father's loving will. The Son's great victory is to yield to what happened to him as the will of his Father. Thus they are united over the great span of distance since there is love at both ends. Their distance from one another thus becomes a measure of the extent of their love; the extent of their love is expressed by the very medium of their separation. Christ's pain is pain; his affliction is horrible. Yet it is responded to as the will of the Father and as itself contact with his Father in and through the medium of created forces.

Earlier we saw that contact between the love of God and a human being is possible through the medium of the created world. We saw that by an act of yielding to nature's power *as subject to the rule of God*, a person, it is claimed, experiences a gracious presence. Now we are considering how *in* the suffering itself one can find God's love. This can be done by seeing that 'distance', when conceived of as the ordered cosmos between us and God, is also a form of nearness. It is thus a medium of contact between us and God. The pressure of the world on us is an indirect contact with God, its ruler. When it is not pleasant, it is nonetheless an indirect contact with the Father. However horrible the pressure may be, one can have faith that it is still contact with a loving Father because his Son went the greatest distance possible and was not by that very distance separated from his Father's love.

Thus God's love can reach people at any *intermediate* distance—whether that distance be experienced positively or negatively; both are indirect contact with him. One can easily be thought of as the touch of a benevolent Father, because it is positive; the other is not easy to so conceive or to receive by oneself. But for the person who has performed the previous two acts that we have described, the affliction of Christ gives that person reason to accept unavoidable adversities caused by the working of nature and other creatures as an indirect contact with God. It is to be roughly handled—as was his Son—but still it is to be handled, even if indirectly through the medium of this world, by God.

Therefore through Christ it is possible to understand how the Father's love is present in all things, even in suffering. Suffering can be regarded as a mark of our distance from God because we are subject to the cosmos simply by being creatures. Yet, depending on a person's response to suffering, a person can be in contact with God *through* suffering and *in* suffering. To be in touch with the reality God has made, even when it is a painful touch, is to have indirect contact with him who is above it and who is above all else, love. Insofar as it is contact, it is good; insofar as it is painful, it is not. But what a difference when the *same* pain results from the grip of a friend, and not the mindless grip of nature.

For those who regard nature as subject to God's providence and rule, their own unavoidable suffering that arises from nature's workings can thus be a way to participate in the suffering of Christ. The created forces to which he is subject and which lead to his crucifixion are forces to which all persons are liable. Sometimes they cause us to suffer. We are not to seek to suffer, any more than the Son sought to be crucified. Indeed, as we know, he prayed to be spared affliction and taught his disciples to pray not to enter temptation. Nonetheless, it came to him, and we too suffer in various lesser degrees. By our response to our suffering, we can become participants in his crucifixion.

This is again not a theoretic matter. It can be formulated by the intellect and such formulation may assist a person in responding to his suffering so as to find God's love even in his worst suffering; but to know the love of God *in* suffering requires action. We are to yield to our suffering as his will, but this time without the recompense of the joyous experience of his presence. To love God *in* our suffering—to receive it as an indirect contact with a loving Father—is to feel in some degree as Christ felt when afflicted on the Cross: forsaken. The contact in this instance is thus not to experience a feeling of joy.

In addition, although good purposes may be served by such suffering, as was the case with Christ's suffering, this is not always knowable or conceivable when we suffer. But it is claimed that contact with the Father's love is taking place in the negative experience itself and that this contact is our good. For it provides us with the opportunity to trust and obey God, that is, to love him for his sake alone by yielding to nature as his servant. This is the final perfection of the soul: to be so grounded in the love of God as to be able to respond with faithful obedience when all joy is absent and no favourable consequences are foreseen as flowing from the suffering. The love of God is veiled by the unpleasant pressure of nature on a person, but to love God is to trust that this is the same love, now veiled, as is present to us when nature is pleasantly experienced or when nature hurts us but we feel the joy of God's presence in the midst of our suffering.

To have reached this very high level of devotion is to have transcended Epictetus' framework for his claim that whatever happens, we can endure it without being crushed or degraded. Here degradation is experienced, and the devotion does not remove its bitterness nor make the pain pleasant. But it does mean that no adversity that comes through nature's working or through social events can separate a person from God's love; for that very suffering is the effect of contact with his love through the created world.

V

Let us now relate this and earlier material to philosophic discussions of the problem of evil. Consider, for example, Anthony Flew's celebrated essay, 'Theology and Falsification',[12] which is so well known that we need not repeat his parable about two explorers who come across a jungle clearing. Whether there is a God is to be determined by the order of nature on the analogy of deciding whether the relative orderliness of a clearing in a jungle warrants belief in an otherwise undetectable gardener. Suffering is treated as analogous to disorder: disorder counts against the existence of a gardener (a designer); suffering counts against the existence of a benevolent God. Suffering causes religious people to qualify what they mean by God's love so as to render our suffering compatible with it. Flew claims that the meaning given to God's love is progressively more and more severely qualified until we may ask whether the term now has been rendered vacuous or meaningless.

Someone tells us that God loves us as a father loves his children. We are reassured. But then we see a child dying of inoperable cancer of the throat. His earthly father is driven frantic in his efforts to help, but his Heavenly Father reveals no obvious sign of concern. Some qualification is made—'God's love is not a merely human love' or it is 'an inscrutable love', perhaps . . . we are reassured again. But then perhaps we ask: What is this assurance of God's (appropriately qualified) love worth, what is this apparent guarantee really a guarantee against?[13]

But we have introduced some data that makes the question, 'What is this apparent guarantee really a guarantee against?' utterly out of place. There is no expectation of a guarantee against *any* of the adverse effects of the

[12] Reprinted in many places, including *Philosophy of Religion*, ed. Basil Mitchell (London: Oxford University Press, 1971), 13–15.
[13] Ibid. 15.

operations of nature for a person such as Epictetus. The only expectation he has is that no matter what happens, we need not be crushed or degraded by it. Suffering is thus not evidence that counts against the goodness of nature, and hence against the goodness of nature's source (should it have one). Suffering is not a kind of 'disorder'. It is part of the orderliness of a cosmos in which each part is used by some other part, and people are subject to its workings as is every other part of the cosmos.

Christians, such as Schlink, Barfoot, and Weil, who have accepted their utter vulnerability to nature's workings, can go further than Epictetus. They have experienced a felicity through their acceptance of their suffering as God's will. In their two acts of submission the meaning of 'love' has not been qualified. That is, they did not begin with 'love' in the sense of protection against adversity, and then keep qualifying the nature of the protection in the face of various adversities until it looks as though there is no protection at all and hence no love. But *divine* love is exhibited by the order of nature—an order that includes animal and human suffering—and the natural world is perceived as praiseworthy. They find nature good. Divine love also refers to the felicity they have experienced in their submission to the workings of nature as God's creation. So they do not begin with the meaning Flew has given to love and then qualify *that* meaning—whittling it down until it is plausible to say that nothing is left. They operate with a different view of love.

What lies at the root of the difference is the issue of human vulnerability to nature's workings. If we are not supposed to be vulnerable to any of it, or only to some of it, then nature's untowardness is perceived as a reason to argue that nature is unconcerned with our welfare and thus gives us a reason to say nature does not have a benevolent source—as we saw with Hume; or as with Flew, a reason to qualify what we mean by God's benevolence because of the adverse effects of the operation of nature upon us. But if we are utterly vulnerable to its workings, and if a person is able to perform the act of accepting this, then he is able, as was Epictetus, to perceive its goodness in spite of the adversity it brings to us and all its other inhabitants. Such a person has also become a person who can perform a further act of submission—an act that enables him to experience the felicity of God's love in the midst of his suffering. Flew has ignored the step Epictetus took—humility before nature—much less considered the second more advanced step we have described.

A more recent work on the problem of evil that does consider the development of a person is John Hick's *Evil and the God of Love*.[14] He

[14] John Hick, *Evil and the God of Love* (New York: Harper & Row, 1966).

emphasizes the role of 'soul-making' in his theodicy. But humility of the kind we have described is not a feature of soul-making as he presents it, and he neglects the role nature can play in the development of humility. Thus it is not accidental that he dismisses what he calls 'the aesthetic theme' in theodicies which point to the present goodness and harmony of the cosmic order. He fails to see nature in that fashion because he has neglected the kind of development that enables a person to make such an evaluation of nature. Thus not only does animal suffering present an insoluble problem for him, but he is left with the need to make a calculation to determine whether soul-making is worth the cost of all the human and animal suffering it involves.

But for one who has accepted our vulnerability to nature's workings and also accepted nature as obedient to God's will, the felicity of God's presence transcends any calculation of the pluses and minuses that are involved in 'soul-making'. It is contact with God's love, and contact through present suffering, that is at the forefront of the experience of those people we have described. That good is incommensurate with the trials and tribulations of life or what benefit they may lead to in this life. Such a present good does not exclude contact with God in a resurrected life, but such a future good is not needed or used to make up for present adversities and thus allow one to maintain God's goodness in spite of present adversities.

Finally, affliction as contact with God's love is relevant to the discussions of natural evil as instrumental to the development of virtue. J. L. Mackie examines this type of argument in his article, 'Evil and Omnipotence'.[15] He argues that on this view pain and disease make possible the existence of sympathy, benevolence, and heroism. Pain and disease are called 'first order evils', and pleasure and happiness are called 'first order goods'. Sympathy and the like are 'second order goods', and they are more important than first order good or evil.

With these distinctions he goes on to argue that just as pain and disease make second order virtues possible, so too do they make second order evils possible—malevolence, cruelty, callousness and cowardice. To justify their existence—on the basis of this line of argument alone—we would have to specify a third order of good. But this opens the way to third order evils; for at every step a lower level evil is the occasion for *both* a higher level good and a higher level evil. He therefore says we must shift from this line of argument by turning to the free will defence.

But Mackie can be challenged before he makes a shift to the free will defence. The instrumental role of evil occupies a major place in Epictetus.

[15] Reprinted in *Philosophy of Religion*, ed. Basil Mitchell, pp. 97–100 [Chapter I in this collection].

The adverse workings of nature bring out various virtues, leading to the highest courage and magnanimity in the face of death. No matter what the adversity, we can face it without being crushed or degraded. It is this ability which gives us our dignity.

It is true that some virtues are connected to adversity, but instead of seeking to maintain the goodness of the cosmos, and hence of its source (should it have one) by moving up a scale from lesser evils to higher goods, and from higher evils to still higher goods (which seems to be involved in Epictetus), we can start at the other end, with the highest good, as does Weil. She does not justify lesser evils with higher goods which in turn raise the question of their counterpart evil. In her justification she takes the most severe suffering and the greatest evil—affliction, and indeed Christ's affliction—and relates this to the love of God. Then all other forms of suffering, from human affliction on down, are described as ways we can participate in Christ's affliction and thereby love God with as near a perfect love as human beings in this life are capable of. Thus we can in any adversity have contact with the love of God, although we must prepare ourselves for this opportunity if we are to make use of it.

This line of approach to the subject of suffering requires the use of specific Christian doctrines—Creation, Trinity, and Cross—which are often ignored in philosophic discussions of evil. Yet it is what is unique and central to Christianity which allows us to conceive of all suffering as the presence of God to us through the world (both natural and social), and enables us to find his love in and through the events of this life.

These applications of what we may learn from suffering to some widely influential philosophic discussions of the philosophic problem of evil allow us to make the following generalization. For a person to reflect on the problem of evil without having performed even the first action we have described, means that he is trying to deal with the logic of certain concepts (such as unlimited power, goodness, and evil) without some of the relevant data.

It also means that it is incorrect to think that a fully satisfactory theodicy must be available for one reasonably to believe in a Christian God. From the point of view of those who have acted at the various levels we have described, all questions concerning how evil arose in a universe created by an all-powerful, good and wise God; whether the amount of evil could or could not have been less; whether the cost of evil is worth the actual or potential good it makes possible; and the like, do not necessarily have to be resolved in order for one reasonably to believe in the goodness of the world and the love of God. For one who has acted as Epictetus, the goodness of the world is evident. For those who have taken the next step, as have

Schlink, Barfoot, and Weil, the love of God is present in the midst of suffering. For the rare person, such as Weil, who has apparently been scarred by affliction, no reward in this life or the next is needed to compensate for what is untoward so that one may praise God; for in suffering such a person has the opportunity to love God with a near perfect love. People who are not afflicted but who know about affliction and the Cross, may bear their lesser adversities as a way of knowing the love of God *in* their sufferings. Thus from the viewpoint of those who have learned from suffering, answers to all the philosophic questions raised by the problem of evil are not necessary in order for belief in the goodness of God to be reasonable.

XII

HORRENDOUS EVILS AND THE GOODNESS OF GOD

MARILYN McCORD ADAMS

1. INTRODUCTION

Over the past thirty years, analytic philosophers of religion have defined 'the problem of evil' in terms of the prima-facie difficulty in consistently maintaining

(1) God exists, and is omnipotent, omniscient, and perfectly good

and

(2) Evil exists.

In a crisp and classic article, 'Evil and Omnipotence',[1] J. L. Mackie emphasized that the problem is not that (1) and (2) are logically inconsistent by themselves, but that they together with quasi-logical rules formulating attribute-analyses—such as

(P1) A perfectly good being would always eliminate evil so far as it could,

and

(P2) There are *no limits* to what an omnipotent being can do—constitute an inconsistent premiss-set. He added, of course, that the inconsistency might be removed by substituting alternative and perhaps more subtle analyses, but cautioned that such replacements of (P1) and (P2) would save 'ordinary theism' from his charge of positive irrationality, only if true to its 'essential requirements'.[2]

Marilyn McCord Adams, 'Horrendous Evils and The Goodness of God', first published in *Proceedings of the Aristotelian Society*, Supplementary Vol. 63 (1989), pp. 297–310, slightly revised by the author for publication in this volume, with the addition of notes that respond to the comments of Professor Stewart Sutherland, commentator at the 1989 Joint Session of the Mind Association and Aristotelian Society at which the paper was presented. © The Aristotelian Society 1989. Reprinted by courtesy of the Editor.

[1] J. L. Mackie, 'Evil and Omnipotence', *Mind*, 64 (1955) [Chapter I in this collection]; repr. in Nelson Pike (ed.), *God and Evil* (Englewood Cliffs, NJ: Prentice-Hall, 1964), 46–60.

[2] Ibid. 47 [pp. 26–7, 37 above].

In an earlier paper, 'Problems of Evil: More Advice to Christian Philosophers',[3] I underscored Mackie's point and took it a step further. In debates about whether the argument from evil can establish the irrationality of religious belief, care must be taken, both by the atheologians who deploy it and by the believers who defend against it, to ensure that the operative attribute-analyses accurately reflect that religion's understanding of divine power and goodness. It does the atheologian no good to argue for the falsity of Christianity on the ground that the existence of an omnipotent, omniscient, pleasure-maximizer is incompossible with a world such as ours, because Christians never believed God was a pleasure-maximizer anyway. But equally, the truth of Christianity would be inadequately defended by the observation that an omnipotent, omniscient egoist could have created a world with suffering creatures, because Christians insist that God loves other (created) persons than Himself. The extension of 'evil' in (2) is likewise important. Since Mackie and his successors are out to show that 'the several parts of the *essential* theological doctrine are inconsistent with *one another*',[4] they can accomplish their aim only if they circumscribe the extension of 'evil' as their religious opponents do. By the same token, it is not enough for Christian philosophers to explain how the power, knowledge, and goodness of God could coexist with some evils or other; a full account must exhibit the compossibility of divine perfection with evils in the amounts and of the kinds found in the actual world (and evaluated as such by Christian standards).

The moral of my earlier story might be summarized thus: where the internal coherence of a system of religious beliefs is at stake, successful arguments for its inconsistency must draw on premises (explicitly or implicitly) internal to that system or obviously acceptable to its adherents; likewise for successful rebuttals or explanations of consistency. The thrust of my argument is to push both sides of the debate towards more detailed attention to and subtle understanding of the religious system in question.

As a Christian philosopher, I want to focus in this paper on the problem for the truth of Christianity raised by what I shall call 'horrendous' evils. Although our world is riddled with them, the biblical record punctuated by them, and one of them—namely, the passion of Christ; according to Christian belief, the judicial murder of God by the people of God—is memorialized by the Church on its most solemn holiday (Good Friday) and in its central sacrament (the Eucharist), the problem of horrendous evils is largely skirted by standard treatments for the good reason that they are

---

[3] Marilyn McCord Adams, 'Problems of Evil: More Advice to Christian Philosophers', *Faith and Philosophy* (Apr. 1988), 121–43.

[4] Mackie, 'Evil and Omnipotence', pp. 46–7 [p. 25 above]. (emphasis mine).

intractable by them. After showing why, I will draw on other Christian materials to sketch ways of meeting this, the deepest of religious problems.

2. DEFINING THE CATEGORY

For present purposes, I define 'horrendous evils' as 'evils the participation in (the doing or suffering of) which gives one reason prima facie to doubt whether one's life could (given their inclusion in it) be a great good to one on the whole'.[5] Such reasonable doubt arises because it is so difficult humanly to conceive how such evils could be overcome. Borrowing Chisholm's contrast between *balancing off* (which occurs when the opposing values of *mutually exclusive* parts of a whole partially or totally cancel each other out) and *defeat* (which cannot occur by the mere addition to the whole of a new part of opposing value, but involves some 'organic unity' among the values of parts and wholes, as when the positive aesthetic value of a whole painting defeats the ugliness of a small colour patch),[6] horrendous evils seem prima facie, not only to balance off but to engulf the positive value of a participant's life. Nevertheless, that very horrendous proportion, by which they threaten to rob a person's life of positive meaning, cries out not only to be engulfed, but to be made meaningful through positive and decisive defeat.

I understand this criterion to be objective, but relative to individuals. The example of habitual complainers, who know how to make the worst of a good situation, shows individuals not to be incorrigible experts on what ills would defeat the positive value of their lives. Nevertheless, nature and experience endow people with different strengths; one bears easily what crushes another. And a major consideration in determining whether an individual's life is/has been a great good to him/her on the whole, is invariably and appropriately how it has seemed to him/her.[7]

I offer the following list of paradigmatic horrors: the rape of a woman and axing off of her arms, psychophysical torture whose ultimate goal is the disintegration of personality, betrayal of one's deepest loyalties,

---

[5] Stewart Sutherland (in his comment 'Horrendous Evils and the Goodness of God—II', *Proceedings of the Aristotelian Society*, suppl. vol. 63 (1989), 311–23; esp. 311) takes my criterion to be somehow 'first-person'. This was not my intention. My definition may be made more explicit as follows: an evil *e* is horrendous if and only if participation in *e* by person *p* gives everyone prima-facie reason to doubt whether *p*'s life can, given *p*'s participation in *e*, be a great good to *p* on the whole.

[6] Roderick Chisholm, 'The Defeat of Good and Evil' [Chapter III in this collection].

[7] Cf. Malcolm's astonishment at Wittgenstein's dying exclamation that he had had a wonderful life, *Ludwig Wittgenstein: A Memoir* (London: Oxford University Press, 1962), 100.

MARILYN McCORD ADAMS

cannibalizing one's own offspring, child abuse of the sort described by Ivan Karamazov, child pornography, parental incest, slow death by starvation, participation in the Nazi death camps, the explosion of nuclear bombs over populated areas, having to choose which of one's children shall live and which be executed by terrorists, being the accidental and/or unwitting agent of the disfigurement or death of those one loves best. I regard these as *paradigmatic*, because I believe most people would find in the doing or suffering of them prima-facie reason to doubt the positive meaning of their lives.[8] Christian belief counts the crucifixion of Christ another: on the one hand, death by crucifixion seemed to defeat Jesus' Messianic vocation; for according to Jewish law, death by hanging from a tree made its victim ritually accursed, definitively excluded from the compass of God's people, *a fortiori* disqualified from being the Messiah. On the other hand, it represented the defeat of its perpetrators' leadership vocations, as those who were to prepare the people of God for the Messiah's coming, killed and ritually accursed the true Messiah, according to later theological understanding, God Himself.

3. THE IMPOTENCE OF STANDARD SOLUTIONS

For better and worse, the by now standard strategies for 'solving' the problem of evil are powerless in the face of horrendous evils.

3.1. Seeking the Reason-Why

In his model article 'Hume on Evil',[9] Pike takes up Mackie's challenge, arguing that (P1) fails to reflect ordinary moral intuitions (more to the point, I would add, Christian beliefs), and traces the abiding sense of trouble to the hunch that an omnipotent, omniscient being could have no reason compatible with perfect goodness for permitting (bringing about) evils, because all legitimate excuses arise from ignorance or weakness. Solutions to the problem of evil have thus been sought in the form of counter-examples to this latter claim, i.e. logically possible reasons-why that would excuse even an omnipotent, omniscient God! The putative logically possible reasons offered have tended to be *generic* and *global*:

[8] Once again, more explicitly, most people would agree that a person *p*'s doing or suffering of them constitutes prima-facie reason to doubt whether *p*'s life can be, given such participation, a great good to *p* on the whole.

[9] 'Hume on Evil', *Philosophical Review*, 72 (1963), 180–97 [Chapter II in this collection]; reprinted in Pike (ed.), *God and Evil*, p. 88 [pp. 40–1 above].

generic in so far as some *general* reason is sought to cover all sorts of evils; global in so far as they seize upon some feature of the world as a whole. For example, philosophers have alleged that the desire to make a world with one of the following properties—'the best of all possible worlds',[10] 'a world a more perfect than which is impossible', 'a world exhibiting a perfect balance of retributive justice',[11] 'a world with as favorable a balance of (created) moral good over moral evil as God can weakly actualize'[12]— would constitute a reason compatible with perfect goodness for God's creating a world with evils in the amounts and of the kinds found in the actual world. Moreover, such general reasons are presented as so powerful as to do away with any need to catalogue types of evils one by one, and examine God's reason for permitting each in particular. Plantinga explicitly hopes that the problem of horrendous evils can thus be solved without being squarely confronted.[13]

3.2. The Insufficiency of Global Defeat

A pair of distinctions is in order here: (i) between·two dimensions of divine goodness in relation to creation—namely, 'producer of global goods' and 'goodness to' or 'love of individual created persons'; and (ii) between the overbalance/defeat of evil by good on the global scale, and the overbalance/ defeat of evil by good within the context of an individual person's life.[14] Correspondingly, we may separate two problems of evil parallel to the two sorts of goodness mentioned in (i).

In effect, generic and global approaches are directed to the first problem: they defend divine goodness along the first (global) dimension by suggesting logically possible strategies for the global defeat of evils. But establishing God's excellence as a producer of global goods does not automatically

[10] Following Leibniz, Pike draws on this feature as part of what I have called his Epistemic Defence ('Problems of Evil: More Advice to Christian Philosophers', pp. 124–5).

[11] Augustine, *On Free Choice of Will*, iii. 93–102, implies that there is a maximum value for created worlds, and a plurality of worlds that meet it. All of these contain rational free creatures; evils are foreseen but unintended side-effects of their creation. No matter what they choose, however, God can order their choices into a maximally perfect universe by establishing an order of retributive justice.

[12] Plantinga takes this line in numerous discussions, in the course of answering Mackie's objection to the Free Will Defence, that God should have made sinless free creatures. Plantinga insists that, given incompatibilist freedom in creatures, God cannot strongly actualize any world He wants. It is logically possible that a world with evils in the amounts and of the kinds found in this world is the best that He could do, Plantinga argues, given His aim of getting some moral goodness in the world.

[13] Alvin Plantinga, 'Self-Profile', in James E. Tomberlin and Peter van Inwagen (eds.), *Profiles: Alvin Plantinga* (Dordrecht, Boston, Mass., and Lancaster, Pa.: Reidel, 1985), 38.

[14] I owe the second of these distinctions to a remark by Keith De Rose in our Fall 1987 seminar on the problem of evil at UCLA.

solve the second problem, especially in a world containing horrendous evils. For God cannot be said to be good or loving to any created persons the positive meaning of whose lives He allows to be engulfed in and/or defeated by evils—that is, individuals within whose lives horrendous evils remain undefeated. Yet, the only way unsupplemented global and generic approaches could have to explain the latter, would be by applying their general reasons-why to particular cases of horrendous suffering.

Unfortunately, such an exercise fails to give satisfaction. Suppose for the sake of argument that horrendous evil could be included in maximally perfect world orders; its being partially constitutive of such an order would assign it that generic and global positive meaning. But would knowledge of such a fact defeat for a mother the prima-facie reason provided by her cannibalism of her own infant to wish that she had never been born? Again, the aim of perfect retributive balance confers meaning on evils imposed. But would knowledge that the torturer was being tortured give the victim who broke down and turned traitor under pressure any more reason to think his/her life worth while? Would it not merely multiply reasons for the torturer to doubt that his/her life could turn out to be a good to him/her on the whole? Could the truck-driver who accidentally runs over his beloved child find consolation in the idea that this middle-known[15] but unintended side-effect was part of the price God accepted for a world with the best balance of moral good over moral evil he could get?

Not only does the application to horrors of such generic and global reasons for divine permission of evils fail to solve the second problem of evil; it makes it worse by adding *generic prima-facie* reasons to doubt whether human life would be a great good to individual human beings in possible worlds where such divine motives were operative. For, taken in isolation and made to bear the weight of the whole explanation, such reasons-why draw a picture of divine indifference or even hostility to the human plight. Would the fact that God permitted horrors because they were constitutive means to His end of global perfection, or that He tolerated them because He could obtain that global end anyway, make the participant's life more tolerable, more worth living for him/her? Given radical human vulnerability to horrendous evils, the ease with which

---

[15] Middle knowledge, or knowledge of what is 'in between' the actual and the possible, is the sort of knowledge of what a free creature *would do* in every situation in which that creature could possibly find himself. Following Luis de Molina and Francisco Suarez, Alvin Plantinga ascribes such knowledge to God, prior in the order of explanation to God's decision about which free creatures to actualize (in *The Nature of Necessity* (Oxford: Clarendon Press, 1974), pp. 164–93 [Chapter V in this collection]). Robert Merrihew Adams challenges this idea in his article 'Middle Knowledge and the Problem of Evil', *American Philosophical Quarterly*, 14 (1977) [Chapter VI in this collection]; repr. in *The Virtue of Faith* (New York: Oxford University Press, 1987), 77–93.

humans participate in them, whether as victim or perpetrator, would not the thought that God visits horrors on anyone who caused them, simply because he/she deserves it, provide one more reason to expect human life to be a nightmare?

Those willing to split the two problems of evil apart might adopt a divide-and-conquer strategy, by simply denying divine goodness along the second dimension. For example, many Christians do not believe that God will ensure an overwhelmingly good life to each and every person He creates. Some say the decisive defeat of evil with good is promised only within the lives of the obedient, who enter by the narrow gate. Some speculate that the elect may be few. Many recognize that the sufferings of this present life are as nothing compared to the hell of eternal torment, designed to defeat goodness with horrors within the lives of the damned.

Such a road can be consistently travelled only at the heavy toll of admitting that human life in worlds such as ours is a bad bet. Imagine (adapting Rawls's device) persons in a pre-original position, considering possible worlds containing managers of differing power, wisdom, and character, and subjects of varying fates. The question they are to answer about each world is whether they would willingly enter it as a human being, from behind a veil of ignorance as to which position they would occupy. Reason would, I submit, dictate a negative verdict for worlds whose omniscient and omnipotent manager permits ante-mortem horrors that remain undefeated within the context of the human participant's life; *a fortiori*, for worlds in which some or most humans suffer eternal torment.

3.3. Inaccessible Reasons

So far, I have argued that generic and global solutions are at best incomplete: however well their account of divine motivating reasons deals with the first problem of evil, the attempt to extend it to the second fails by making it worse. This verdict might seem prima facie tolerable to standard generic and global approaches and indicative of only a minor modification in their strategy: let the above-mentioned generic and global reasons cover divine permission of non-horrendous evils, and find other *reasons* compatible with perfect goodness *why* even an omnipotent, omniscient God would permit horrors.

In my judgement, such an approach is hopeless. As Plantinga[16] points out, where horrendous evils are concerned, not only do we not know God's *actual* reason for permitting them; we cannot even *conceive* of any plausible

---

[16] Alvin Plantinga, 'Self-Profile', pp. 34–5.

candidate sort of reason consistent with worthwhile lives for human participants in them.

4. THE HOW OF GOD'S VICTORY

Up to now, my discussion has given the reader cause to wonder whose side I am on anyway. For I have insisted, with rebels like Ivan Karamazov and John Stuart Mill, on spotlighting the problem horrendous evils pose. Yet, I have signalled my preference for a version of Christianity that insists on both dimensions of divine goodness, and maintains not only (*a*) that God will be good enough to created persons to make human life a good bet, but also (*b*) that each created person will have a life that is a great good to him/her on the whole. My critique of standard approaches to the problem of evil thus seems to reinforce atheologian Mackie's verdict of 'positive irrationality' for such a religious position.

4.1. *Whys Versus Hows*

The inaccessibility of reasons-why seems especially decisive. For surely an all-wise and all-powerful God, who loved each created person enough (*a*) to defeat any experienced horrors within the context of the participant's life, and (*b*) to give each created person a life that is a great good to him/her on the whole, would not permit such persons to suffer horrors for no reason.[17] Does not our inability even to conceive of plausible candidate reasons suffice to make belief in such a God positively irrational in a world containing horrors? In my judgement, it does not.

To be sure, motivating reasons come in several varieties relative to our conceptual grasp: There are (i) reasons of the sort we can readily understand when we are informed of them (e.g. the mother who permits her child to undergo painful heart surgery because it is the only humanly possible way to save its life). Moreover, there are (ii) reasons we would be cognitively, emotionally, and spiritually equipped to grasp if only we had a larger memory or wider attention span (analogy: I may be able to memorize small town street plans; memorizing the road networks of the entire country is a task requiring more of the same, in the way that proving Gödel's theorem is not). Some generic and global approaches insinuate that divine permission of evils has motivating reasons of this sort. Finally, there are (iii) reasons

---

[17] This point was made by William Fitzpatrick in our Fall 1987 seminar on the problem of evil at UCLA.

that we are cognitively, emotionally, and/or spiritually too immature to fathom (the way a two-year-old child is incapable of understanding its mother's reasons for permitting the surgery). I agree with Plantinga that our ignorance of divine reasons for permitting horrendous evils is not of types (i) or (ii), but of type (iii).

Nevertheless, if there are varities of ignorance, there are also varieties of reassurance.[18] The two-year-old heart patient is convinced of its mother's love, not by her cognitively inaccessible reasons, but by her intimate care and presence through its painful experience. The story of Job suggests something similar is true with human participation in horrendous suffering: God does not give Job His reasons-why, and implies that Job isn't smart enough to grasp them; rather Job is lectured on the extent of divine power, and sees God's goodness face to face! Likewise, I suggest, to exhibit the logical compossibility of both dimensions of divine goodness with horrendous suffering, it is not necessary to find logically possible reasons *why* God might permit them. It is enough to show *how* God can be good enough to created persons despite their participation in horrors—by defeating them within the context of the individual's life and by giving that individual a life that is a great good to him/her on the whole.

4.2. What Sort of Valuables?

In my opinion, the reasonableness of Christianity can be maintained in the face of horrendous evils only by drawing on resources of religious value theory. For one way for God to be *good to* created persons is by relating them appropriately to relevant and great goods. But philosophical and religious theories differ importantly on what valuables they admit into their ontology. Some maintain that 'what you see is what you get', but nevertheless admit a wide range of valuables, from sensory pleasures, the beauty of nature and cultural artefacts, the joys of creativity, to loving personal intimacy. Others posit a transcendent good (e.g. the Form of the Good in Platonism, or God, the Supremely Valuable Object, in Christianity). In the spirit of Ivan Karamazov, I am convinced that the depth of horrific evil cannot be accurately estimated without recognizing it to be incommensurate with any package of merely non-transcendent goods and so unable to be balanced off, much less defeated, thereby.

[18] Contrary to what Sutherland suggests ('Horrendous Evils', pp. 314–15), so far as the compossibility problem is concerned, I intend no illicit shift from reason to emotion. My point is that intimacy with a loving other is a good, participation in which can defeat evils, and so provide everyone with reason to think a person's life can be a great good to him/her on the whole, despite his/her participation in evils.

Where the *internal* coherence of Christianity is the issue, however, it is fair to appeal to its own store of valuables. From a Christian point of view, God is a being a greater than which cannot be conceived, a good incommensurate with both created goods and temporal evils. Likewise, the good of beatific, face-to-face intimacy with God is simply incommensurate with any merely non-transcendent goods or ills a person might experience. Thus, the good of beatific face-to-face intimacy with God would *engulf* (in a sense analogous to Chisholmian balancing off) even the horrendous evils humans experience in this present life here below, and overcome any prima-facie reasons the individual had to doubt whether his/her life would or could be worth living.

4.3. Personal Meaning, Horrors Defeated

Engulfing personal horrors within the context of the participant's life would vouchsafe to that individual a life that was a great good to him/her on the whole. I am still inclined to think it would guarantee that immeasurable divine goodness to any person thus benefited. But there is good theological reason for Christians to believe that God would go further, beyond engulfment to defeat. For it is the nature of persons to look for meaning, both in their lives and in the world. Divine respect for and commitment to created personhood would drive God to make all those sufferings which threaten to destroy the positive meaning of a person's life meaningful through positive defeat.[19]

How could God do it? So far as I can see, only by integrating participation in horrendous evils into a person's relationship with God. Possible dimensions of integration are charted by Christian soteriology. I pause here to sketch three:[20] (i) First, because God in Christ participated in horrendous evil

[19] Note, once again, contrary to what Sutherland suggests ('Horrendous Evils', pp. 321–3) 'horrendous evil *e* is defeated' entails *none* of the following propositions: '*e* was not horrendous', '*e* was not unjust', '*e* was not so bad after all'. Nor does my suggestion that even horrendous evils can be defeated by a great enough (because incommensurate and uncreated) good, in any way impugn the reliability of our moral intuitions about injustice, cold-bloodedness, or horror. The judgement that participation in *e* constitutes prima-facie reason to believe that *p*'s life is ruined, stands and remains a daunting measure of *e*'s horror.

[20] In my paper 'Redemptive Suffering: A Christian Solution to the Problem of Evil', in Robert Audi and William J. Wainwright (eds.), *Rationality, Religious Belief, and Moral Commitment: New Essays in Philosophy of Religion* (Cornell University Pres,, 1986), 248–67, I sketch how horrendous suffering can be meaningful by being made a vehicle of divine redemption for victim, perpetrator, and onlooker, and thus an occasion of the victim's collaboration with God. In 'Separation and Reversal in Luke–Acts', in Thomas Morris (ed.), *Philosophy and the Christian Faith* (Notre Dame, Ind.: Notre Dame University Press, 1988), 92–117, I attempted to chart the redemptive plot-line whereby horrendous sufferings are made meaningful by being woven into the divine redemptive plot. My considered opinion is that such collaboration would be too strenuous for the human condition were it not to be supplemented by a more explicit and beatific divine intimacy.

through His passion and death, human experience of horrors can be a means of *identifying* with Christ, either through *sympathetic* identification (in which each person suffers his/her own pains, but their similarity enables each to know what it is like for the other) or through *mystical* identification (in which the created person is supposed literally to experience a share of Christ's pain[21]). (ii) Julian of Norwich's description of heavenly welcome suggests the possible defeat of horrendous evil through divine gratitude. According to Julian, before the elect have a chance to thank God for all He has done for them, God will say, 'Thank you for all your suffering, the suffering of your youth.' She says that the creature's experience of divine gratitude will bring such full and unending joy as could not be merited by the whole sea of human pain and suffering throughout the ages.[22] (iii) A third idea identifies temporal suffering itself with a vision into the inner life of God, and can be developed several ways. Perhaps, contrary to medieval theology, God is not impassible, but rather has matched capacities for joy and for suffering. Perhaps, as the Heidelberg catechism suggests, God responds to human sin and the sufferings of Christ with an agony beyond human conception.[23] Alternatively, the inner life of God may be, strictly speaking and in and of itself, beyond both joy and sorrow. But, just as (according to Rudolf Otto) humans experience divine presence now as *tremendum* (with deep dread and anxiety), now as *fascinans* (with ineffable attraction), so perhaps our deepest suffering as much as our highest joys may themselves be direct visions into the inner life of God, imperfect but somehow less obscure in proportion to their intensity. And if a face-to-face vision of God is a good for humans incommensurate with any non-transcendent goods or ills, so any vision of God (including horrendous suffering) would have a good aspect in so far as it is a vision of God (even if it has an evil aspect in so far as it is horrendous suffering). For the most part, horrors are not recognized as experiences of God (any more than the city slicker recognizes his visual image of a brown patch as a vision of Beulah the cow in the distance). But, Christian mysticism might claim, at least from the post-mortem perspective of the beatific vision, such sufferings will be seen for what they were, and retrospectively no one will wish away any intimate encounters with God from his/her life-history in this world. The created person's experience of the beatific vision together with his/her knowledge

---

[21] For example, Julian of Norwich tells us that she prayed for and received the latter (*Revelations of Divine Love*, ch. 17). Mother Theresa of Calcutta seems to construe Matthew 25: 31–46 to mean that the poorest and the least *are* Christ, and that their sufferings *are* Christ's (Malcolm Muggeridge, *Something Beautiful for God* (New York: Harper & Row, 1960), 72–5).

[22] *Revelations of Divine Love*, ch. 14. I am grateful to Houston Smit for recognizing this scenario of Julian's as a case of Chisholmian defeat.

[23] Cf. Plantinga, 'Self-Profile', p. 36.

that intimate divine presence stretched back over his/her ante-mortem life and reached down into the depths of his/her worst suffering, would provide retrospective comfort independent of comprehension of the reasons-why akin to the two-year-old's assurance of its mother's love. Taking this third approach, Christians would not need to commit themselves about what in any event we do not know: namely, whether we will (like the two-year-old) ever grow up enough to understand the reasons why God permits our participation in horrendous evils. For by contrast with the best of earthly mothers, such divine intimacy is an incommensurate good and would cancel out for the creature any need to know why.

5. CONCLUSION

The worst evils demand to be defeated by the best goods. Horrendous evils can be overcome only by the goodness of God. Relative to human nature, participation in horrendous evils and loving intimacy with God are alike disproportionate: for the former threatens to engulf the good in an individual human life with evil, while the latter guarantees the reverse engulfment of evil by good. Relative to one another, there is also disproportion, because the good that God *is*, and intimate relationship with Him, is incommensurate with created goods and evils alike. Because intimacy with God so outscales relations (good or bad) with any creatures, integration into the human person's relationship with God confers significant meaning and positive value even on horrendous suffering. This result coheres with basic Christian intuition: that the powers of darkness are stronger than humans, but they are no match for God!

Standard generic and global solutions have for the most part tried to operate within the territory common to believer and unbeliever, within the confines of religion-neutral value theory. Many discussions reflect the hope that substitute attribute-analyses, candidate reasons-why, and/or defeaters could issue out of values shared by believers and unbelievers alike. And some virtually make this a requirement on an adequate solution. Mackie knew better how to distinguish the many charges that may be levelled against religion. Just as philosophers may or may not find the existence of God plausible, so they may be variously attracted or repelled by Christian values of grace and redemptive sacrifice. But agreement on truth-value is not necessary to consensus on internal consistency. My contention has been that it is not only legitimate, but, given horrendous evils, necessary for Christians to dip into their richer store of valuables to exhibit the consistency of (1) and (2).[24] I would go one step further: assuming the pragmatic and/or moral (I would prefer to say, broadly speaking, religious) importance of believing that (one's own) human life is worth living, the ability of Christianity to exhibit how this could be so despite human vulnerability to horrendous evil, constitutes a pragmatic/moral/religious consideration in its favour, relative to value schemes that do not.

To me, the most troublesome weakness in what I have said lies in the area of conceptual under-development. The contention that God suffered in Christ or that one person can experience another's pain requires detailed analysis and articulation in metaphysics and philosophy of mind. I have shouldered some of this burden elsewhere,[25] but its full discharge is well beyond the scope of this paper.

[24] I develop this point at some length in 'Problems of Evil: More Advice to Christian Philosophers', pp. 127–35.

[25] For example in 'The Metaphysics of the Incarnation in Some Fourteenth Century Franciscans', in William A. Frank and Girard J. Etzkorn (eds.), *Essays Honoring Allan B. Wolter* (St. Bonaventure, NY: The Franciscan Institute, 1985), 21–57.

In the development of these ideas, I am indebted to the members of our Fall 1987 seminar on the problem of evil at UCLA—especially to Robert Merrihew Adams (its co-leader) and to Keith De Rose, William Fitzpatrick, and Houston Smit. I am also grateful to the Very Revd. Jon Hart Olson for many conversations in mystical theology.

NOTES ON THE CONTRIBUTORS

MARILYN MCCORD ADAMS is Professor of Philosophy at UCLA. Her publications divide between philosophy of religion and medieval philosophy, and include her two-volume book *William Ockham*.

ROBERT MERRIHEW ADAMS is Professor of Philosophy at UCLA. His articles range over philosophy of religion, metaphysics, ethics, and Leibniz. Some essays in the first of these fields have been collected in the volume *The Virtue of Faith*.

DIOGENES ALLEN is Stuart Professor of Philosophy at Princeton Theological Seminary. His books on philosophical theology include *The Reasonableness of Faith*; *Finding Our Father*; *Traces of God in a Frequently Hostile World*; and *Three Outsiders: Pascal, Kierkegaard, Simone Weil*.

RODERICK M. CHISHOLM is Emeritus Professor of Philosophy and Andrew W. Mellon Professor of Humanities at Brown University. A leader in the fields of epistemology and metaphysics, Chisholm is the author of many publications, including the following books: *Perceiving: a Philosophical Study*; *Theory of Knowledge*; *Person and Object: A Metaphysical Study*; and *Brentano and Intrinsic Value*.

JOHN HICK is Danforth Professor of Philosophy of Religion at the Claremont Graduate School, California. Earlier in his career, he taught at Cambridge University, Princeton Theological Seminary, and Cornell University, before becoming H. G. Wood Professor of Theology at the University of Birmingham. His many books include *Faith and Knowledge*; *Evil and the God of Love*; *Death and Eternal Life*; *Problems of Religious Pluralism*; and *An Interpretation of Religion*.

JOHN L. MACKIE was, at the time of his death in 1982, a Fellow of University College and a Reader in Philosophy at the University of Oxford, and a Fellow of the British Academy. Besides producing many influential articles, Mackie wrote numerous books during his last decade, including *The Cement of the Universe: a Study of Causation*; *Problems from Locke*; *Ethics: Inventing Right and Wrong*; *Hume's Moral Theory*; *The Miracle of Theism: Arguments for and against the Existence of God*; and *Logic and Knowledge*.

TERENCE M. PENELHUM is Professor Emeritus of Philosophy and Religious Studies at the University of Calgary. In addition to widely ranging articles in the philosophy of religion, Penelhum has authored *Survival and Disembodied Existence*; *Religion and Rationality*; *Problems of Religious Knowledge*; and *God and Scepticism*.

NELSON C. PIKE has been for many years Professor of Philosophy at University of California, Irvine; his earlier positions included UCLA and Cornell University. In addition to his widely anthologized articles on the problem of evil and the attributes of God, Pike has authored *God and Timelessness* and edited *God and Evil* and *David Hume (1711–1776): Dialogues concerning Natural Religion* (with commentary).

ALVIN PLANTINGA taught at Wayne State, then for many years at Calvin College, before becoming O'Brien Professor of Philosophy of Religion at the University of Notre Dame. His writings on philosophy of religion, metaphysics, and 'reformed' epistemology have been widely influential. He has authored *God and Other Minds*; *The Nature of Necessity*; and *God, Freedom, and Evil*.

WILLIAM L. ROWE is Professor of Philosophy at Purdue University. He has written many articles on philosophy of religion, metaphysics, and epistemology. His books include *Religious Symbols and God: a Philosophical Study of Tillich's Theology* and *The Cosmological Argument*.

STEPHEN J. WYKSTRA is Professor of Philosophy at Calvin College. His articles range over topics in the philosophy of science, epistemology, and philosophy of religion.

BIBLIOGRAPHY

This is a selection of books and articles on the problem of evil. Almost all of them have appeared since 1960 and represent contemporary 'analytical' philosophy of religion. The essays reprinted in this anthology are not listed here. A most useful guide to further reading is William J. Wainwright, *Philosophy of Religion: An Annotated Bibliography of Twentieth-Century Writings in English* (New York: Garland Publishing, 1978); pp. 272–367 are devoted to the problem of evil. Numbers in square brackets cross-refer to items in the present Bibliography.

1. General

1. ADAMS, MARILYN McCORD, 'Problems of Evil: More Advice to Christian Philosophers', *Faith and Philosophy*, 5 (1988), 121–43.
2. BOWKER, JOHN, *Problems of Suffering in the Religions of the World* (Cambridge: Cambridge University Press, 1970).
3. FARRER, AUSTIN MARSDEN, *Love Almighty and Ills Unlimited* (London: Collins, 1961).
4. HICK, JOHN HARWOOD, *Evil and the God of Love*, rev. edn. (New York: Harper & Row, 1978).
5. MADDEN, EDWARD H., and HARE, PETER H., *Evil and the Concept of God* (Springfield, Ill. Charles C. Thomas, 1968).
6. McCLOSKEY, HENRY JOHN, 'God and Evil', *Philosophical Quarterly*, 10 (1960), 97–114.
7. PETERSON, MICHAEL L., 'Recent Work on the Problem of Evil', *American Philosophical Quarterly*, 20 (1983), 321–40.
8. PIKE, NELSON CRAFT (ed.), *God and Evil: Readings on the Theological Problem of Evil* (Englewood Cliffs, NJ: Prentice-Hall, 1964).
9. REICHENBACH, BRUCE P., *Evil and a Good God* (New York: Fordham University Press, 1982).
10. SCHLESINGER, GEORGE, *Religion and Scientific Method* (Dordrecht: Reidel, 1977), chs. 1–10 (cf. Schlesinger [16] and Morris [14]).
11. SWINBURNE, RICHARD, *The Existence of God* (Oxford: Clarendon Press, 1979), chs. 10–12.

2. The Best of All Possible Worlds

12. ADAMS, ROBERT MERRIHEW, 'Must God Create the Best?' *Philosophical Review*, 81 (1972), 317–32 (cf. Grover [13] and Quinn [15]).
13. GROVER, STEPHEN, 'Why Only the Best Is Good Enough', *Analysis*, 48 (1988), 224.
14. MORRIS, THOMAS V., 'A Response to the Problem of Evil', *Philosophia* (Israel), 14 (1984), 173–86 (on Schlesinger [16] and [10]).
15. QUINN, PHILIP L., 'God, Moral Perfection, and Possible Worlds', in Frederick Sontag and M. Darrol Bryant (eds), *God: The Contemporary Discussion* (New York: Rose of Sharon Press, 1982), 197–215 (on Adams [12]).
16. SCHLESINGER, GEORGE, 'The Problem of Evil and the Problem of Suffering', *American Philosophical Quarterly*, 1 (1964), 244–7 (updated in Schlesinger [10], chs. 9–10; cf. Morris [14]).

3. The Defeat of Evils

17. CHISHOLM, RODERICK, *Brentano and Intrinsic Value* (Cambridge: Cambridge University Press, 1986), chs. 7–8.
18. FLEW, ANTONY, 'Are Ninian Smart's Temptations Irresistible?', *Philosophy*, 37 (1962), 57–60 (on Smart [21]).
19. MACKIE, JOHN LESLIE, 'Theism and Utopia', *Philosophy*, 37 (1962), 153–8 (on Smart [21]).
20. MORA, FREYA, 'Thank God for Evil?' *Philosophy*, 58 (1983), 399–401.
21. SMART, NINIAN, 'Omnipotence, Evil, and Supermen', *Philosophy*, 36 (1961), 188–95; (discussed in Flew [18], Mackie [19]).
22. —— 'Probably', *Philosophy*, 37 (1962), 60 (reply to Flew [18]).
23. WISDOM, JOHN, 'God and Evil', *Mind*, 44 (1935), 1–20.

4. Free Will and Theodicy

24. ADAMS, MARILYN MCCORD, 'Theodicy without Blame', *Philosophical Topics*, 16 (1988), 215–45.
25. ADAMS, ROBERT M., 'Plantinga on the Problem of Evil', in James E. Tomberlin and Peter van Inwagen, (eds.), *Profiles: Alvin Plantinga* (Dordrecht: Reidel, 1985), 225–55.
26. DAVIES, MARTIN, 'Determinism and Evil', *Australasian Journal of Philosophy*, 58 (1980), 116–27.
27. FLEW, ANTHONY, 'Divine Omnipotence and Human Freedom', in Antony Flew and Alasdair MacIntyre (eds.), *New Essays in Philosophical Theology* (London: SCM Press, 1955), 144–69.
28. PIKE, NELSON, 'Plantinga on Free Will and Evil', *Religious Studies*, 15 (1979), 449–73.
29. —— 'Over-Power and God's Responsibility for Sin', in Alfred J. Freddoso (ed.), *The Existence and Nature of God* (Notre Dame, Ind.: University of Notre Dame Press, 1983), 11–36.
30. PLANTINGA, ALVIN, *God and Other Minds: A Study of the Rational Justification of Belief in God* (Ithaca, NY: Cornell University Press, 1967), chs. 5–6.
31. —— *God, Freedom and Evil* (New York: Harper & Row, 1974), 7–64.
32. —— 'Tooley and Evil: A Reply', *Australasian Journal of Philosophy*, 60 (1982), 66–75 (reply to Tooley [35]).
33. —— 'Self-Profile', in James E. Tomberlin and Peter van Inwagen (eds.), *Profiles: Alvin Plantinga* (Dordrecht, Boston, Mass., and Lancaster, Pa.: Reidel, 1985), 36–55.
34. RICHMAN, ROBERT, 'Plantinga, God and (Yet) Other Minds', *Australasian Journal of Philosophy*, 50 (1972), 46–50 (on Plantinga [30]).
35. TOOLEY, MICHAEL, 'Alvin Plantinga and the Argument from Evil', *Australasian Journal of Philosophy*, 58 (1980), 360–76 (reply by Plantinga [32]).

5. Middle Knowledge and Counterfactuals of Freedom

36. BASINGER, DAVID, 'Middle Knowledge and Human Freedom: Some Clarifications', *Faith and Philosophy*, 4 (1987), 330–6 (on Hasker [38]).
37. FREDDOSO, ALFRED J., 'Introduction', in *Luis de Molina: On Divine Foreknowledge: Part IV of the Concordia* (Ithaca, NY: Cornell University Press, 1988), 1–81.
38. HASKER, WILLIAM, 'A Refutation of Middle Knowledge', *Noûs*, 20 (1986), 545–57 (discussed in Basinger [36] and Hasker [39]).
39. —— 'Reply to Basinger on Power Entailment', *Faith and Philosophy*, 5 (1988), 87–90 (reply to Basinger [36]).
40. KENNY, ANTHONY, *The God of the Philosophers* (Oxford: Clarendon Press, 1979), 61–71.

41. PLANTINGA, ALVIN, 'Replies to My Colleagues', in James E. Tomberlin and Peter van Inwagen (eds.), *Profiles: Alvin Plantinga* (Dordrecht: Reidel, 1985), 372–82.
42. WINDT, PETER YALE, 'Plantinga's Unfortunate God', *Philosophical Studies*, 24 (1973), 335–42.

6. Natural Evil and its Relation to Moral Evil

43. BOËR, STEVEN E., 'The Irrelevance of the Free Will Defense', *Analysis*, 38 (1978), 110–12.
44. COUGHLAN, M. J., 'Moral Evil without Consequences?' *Analysis*, 39 (1979), 58–60.
45. O'CONNOR, DAVID, 'Swinburne on Natural Evil', *Religious Studies*, 19 (1983), 65–73.
46. SAINSBURY, R. M., 'Benevolence and Evil', *Australasian Journal of Philosophy*, 58 (1980), 128–34.
47. STUMP, ELEONORE, 'Knowledge, Freedom, and the Problem of Evil', *International Journal for Philosophy of Religion*, 14 (1983), 49–58 (on Swinburne [11]).
48. SWINBURNE, RICHARD, 'Knowledge from Experience and the Problem of Evil', in William J. Abraham and Steven W. Holtzer (eds.), *The Rationality of Religious Belief: Essays in Honour of Basil Mitchell* (Oxford: Clarendon Press, 1987), 141–67.

7. The Evidential Problem of Evil

49. PERKINS, R. K., 'An Atheistic Argument from the Improvability of the Universe', *Noûs*, 17 (1983), 239–50.
50. PLANTINGA, ALVIN, 'The Probabilistic Argument from Evil', *Philosophical Studies*, 35 (1979), 1–53.
51. RICHMAN, ROBERT J., 'The Argument from Evil', *Religious Studies*, 4 (1969), 203–11.
52. ROWE, WILLIAM LEONARD, 'The Empirical Argument from Evil', in Robert Audi and William Wainwright (eds.), *Rationality, Religious Belief, and Moral Commitment* (Ithaca, NY: Cornell University Press, 1986), 227–47.
53. —— 'Evil and Theodicy', *Philosophical Topics*, 16 (1988), 119–32.
54. RUSSELL, BRUCE, 'The Persistent Problem of Evil', *Faith and Philosophy*, 6 (1989), 121–39.
55. SWINBURNE, RICHARD, 'Does Theism Need a Theodicy?' *Canadian Journal of Philosophy*, 18 (1988), 287–311 (on Wykstra [Chapter VIII of this collection] and Plantinga [50]).

8. Moral Education (Soul-Making) and Theodicy

56. HASKER, WILLIAM, 'Suffering, Soul-Making, and Salvation', *International Philosophical Quarterly*, 28 (1988), 3–19 (on Stump [60]).
57. HICK, JOHN H., 'God, Evil and Mystery', *Religious Studies*, 3 (1968), 539–46 (a reply to Puccetti [59]).
58. KANE, GORDON STANLEY, 'The Failure of Soul-Making Theodicy', *International Journal for Philosophy of Religion*, 6 (1975), 1–22.
59. PUCCETTI, ROLAND, 'The Loving God—Some Observations on John Hick's *Evil and the God of Love*', *Religious Studies*, 2 (1967), 255–68 (cf. Hick's reply [57]).
60. STUMP, ELEONORE, 'The Problem of Evil', *Faith and Philosophy*, 2 (1985), 392–423 (cf. Hasker [56]).

9. Religious Goods and the Problem of Evil

61. ADAMS, MARILYN McCORD, 'Duns Scotus on the Goodness of God', *Faith and Philosophy*, 4 (1987), 468–505.
62. —— 'Redemptive Suffering: A Christian Solution to the Problem of Evil', in Robert Audi and William Wainwright (eds.), *Rationality, Religious Belief, and Moral Commitment* (Ithaca, NY: Cornell University Press, 1986), 248–67.
63. ALLEN, DIOGENES, *The Traces of God in a Frequently Hostile World* (Cambridge, Mass.: Cowley, 1981).
64. SPRINGSTED, ERIC O., 'Is There a Problem with the Problem of Evil?' *International Philosophical Quarterly*, 24 (1984), 303–12.
65. STEWART, MELVILLE, 'O Felix Culpa, Redemption and the Greater Good Defense', *Sophia* (1986), 18–31.

10. Theodicy Without Omnipotence

66. GRIFFIN, DAVID RAY, *God, Power, and Evil: A Process Theodicy* (Philadelphia: Westminster Press, 1976).
67. —— 'Actuality, Possibility, and Theodicy: A Response to Nelson Pike', *Process Studies*, 12 (1982), 168–79 (reply to Pike [70]).
68. HARE, PETER HEWITT, and MADDEN, EDWARD H., 'Evil and Persuasive Power', *Process Studies*, 2 (1972), 44–8.
69. HOLMES, ARTHUR F., 'Why God Cannot Act' in Ronald H. Nash (ed.), *Process Theology* (Grand Rapids: Baker Books, 1987), 177–95.
70. PIKE, NELSON, 'Process Theodicy and the Concept of Power', *Process Studies*, 12 (1982), 148–67 (cf. Griffin [66, 67]).

11. Other Approaches to Theodicy

71. ADAMS, ROBERT MERRIHEW, *The Virtue of Faith and Other Essays in Philosophical Theology* (New York: Oxford University Press, 1987), ch. 5: 'Existence, Self-Interest, and the Problem of Evil' (cf. Hasker [72] and Morriston [74]).
72. HASKER, WILLIAM, 'On Regretting the Evils of This World', *Southern Journal of Philosophy*, 19 (1981), 425–38 (cf. Morriston [74]).
73. HITTERDALE, LARRY, 'The Problem of Evil and the Subjectivity of Values are Incompatible', *International Philosophical Quarterly*, 18 (1978), 467–9.
74. MORRISTON, WESLEY, 'Gladness, Regret, God, and Evil', *Southern Journal of Philosophy*, 20 (1982), 401–7 (on Hasker [72]).
75. ROSS, JAMES FRANCIS, *Philosophical Theology* (Indianapolis and New York: The Bobbs-Merrill Co., Inc., 1969), 222–78.

INDEX OF NAMES